FIELD WORK

An Introduction to the Social Sciences

By

BUFORD H. JUNKER

With an Introduction by

EVERETT C. HUGHES

THE UNIVERSITY OF CHICAGO PRESS

CHICAGO & LONDON

International Standard Book Number: 0-226-41666-6

Library of Congress Catalog Card Number: 60-7238

THE UNIVERSITY OF CHICAGO PRESS, CHICAGO 60637
The University of Chicago Press, Ltd., London

INTRODUCTION: THE PLACE OF FIELD WORK
IN SOCIAL SCIENCE

Field work refers, in this volume, to observation of people in situ;
finding them where they are, staying with them in some role which, while
acceptable to them, will allow both intimate observation of certain parts
of their behavior, and reporting it in ways useful to social science but not
harmful to those observed. It is not easy to find a suitable formula in the
best case; it may be impossible in some cases: say, a secret society devoted to crime or revolution or simply espousing "dangerous" ideas. But
most people can be studied and most can do more field work than they believe. It is a strenuous, but exciting and satisfying business to expand one's
own social perceptions and social knowledge in this way, and to contribute
thereby to general social knowledge. Learning to do it—both parts of it,
observing and reporting—can have some of the quality of a mild psycho-
analysis. But, as in other kinds of self-discovery, one cannot learn more
about one's self unless he is honestly willing to see others in a new light,
and to learn about them, too.

But perhaps I should say something of the history of the project out of
which this volume came. Dr. Junker, a man of much and varied field experience—in Yankee City, in a prison, in southern and midwestern communities, in various professions and institutions, among various racial and ethnic groups, in the United States Army both at home and in Europe—has
thought about this subject for a good many years. He has done field work
on field work. In 1951 he joined me in a project whose aim was to do just
that.[1]

How did I come to initiate such a project? Certainly not because I ever
found field observation easy to undertake. Once I start, I am, I believe, not
bad at it. But it has always been a torture. Documents are so much easier
to approach; one simply blows the dust off them, opens them up, and may
have the pleasure of seeing words and thoughts on which no eye has been
set these many years. Yet, in every project I have undertaken, studying
real estate men, the Catholic labor movement in the Rhineland, and newly

1. The project was supported from a grant made by the Ford Foundation to the Division of the Social Sciences of the University of Chicago.
Professor W. Lloyd Warner and the late Professor Robert Redfield served
as advisers.

industrialized towns in Quebec, the time came when I had to desert statistical reports and documents and fare forth to see for myself. It was then that the real learning began, although the knowledge gained in advance was very useful; in fact, it often made possible the conversations which opened the field. One who has some information and asks for more is perhaps less likely to be refused than one who has no advance information; perhaps the best formula is to have advance knowledge, but to let it show only in the kind of questions one asks. But if I have usually been hesitant in entering the field myself and have perhaps walked around the block getting up my courage to knock at doors more often than almost any of my students (I have been doing it longer), I have sent a great many students into the field. Listening to them has given me sympathy with their problems; it has also convinced me that most students can learn to do field observation and will profit from it.

When I came to the University of Chicago in 1938, my colleagues assigned me an introductory course in sociology. It was a course taken mainly by young people who had had two or more years of social science in the College of the University of Chicago. They were probably better read in the social sciences than their peers in any other college on this continent. But many of them had not yet come to that point in education where one sees the connection between small things and great. They liked everything to be great—events as well as ideas. They were inclined to be impatient with the small observations which, accumulated, are the evidence on which theories of culture and society are built. To quite a number of them real life seemed banal, trivial, and often misguided.

I used various devices to get some of the students to collect social data themselves, in the hope that the experience would give them a livelier sense of the problems of gathering social data and turning them, by analysis, into social facts. Eventually I took a bolder step. Since there was no danger that these students would miss adequate exposure to social theories, I, with the approval of my colleagues, replaced the general course with a full term of introduction to field work.

While we never set the form of the course in any inflexible way, there was a general pattern which did not change greatly. Each student, alone or with another, made a series of observations in a Census Tract or other small area of Chicago outside his everyday experience and reported on these observations almost week by week. We discussed the problems the students met in the field. They were asked to notice especially whom they were taken for by people in the areas where they studied and to find an explanation for the peculiar roles attributed to them. When they had done the several assigned kinds of observation, they were asked to draw up a proposal for a study which might be done in such an area, by a person of small resources.

After some years in which nearly all students of sociology, many students of anthropology, and some others went through this experience, I asked for and received a small grant to be used in putting together what we had learned from these several hundred students about the learning and doing of field work and to learn how people of greater experience and sophistication had gone about field observation.

Dr. Junker took charge of the project. Dr. Ray Gold interviewed the current crop of students about their field experiences. Together we held a seminar in which people who had done field observation on a great variety of problems and in many different situations reported on their experiences. A record was kept of their reports. Miss Dorothy Kittel, a bibliographer, helped us in finding documents which reported experiences of people in the field. We put some of the resulting material into a privately circulated document, "Cases on Field Work." What Dr. Junker has put into the present book is in part a more succinct and readable distillate of that volume. But it is more than that. This book has evolved through eight more years of his thought and work.

Those of us who had a part in this project have been strengthened in our conviction that field work is not merely one among several methods of social study but is paramount. It is, more than other methods of study, itself a practice, consciously undertaken, in sociology itself—in the perceiving and predicting of social roles, both one's own and those of others. It consists of exchanges of tentative social gestures, to use the terms of George Herbert Mead. That theme is developed by Dr. Junker. I shall confine myself to some general remarks on the place of field work in the social sciences.

Field work, when mentioned as an activity of social scientists, calls to mind first of all the ethnologist or anthropologist far afield observing and recording the ways, language, artifacts, and physical characteristics of exotic or primitive people. He is presumably there because the people he is interested in have never written down anything about themselves or because, if they do write, they have not had the habit of recording the things the ethnologist wants to know. The early manuals issued to aid ethnologists told the prospective observer what to look for, not how to look for it. Later anthropologists—Malinowski, Margaret Mead, and others—have told of their field experiences in a penetrating way.

Until a generation ago the phrase field work might also have brought to mind what was then called the "social survey." At the turn of the century the social surveyors were going to the slums of the great cities of

Britain and North America to observe the "conditions" in which the new urban industrial poor lived. They then reported them in simple statistical
tables on consumption of food and clothing, on wages, housing, illness and
crime. But they also described what they found, "fully, freely and bitter-
ly," as Robert E. Park used to say, in the hope that an aroused public
would change things. Their work had its journalistic and literary counter-
part in "muck-raking." The seventeen volumes of Charles Booth's The
Life and Labour of the People of London report several years of observation of the kind known then and for several decades afterwards as "social
survey." Among Booth's collaborators were school "visitors," who went
from door to door to see conditions and to talk to people. They also visited
churches, clubs, public houses, parks, and pawnshops. They got acquainted
with the factories, docks, and other places of work of the poor of East London. The work continued for several years; when at last they did the field
work for a series of volumes entitled Religious Influences, they described
not merely the feeble religious institutions of East London, but also the
recreational institutions—including public houses—which seemed to have
supplanted the church in the lives of working people. They had become
rather more sympathetic reporters than muck-rakers. They had also established a tradition of social observation with two facets: (1) the kinds of
data which were thought important to description of the social life of the
poor, and (2) a way of gathering them. In North America, the tradition was
carried on and developed; the Pittsburgh Survey (Kellogg, 1909-14), reporting the conditions of life and work of immigrant steelworkers, was the
most voluminous and notorious of such projects in this country. LePlay, in
France, had gone about getting data from families concerning their in-
comes and expenditures. In all of these enterprises, investigators went
among the industrial and urban poor to gather information which was not,
at that time, to be found in the censuses taken by public authorities. In
many of them, the surveyors were betrayed by their humanity and curiosity into noting other kinds of information, into becoming, in effect, the ethnologists of social classes and other social groups than their own.

   For the older social surveys discovered and described customs and
institutions as well as opinions. Bosanquet, in the course of surveying the
standards of living in London, learned the peculiar functions of the pawn-
shop among the poor of London.[2] Booth described the institutions of East
London and came to the conclusion that no recreational or religious institution could survive there without a subsidy: it might be from gambling or
the sale of beer, or it might be subsidy from the middle classes in other

   2. Helen D. Bosanquet, The Standard of Life and Other Studies (London: Macmillan & Co., 1895).

parts of town. He also described in detail the habits of drinking, by age and sex, among working people, and came to the conclusion that the sending of children to fetch a bucket of beer for their father's tea did not have the horrible consequences the middle class attributed to it.[3]

Although the surveys were not, in Europe, associated with the name of sociology, in England and America the survey movement became part of the peculiar sociological mix. Social workers, important in the earlier surveys, turned more and more to individual case work and seemed to lose interest in communities, groups, and styles of life. "Professionalized" social work abandoned the social survey for psychiatry, which uses a quite different research role and collects information of a different kind.

The unique thing about the early department of sociology at the University of Chicago was that it brought together Albion W. Small, who was both a devotee of German theoretical sociology and of the American social gospel of reform, and a number of people who were even more closely identified with social surveys, social problems, and social reform. W. I. Thomas, who inspired and carried out the great study of The Polish Peasant in Europe and America with the collaboration of Florian Znaniecki, was following the tradition of the social survey, but he was also leading it in a new direction, that of a more self-conscious and acute theoretical analysis. Robert E. Park, who eventually joined the department, combined even more than the others, the two facets of American sociology. For he had a Heidelberg degree in philosophy, got by writing a theoretical treatise on collective behavior in the crowd and the public.[4] His interest in the behavior of crowds and publics was, however, developed during twelve years of work as a newspaper reporter and city editor. He did more perhaps than any other person to produce the new American sociology in which people went out and did field observations designed to advance theoretical, as well as practical, knowledge of modern, urban society.

Under his influence, and that of his colleagues, hundreds of students of sociology at the University of Chicago went to the field in various areas of Chicago. Their work was co-ordinated, for some years, by Dr. Vivien Palmer, who then published a book on how to do such observation.[5] With

---

3. For an account of the further development of the social survey in Great Britain see D. Caradog Jones, Social Surveys (London: Hutchinson's University Library, 1949); also his article, "Evolution of the Social Survey in England since Booth," American Journal of Sociology, XLVI, 818-25.

4. Masse und Publikum, eine methodologische und soziologische Untersuchung (Bern, 1904).

5. Field Studies in Sociology (Chicago: University of Chicago Press,

the development of better quantitative methods of handling social data, the practice of field work declined. It became known, with a certain condescension, as the "anthropological" method. Eventually the very term "survey" took on a new meaning. "Survey research" now means the study of political or other opinions, including consumers' preferences, by interviewing, with set questions, individuals so chosen as statistically to represent large populations about which the information is wanted. Going to the field means getting out to interview the sample. Some place is given to less formal field observation, but it is called "pilot study" or "exploratory study," and is considered preparatory to the main business of getting a questionnaire on the road. Its aim is to learn how to standardize the questions one wants to ask, not generally to learn what questions to ask. Great ingenuity is sometimes shown in such exploration and pretesting, but it is usually done with a certain impatience, since it delays the real work of "administering" the questionnaire. Once the questionnaire is settled upon, any doubts about the questions must be explained away, as it is too expensive and too disturbing to change anything at that point. The survey research of today, valuable as it is, conceives of field observation in quite a different way from that presented in this book.

For one thing, the sample survey still must work on the assumption that some very large population speaks so nearly the same language, both in letter and figure of speech, that the differences in answers will not be due in significant degree to differences in the meaning of words in the questions. This is a condition hard to meet even in Western literate countries: in many parts of the world, it cannot be met at all. The survey method, in this new sense of the term, must work with small variation in the midst of great bodies of common social definition. The preparatory field work is used to determine the limits of common meaning within which one can conduct the survey. Very often, groups of people not in the common social world have to be left out of consideration. In this country many surveys omit Negroes and other "deviant" groups. It is part of the merit of field work of the kind we are discussing in this book that it does not have to limit itself to minor variations of behavior within large homogeneous populations. But even within such populations, field observation is more than a preparatory step for large statistical surveys. It is an ongoing part of social science. Most surveys, again in the new sense, would be much more useful if they were followed by even more intensive field work than that which precedes them. There is a tendency for the statistical concen-

_____

1928).
The Webbs wrote a classic in this field under the title, Methods of Social Study (London: Longmans, Green & Co., 1932).

trations and relationships found in a questionnaire survey to be explained
in a text which merely presents alternative speculations. It is at that point
that good field work, instead of getting "soft" data, would give firmer stuff.
In fact, this is what was done in a recent study of anxiety among college
professors.[6] A field team followed the interviewers. The social science of
today requires, in fact, a great many arts of observation and analysis.
Field observation is one of them.

There were some important differences between the field work of the
ethnologists and that of the sociologists who followed the tradition of the
social survey. The ethnologist was always an exotic to the people he studied; clearly a stranger in every way except his humanity, and perhaps he
had to establish even that. The sociologist observed and reported upon a
segment of his own world, albeit a poverty-stricken and socially powerless
one. He was usually a class stranger to the people he studied; often, in
some measure, an ethnic, religious, or racial stranger. Still, he was among
people of kinds whom he might see any day in public places and who might
read the same newspaper as himself. In due time, some of the sociologists
themselves came from the segments of society which had been, or still
were, objects of study and began to report on the very minorities—racial,
sectarian, ethnic—of which they were members. The sociologist came to
be less and less a stranger studying strangers and reporting to still other
strangers. Student, object of study, and member of audience for the study
tended to overlap and merge more and more. The sociologist was now reporting observations made, not as a complete stranger, but in some measure as a member of an in-group, although, of course, the member becomes
something of a stranger in the very act of objectifying and reporting his experiences.

The unending dialectic between the role of member (participant) and
stranger (observer and reporter) is essential to the very concept of field
work. It is hard to be both at the same time. One solution is to separate
them in time. One reports, years later and when one is at a distance in
mind and spirit, what he remembers of social experiences in which he was
a full participant.

It is doubtful whether one can become a good social reporter unless he
has been able to look, in a reporting mood, at the social world in which he
was reared. On the other hand, a person cannot make a career out of the

---

6. Paul F. Lazarsfeld and Wagner Thielens, Jr., The Academic Mind:
Social Scientists in a Time of Crisis (Glencoe, Ill.: Free Press, 1958), with
a field report by David Riesman.

reporting of reminiscences unless he is so far alienated from his own background as to be able to expose and exploit it before some new world with which he now identifies himself. One has to learn to get new data and to get them in a great variety of settings as demanded by new problems he wants to solve. Other ways of solving this dialectic include being a part-time participant and part-time reporter, privately participant and publicly reporter, or publicly participant and secretly reporter. All these are practiced. All have their moral, personal, and scientific pitfalls. But the dialectic is never fully resolved, for to do good social observation one has to be close to people living their lives and must be himself living his life and must also report. The problem of maintaining good balance between these roles lies at the very heart of sociology, and indeed of all social science.

Each of the two disciplines, anthropology and sociology, which have made most use of field work, has its own history. In each, the field situation has tended to be different from that of the other. The ethnologist reported upon a whole community; the sociologist generally observed and reported only upon people of some segment, usually a poor and socially powerless one, of a community. In due time, it came about that some of the sociologists themselves came from odd and less-known corners of society or from minorities and began to report upon their own people to their new associates in the academic and larger society. This introduced a new element of distinction from the older ethnology. For the sociologist was now reporting upon observations made, not in the role of the stranger, but as a full member of the little world he reported on. He observed as a member of an in-group but, in the act of objectifying and reporting his experience, became of necessity a sort of outsider.

As one reads into the analyses and the documents included herein, he will see the meaning of this. For it comes out clearly, I believe, that the situations and circumstances in which field observation of human behavior is done are so various that no manual of detailed rules would serve; it is perhaps less clear, but equally true, that the basic problems are the same in all situations. It is the discovery of this likeness inside the shell of variety that is perhaps the greatest and most important step in learning to be an effective and versatile observer.

In the foregoing I have said nothing about the logic of field observation in social science. One reason I have not done so up to this point is that I wanted to emphasize that the departments of social science are as much historic institutions as logical divisions. Each one is the product either of social movements inside the academic world or of movements outside which later got into the academic world. While some of the departments have or claim a peculiar subject matter which sets them off from the others, this subject matter is perhaps more often a product of history, become convention and prerogative, than of pure logic. One might imagine a university in which there would be no divisions of subject matter except those dictated by clear differences of method. Economists would study all phenomena which could profitably be studied by the methods developed for analysis of the behavior of men playing the game of maximizing their share of scarce, but desired, goods. Some other branch would study all phenomena which yield well to analyses based upon skilled observation of power relations among men, and so on. I think it is obvious that this is not the situation at present. Each branch of social science appears to be some mixture of a concern with a basic logic or method with a somewhat monopolistic and jealous concern with some set of institutions or practical problems.

One should add that each, whatever its basic logic or method, has its favorite kinds of data. The historian loves to get his hands on a manuscript that no one has seen before. He wants to sit down in a quiet and musty corner of the archives and copy out parts of it by hand. He is preoccupied with manuscripts and prides himself on his skill in reading both the lines and what is between the lines. The political scientist shares this interest or preoccupation somewhat, with the variation that he especially loves a secret rather than a merely rare document. The psychologist has, more than others engaged in the study of social behavior, set himself the model of the natural scientist making stylized observations in a prepared situation, that is, in a laboratory. The economist and some sociologists like to get their data already in quantitative form and in massive numbers. Their love is the manipulation of such data to create situations with a maximum of chance and then to discover departures from it.

Now there may be some relation between the number of possible fruitful kinds of data and ways of getting and handling them and the number of departments of social science in an American university, but I doubt it. We may discover in due time that there are only a few basic ways of getting human data and a few basic skills for analyzing them. While it may for a long time be true that the departments will be distinguished more by their preoccupations than by their method, conceived in terms of pure logic, it may also be that we can sort out these basic skills of observation and analysis and work on them irrespective of conventional disciplinary lines.

One of these areas of skill will be that of observing and recording the behavior of human beings "on the hoof." Men deposit some of their thoughts and actions in artifacts and documents which historians learn to read with consummate skill. Some of their actions yield to analysis of small items of behavior recorded in astronomical numbers of cases. But others, I am

convinced, yield only to close observation at the time, observation sometimes of the passive bystander, sometimes of the active participant, sometimes of the active intervener, as in the case of the group experimenter
and of the psychoanalyst who rends painful hidden memories from the unwilling patient. It is observation "on the hoof" that we refer to as field observation.

It is a method increasingly used by students of many modern institutions (unions, industries, hospitals, armies) as well as by students of communities, near or far from home. The outstanding peculiarity of this method is that the observer, in greater or less degree, is caught up in the very
web of social interaction which he observes, analyzes, and reports. Even
if he observes through a peephole, he plays a role: that of spy. And when
he reports his observations made thus he becomes a kind of informer. If
he observes in the role of a member of the group, he may be considered a
traitor the moment he reports. Even the historian, who works upon documents, gets caught in a role problem when he reports, unless there is no
person alive who might identify himself with the people or social group
concerned. The hatred occasionally visited upon the debunking historian is
visited almost daily upon the person who reports on the behavior of people
he has lived among; and it is not so much the writing of the report, as the
very act of thinking in such objective terms that disturbs the people observed. It is a violation of apparently shared secrets and sentiments. The
reader will see that in the discussions and documents which follow we have
all become very much occupied with the dimensions of this problem, of the
on-going social and personal dilemmas of the man who observes and analyzes, more than is necessary for survival and good participation, the behavior of people about him and reports it to some audience.

The usefulness of field observation is not confined to one institution or
aspect of life—religious conduct, economic, familial, political, or any other
institutional aspect of behavior will yield in some measure to field observation. Insofar as it does, the observer, no matter what his formal field or
academic fraternity, will share problems of skill, role, and ethic with all
others who use the method. The aim of the project from which this book
grew was not to sell this idea to people in sociology or in other fields, but
to assemble what knowledge and insight we could on problems of learning
and using the method of field observation, without limiting ourselves to any
conventional confines.

If there is any sense in which field method is peculiarly sociological
it is in this. If sociology is conceived as the science of social interaction
and of the cultural and institutional results of interaction (which become
factors conditioning future interaction), then field observation is applied

sociology. Insofar as the field observer becomes a conscious observer and analyst of himself in the role of observer, he becomes also a pure sociologist. For the concepts which he will need for this observation of the observer are the very concepts needed for analysis of any social interaction. The very difficulties of carrying out field observation—the resistance of his subjects, the danger that his very success as a participant may later prevent him from full reporting, even the experience of getting thrown out of town—are facts to be analyzed sociologically. It was the realization of these points that made our little research group exclaim one day, almost as one man, "We are studying the sociology of sociology."

This has a peculiar corollary. The problem of learning to be a field observer is like the problem of learning to live in society. It is the problem of making enough good guesses from previous experience so that one can get into a social situation in which to get more knowledge and experience to enable him to make more good guesses to get into a better situation, ad infinitum.

The problem of any field observer is to learn how he, even he, can keep expanding this series as long as possible and in what situations he can do so. The part of theoretical analysis and the part of insightful experience, and the relation of the two to each other, are, in a sense, what we set out to discover.

EVERETT C. HUGHES

ACKNOWLEDGMENTS

The present work was written largely in the spring of 1959 while I was on the staff of the Administrative Science Center at the University of Pittsburgh. Acknowledgments are due the Director of the Center, Dr. James D. Thompson, for his sympathetic interest and support of this effort; to staff members, Dr. Robert Hawkes, Dr. Peter B. Hammond, and Dr. Arthur Tuden, for their helpful suggestions and criticisms of the manuscript; and to the staff members who first produced these chapters in readable form, Mrs. Augusta Moretti, Miss Judith Brugh, and Miss Marian Hatok. As every author enjoying secretarial services knows, the young ladies who turn out the first clean draft make a very real contribution to the making of a book. Thanks are also due an anthropologist who visited the Center one day and who volunteered to read the manuscript, namely, Professor William J. McEwen, of the Downstate Medical Center, State University of New York.

The reader will find, in the several chapters and the Selected Bibliography, other acknowledgments—to authors and publishers, to university and foundation support of field work, including field work on field workers, and to a number of my own principal teachers and colleagues, including especially students.

To all of these, named and anonymous, and to my wife, my many thanks for their encouragement, stimulation, and very effective help.

CONTENTS

I

THE MEANING OF FIELD WORK

Field work for a social science—one concerned with learning first-hand from living people about themselves and their society—is in itself an application of that science. Field work viewed as applied sociology, for example, provides one way to learn what sociology is about and what it means in its simplest and most vital terms.

The student, after his first interview for a social science purpose and as he writes a full and free acount of what occurred (not merely what was said, verbatim, and done, in context, by both participants, but also what seemed to be felt and implied), will come to realize that for him in some sense and even for others, perhaps, the single interview illuminates what society is, in microcosm.[1] He has available for study and reflection leading to his further development, intellectual and otherwise, a report of an instance of interaction in a certain period of time in a given setting in which he and another person created a learning situation for each other and accomplished some kind and amount of communication of information that may be relevant to the knowledge sought by a social science. He can henceforth engage himself actively in the endless interplay between concept and percept, percept and concept, and so on, which make up and sustain what is known about man as a social animal.

Field work, as practiced occasionally or routinely in education, social work, and other enterprises involving human relations in applied fields, is distinguished by a less direct concern for its contributions to knowledge and a more immediate concern for changing people or their situations or both. In certain kinds of action research, there may occur applications of social science at two levels, sometimes almost simultaneously: (1) at the level of discovering and helping to define the nature and rate of changes desired by the people in the situation; (2) at the level of participating with the people to assist them in making changes. Such field work may be supplemented by the kind of field work with which this book is largely concerned, but the distinction is worth making if only because there may be a serious underlying difference in attitude towards "the facts." If one is primarily concerned to change the latter, his interest may contaminate his

---

1. See Selected Bibliography, Part III, D-4 (The Interview), especially Riesman and Benney (eds.) (September, 1956).

1

contributions to knowledge. In contrast, if one is so opposed to changing
"the facts" because this would materially intervene in the natural processes being studied, his concern may block his perceptions of what the full
natural process really is, and so diminish his contributions to knowledge.
The resolution of this conflict, if it is as crucial to the advance of social
science as these blunt opposing statements make it appear, is not to be
concluded in a paragraph or even one lifetime. Concerned we must be, but
our goal should be to rise above pre-judgment of a social science problem
like this one on the basis of narrow concern either way.

Our concern in this book is to deal with field work for a social science
—that is, the tasks of observing and recording and reporting the behavior
of living people in contemporary situations with no intention of changing
them or their situations, in any direct way, and with, rather, every intention of avoiding disturbance to their natural activities. Such field work
aims to influence only those committed to the advancement of knowledge in
the social sciences.

It is assumed that improving such knowledge is a good thing, on the
whole, and that human beings need not fear the even more general public
dissemination of what science can learn about ourselves, our fellows, and
our common fates. The basic and important ethical questions about the
uses to which this improved knowledge should be put are not different from
those which mankind has faced through the centuries. Modern social sciences did not invent the evil use of superior weapons of propaganda any
more than did the modern physical sciences invent the use of superior
weapons of war. Neither, in fact, invented either lying or murder, or even
their current definitions in modern civilizations. Nor can any modern science claim to have invented goodness and love. If understanding and insight
can lead some people to perfections, it can also lead other people into evil
ways. It is much more likely that insight and understanding make good or
wicked tendencies merely more efficient.

The matter ultimately comes down to the facts about how people conduct themselves and why. And this includes social scientists doing field
work: they have the initiative and the responsibility when it comes to reporting, especially in the sense of publishing. Even if the people from
whom the field worker learns have the first choice about helping him, once
they have given him anything, whether it is all the information he desires
or a blank stare of refusal to help him at all, he is under an ethical obligation to them in their terms. The social scientist field worker also has a
set of obligations to his science, to his colleagues, and perhaps ultimately
the world. In the long run, the survival of the social sciences concerned
with living people may hinge upon society's judgments upon the ways in

which social scientists have weighed their prior direct obligations incurred in field work situations against their other obligations, incurred before or after field work, to report as social scientists. Unlike the historian, the social scientist concerned with people can't wait until they are dead, and he need not expect his unpublished observations to be printed after he is dead. It is not a simple task for a thoughtful field worker to weigh these obligations and decide his course in the immediate case. Indeed, his dilemma may be excruciating. A continued theme in this book therefore is the ethics of reporting.

Some years ago it may have been possible to consider field observation as a magic bundle of techniques to obtain data that would have a direct bearing upon the verification of natural laws about human nature and society. Alas! we have social evolution in social science itself, or at least change, and must now recognize that scientific knowledge about social life will require a vast collaboration of many persons for a long time to come.

Knowledge in a social science may be regarded as resting upon data, which in this book is to be read "data-about-society." The latter in turn rest upon "information-in-society," hereafter simply called information. Information, in turn, consists of what is and can be recorded of all the things that people do and say. Of all that can be recorded with modern equipment (photographic, phonographic, and otherwise), we are primarily concerned with what can be recorded and later reported in the words, charts, and tables of scientific symbolism.

Knowledge in this context refers to statements at the higher orders of generalization which approach the standing of natural laws. Data are facts based upon information: they are summaries of real-life phenomena, and they stand at that level of generalization called classification. Natural laws state general relationships; classifications merely suggest them. Information at the bottom of the pyramid is what "everybody knows," or what "some know" or "few know," or what "I alone know." Information is the record of "life in the raw," and in field-worker circles it is sometimes carelessly referred to as "the raw data."

Part of field work consists of making observations, including those of interviewing, but the major part of the field worker's time and effort is put into the recording of these observations. Even if he edits a stenographer's transcript of a tape recording, to turn it into information usable at the next step—classification into data—he will find this to be true. Modern conveniences can sometimes make more labor than they save.

More important for our immediate purposes is to recognize the interdependence of the several levels of communication we may call knowledge, data, and information. It is in the nature of scientific communication or any other kind of discursive symbolism that it requires a speaker with at least one listener and that it requires a somewhat larger audience, to say the least, before the communication can become scientific knowledge. It should never be forgotten, however, that knowledge in the social sciences rests upon at least one field worker's having observed and recorded some information in such a way that his data, properly reported, can be compared with others' data. Only if these activities are replicated many times can a speaker eventually declare to an audience that "We know" and have some hope that some of them will join in his "we-group." There is no intention here to argue that all social scientists should or could reach agreement. Yet the plain fact is that a science rests upon substantial agreement among observers about what they observe and how to observe it.

Field work results, therefore, consist of recorded items of information which gain in scientific interest in proportion to how well they can be communicated at the more general levels of theoretical analysis. The criteria of effective communication in this context are two: (1) that there be true (correct and adequate) connections between observation and record of information, between information and its classification as datum, and between datum and its use in higher-order generalization; and (2) that, in addition to this clear and economical delineation of what was observed and its scientific meanings, there also be an adequate and correct description of the research operations—in short, of how to observe the same sort of thing. With these two criteria in mind, one can ascertain the relevance of "raw data" to theory, or of theory to observable behavior, and one can relate one's own direct experience and insights to the reported observations of others, or even to a line of theoretical analysis that appears worth testing. In short, one can practice a high degree of literacy in reading or writing any book or article in the social sciences by keeping in mind these ideal standards of discourse.[2] The two short questions to keep in mind might be: "What is he talking about?" and "How does he know it?"

Insofar as these questions can be answered satisfactorily, there is a real possibility that a scientific rationale for a piece of field work can be communicated along with its results in forms of information, data, and contribution to knowledge. If all social science knowledge were based upon field work so performed and reported, then we should not have to say that in the social sciences there are no unchallenged statements at the level of generalization called natural law. Instead, we must admit that we have

---

2. See full reference in Selected Bibliography, Part II, to Ogden and Richards, The Meaning of Meaning. See also chapter ii, section on Semantics and Field Work, which includes an excerpt from B. Malinowski in the book by Ogden and Richards.

nothing like the formulations in the physical sciences. For the most part, the highest-order generalizations in the social sciences turn out to be, on re-examination by succeeding generations, something in the nature of classifications. By that time, they have become established concepts—and succeeding generations of students, if they are lucky and well led, learn them in a mental process involving an interweaving of concept and percept, and in this way they may rapidly internalize the hard-won results of human learning. Since they did not have to learn "the hard way," it is of some advantage to the social sciences that each generation of students adds to the audience composed of those who have at least "heard the words" and can look bright and attentive when the terms pass into common enough parlance. In the long run, however, it is a disadvantage to the social sciences, and a misguided direction of their true educational mission, that their growing audience does not also include a growing proportion of those who can ask, "What is known and how is it known?" and who can seek the answers each with his own tenacious and respected intellectual integrity.

Although the larger social situation surrounding the social sciences, as well as the specific preoccupations of their current leaders, should not be ignored, the reader is asked to center his attention upon the major dimensions of the immediate situation of field work, from the individual field worker's point of view. This focusing of attention may need some explanation. For one thing, there is the concern with field work training for future social scientists as individuals. These younger people will experience something given to few others in a well-ordered society, namely, an opportunity to escape from the particular variety of ethnocentrism to which each, in his own way, is very likely to be bound. For another, there is the debt owing to all field workers who have reported, over and beyond the expectations of their audiences at the time, what went on during their field work, in the immediate situation, in the minds of the people studied, and in their own minds, so far as it could be learned and narrated in the final account.

For a third reason, I am focusing upon the immediate situation from the field worker's point of view, because there is little or nothing in print (or otherwise suited to be called "known") about the experience of the living people in the field work situation, those who are sometimes called "subjects" and sometimes referred to as "good friends" but also often described in terms that express the field worker's relief at the parting. The people are rarely heard from, so far at least, but there is reason to believe that the widening web of social science communications will eventually include us all, and it is no secret among field workers that this is an important item in their lists of concerns. There is no published case, to my knowledge, of a field worker's accompanying another field worker to get their side of the story from the people he learns from. The unpublished informal evidence suggests that trying to find out from two observers what happened may be more difficult than getting what one can from a single field worker himself. At any rate the latter is, in most cases, the one best and often the only reporter of the social processes and personal experiences important in the field work.

Field work is a highly complex activity, and its description is a very difficult task. Even in our focusing upon the immediate situation, putting in the background the larger scientific context affecting the field worker's theoretical orientation, choice of site, definition of research problems, and so on, we find we must pay attention to a multitude of variables.

The immediate situation of field work may be generally characterized as a learning situation, and the kind of learning that goes on, when it does, is quite different from learning the multiplication tables, let us say. The field worker undertakes not to do the learning all by himself—as if his entire task were merely to read the handwriting on some wall—but instead he aims to create a series of learning situations within the larger one, so that the various persons concerned learn, in a very important sense, to act toward each other in such ways that permit him, as one among them, to continue to make the observations essential to his study. Each interview, each reported bit of participant observation, each interaction of the field worker with others, must be something of a learning situation for those present.

The field worker whose aims include avoiding changes in persons or their situations that would disrupt the ongoing social processes to be studied has a peculiar task: he must in fact "change" the persons so that they act appropriately in the learning situations he has had to select or create, and maintain, but he must do this with minimal, and if possible no, change in the ongoing processes. If disruptions and reorganization cannot be avoided, the social scientist must find ways to make his field study a useful inquiry into such phenomena as a part of the social process. Some effect on a small group's equilibrium is inevitable when a field worker enters the situation; his task is to understand that effect, make it as slight as possible by minimizing his own interventions, and do his best to help the group achieve either an approximation of their original equilibrium or some new one equally worth analyzing.

The training of field workers to gain skills and experience in dealing with such delicate matters is likewise a complicated task, for it necessarily goes on while the student is not only living as himself in society, but is also engaging in a larger learning experience aimed to help him develop as an educated person, an independent thinker, and even perhaps as a creative social scientist. No two students could possibly have the same learning experiences with the same results, no matter what standardized assignments were required. Learning to do field work as an individual enterprise is therefore inevitable, and this can and should be given positive value by rewards for improvement in effective communication with others about experiences that cannot help being idiosyncratic but that nevertheless may be brought to useful explicit statement as the student's own contribution to the improvement of his social science.

Field work as an individual enterprise requires first attention for another reason. Even with its complexity it is still the simpler case that a sound rule of science bids us seek in order that we may build from this toward an understanding of more complex phenomena. The latter appear in what may be called cases of field work as a group enterprise. This is becoming more common in the social sciences, both in the study of modern civilization and its problems, because the society is more complex and the population larger, and in the study of simpler societies because of increasing interest in the multidimensional nature of the phenomena which social scientists now seek to investigate.

While interdisciplinary and other kinds of group research are increasingly important, it remains true that even within them the basic processes of field work go on: that observations must be made and information translated into data, by a series of operations each performed by one individual at a given moment, no matter what the particular division of labor may be.

In the inquiry upon which this book is based[3] I found very few published reports of what went on within organizations making large-scale field studies. Such reports suggest that there is a whole field of research management to be explored. The individual in such a group enterprise necessarily participates in a more complicated set of relationships, with colleagues and perhaps with superiors and subordinates. He must maintain these, as well as relations with people in the field work situation, and he may be sustained by them as well. If the research group is closely knit (and it may be, in the case of a husband-wife team), their solidarity and state of morale doubtless affect their relations with people in the field situation, and vice versa. The individual field worker might never feel lonely and unprotected under such circumstances, but their effects upon his operations of observation and recording might be considerable. Such matters

---

3. See Introduction. Also see Selected Bibliography for references to publications on this topic: especially M. F. Luszki (ed.) (1958) and others under the classification, D-1 (Methods and Techniques—General discussions and texts).

as these are not so well reported for group enterprises as are the down-
to-earth experiences of individual field workers on their own.

As a learning situation for the student, the group enterprise is characterized by two important features: (1) there is a hierarchy, with a leader
or director, who has one or more lieutenants and, working under supervision, a number of observers as well as translators of information into data
(such as coders); and (2) the data sought, and the means by which the information gatherers are more or less constrained to obtain it, must usually
be controlled and standardized. All this means that the costs of such a
study are large enough to make it necessary to justify it in advance, not as
an exploration into the relatively unknown, but as a project whose results
will quite clearly be worth the effort because they will establish as facts
about a significant population what are already known or strongly sus-
pected to be truths. A group enterprise may start this way and push or be
pushed beyond the expected limits of the study as planned. It is a rare beginner, however, who is permitted by the circumstances to experience in
depth the higher-level work of relating insight to theoretical analysis.
There is no doubt, however, that this can happen, but when it does, the
learning process involved is essentially the same as that from which the
individual field worker profits on his own. Learning to do field work, and
developing a comprehension of it as in itself an applied science, remains
to a high degree a personal educative task.

Insofar as the social sciences dependent upon field work seek to develop a more communicable rationale for these operations, on a broad base
of participation by learners and doers, they may also hope to build firmer
foundations for the kind of knowledge to which they aspire as sciences,
namely, that which makes systematic use of data about society firmly
rooted in the information in society obtained by observers who can communicate as well as perform their scientific operations more effectively than
ever before.

The training of students to do field work for social science purposes
might emphasize a development of technical skills, such as interviewing.
In this case, a manual of technique, carefully practiced in contrived situations, might suffice to protect both students and defenseless society from
unpleasant experiences, before the student is allowed to take his chances
or before any door is knocked upon. If the town environs of the classroom
are so easily saturated by student field workers and if more favorable
field training sites are too inaccessible, then indeed contrived situations
may be the only resource for instruction and practice in field work.

Alternatively, the education of social scientists can aim at growth of
understanding of the nature of field work in its relevant framework—the

enlarging matrix of knowledge about mankind and the development of the student himself as a social scientist and a person living in society.

This book aims to help in the learning of field work skills in ways that reinforce deepening awareness of what is known, what is being added or may be added to our knowledge, and how this knowing comes about. By helping its readers to develop their own more useful ways of thinking about field work, the pages which follow may serve to bring a social science into the living experience of the student, so that even a dusty text can gain in meaning.

The outstanding peculiarity of field work for a social science, and similarly that of a social science which declares and maintains its lively dependence upon field work, is what distinguishes its simplest step of observation of any bit of social reality from the essentials of observation of more concrete realities elsewhere in the natural realm. Let us see how the situations of observation differ in the two groups of sciences—physical and social.

Observation in the laboratory for the student of physics, chemistry, and the like can be and ideally is performed as a set of operations which define and measure certain phenomena only and systematically exclude other phenomena as either irrelevant or as safely to be assumed to provide standard conditions for the observations required. The latter demand that the student act in a determinate role (one that can be operationally defined as suited to the task) and that he perform specified operations with certain objects of a material nature and record certain of his observations as information or, more commonly, directly as data. For example, he may observe a gross or obvious change in a metal bar after he subjects it to heat, but his science, already well supplied with such simple information, requires him to record as data certain measurements and his computations from them, accurate to some established degree of tolerance. The physics student's science as a body of knowledge and a manual of operations, provides a matrix for evaluating such data as he collects so that he and his colleagues can quickly decide if the data fit and can also plan further observations to correct them if they do not or to explore their implications if they do indeed represent something new.

The interaction between percept and concept is one of circular reinforcement in all the forms of seeking to know that we call sciences. But it appears to be a more complex process in the social sciences because the situation of observation not only has more parts and processes but also must, especially for purposes of exploring the unknown, be accepted as "natural," something not to be standardized as in the physics laboratory, but rather to be watched as undisturbed as possible. For such sciences as sociology or social anthropology especially, the situation of observation is itself subject to observation and to all the tasks of field work ideally all the way through to full publication of the whole "story."

For any science the situation of observation evidently always has at least four parts: (1) the observer; (2) the phenomena observed; (3) the information sought (more or less loosely defined by the science to be served: the matrix of knowledge which gives the data their place and which indicates the information to be secured as well as the operations for making observations, turning them into data, and for using them as data later on); and (4) the role of the observer.

In the physics laboratory, parts 2 and 3 can be specified in a manual of instruction that might be followed by the expert as well as the student. The observer, as an individual (a "Self," in George H. Mead's sense), adopts the role of a standard observer—thus merging parts 1 and 4—and the situation of observation can be comprehended by paying attention henceforth to parts 2 and 3.

In the social science field-work situation of observation, however, there is lively interaction between all the components given the short la-

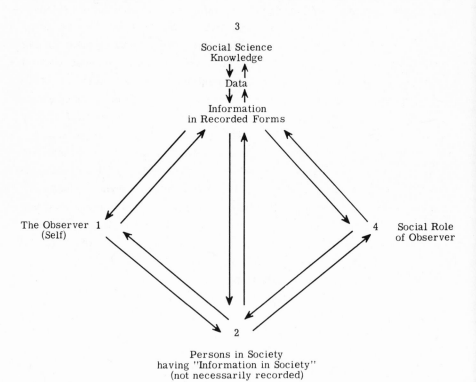

Chart 1. The Field Work Situation of Observation

bels above. With the parts numbers indicated in the foregoing, this situation can be diagramed as in Chart 1. The manifold task of the field worker
includes: (a) learning what information in society is needed for his social
science (3); (b) learning from persons in society (2) what social role as observer will permit him to get from them (by interviews and other observations of behavior) the relevant information in society; (c) accommodating
himself in that role, "getting-in" (into the situation itself), "staying in"
(surviving in his role as observer) and "easing out" (leaving the situation
undamaged and, with himself unhurt, free to report, to turn information into data for a contribution to his social science).

In the chapters which follow, different aspects of the social science
situation of observation are emphasized, one at a time. Chapter ii, "Observing, Recording, and Reporting," as its title indicates, is devoted to illustrating the interconnectedness of the parts in the vertical dimension
leading from 2 up to 3.

II

OBSERVING, RECORDING, AND REPORTING

Field observation for a social science can be as much fun as any other social activity, simply as a matter of pure exercise in sociability. And field work—which adds recording, analyzing, and reporting to the activities of observing—can be as rich in rewards as any other creative effort, as a matter of satisfying intellectual curiosity.

A large proportion of the field worker's time must be devoted to recording. If a piece of field work carried through to completion with a final report published for an appropriate audience takes a total of 600 working hours, it should not be surprising that this may include: 100 hours of observing, 200 hours of recording, 200 hours of analyzing, and 100 hours of reporting (in the sense of finishing a manuscript for publication). But another piece of field work might be so designed that 100 hours of combined observing and recording (such as making check marks in a simple schedule) could be followed by 20 hours of analyzing and 1 hour of reporting (in the sense of writing a very short paper explaining results shown in tables or charts).

For our purposes, however, the first example gives us a useful though very broad rule-of-thumb for timing the four stages of field work: (1) observing, 1/6; (2) recording, 1/3; (3) analyzing, 1/3; and (4) reporting, 1/6 of the total time.

In terms of a forty-hour week—which may sound absurdly short for creative work but may be realistic as a figure for average actual productivity in tasks involving listening attentively and writing carefully—the hypothetical example given covers a total span of fifteen weeks. Since observing and recording, as well as some analyzing, proceed concurrently, and since it is always wise to reserve time for analyzing and reporting, the total period may be divided into eight weeks in the field—allowing the total of 300 hours for observing and recording and allocating 20 hours of analyzing time to spread thinly throughout this period—and seven weeks for the remaining tasks.

The foregoing is not based upon any time study of what creative social scientists actually do. It is possible, and even economically necessary, in many contemporary projects involving field observation, to plan the use of salaried manpower in a bookkeeping context that includes field expenses, overhead, clerical costs, and the like, so that fairly precise limits may be set on the man-hours per task in observing, recording, analyzing, etc. In such a case, time study would very probably provide quite different allocations of field worker time from those we have suggested. This is because I am talking about field inquiry in the situation where either the phenomena are new to the science, or the observer is a learner, new to his task.

Writing a communicable account of a complex event in a social situation requires not only a high degree of literacy but at least some apprehension of the social science purposes for which the record may have its uses. It is a task in the course of which both beginner and professional social scientist, if they were to compare notes, might find that they have more in common than either would suppose. In the one case we see the experienced observer encountering new phenomena and therefore dealing with a social rhetoric that he aims to record in its natural freshness—not as something to be assimilated immediately to a theoretical system which usefully compares analogues but which, if imposed upon the situation of observation, may rob it of the opportunity to reveal something new. In the other case, the task is not greatly different for the beginner who, despite any social science theoretical system to which he has been exposed, has after all not had so many direct experiences with textbook analogues that they threaten to intervene between his recording and his observation or between his perception and the event, but who has, in their place, the handicaps of at least his cultural training to overcome if he is to learn to do field work for a social science.

For expert or student, therefore, the whole point of devoting time to recording is not merely to make sure he will have materials down in black and white upon which to base his final report, but also to insure that he has the opportunity, while in the field or fresh from it, to relate insightful experience to theoretical analysis, percept to concept, back and forth, in a kind of weaving of the fabric of knowledge.

The vertical dimension of the field work situation of observation ranges upward from the phenomena (people, their behavior, their interactions in social situations, their verbalizations, the items of their material culture including graphic records, if any) to information (what the field worker records of his observations) to data (the products of reviewing, reordering, classifying, collating, and otherwise reducing information to forms suited to further analysis and description at a higher level of generalization) to knowledge. The latter is the level at which the field worker seeks ultimately to report—that is, to describe what he has learned, including how he learned it, as having a certain place in an established matrix of what is known, or as suggesting modification of such a matrix, or as being perhaps a discovery fundamental to building a new one.

Each of these steps involves multiple claims, on the part of one or many persons, to have some possession of "scientific truth" or at least a bit of it. If for convenience and simplicity we look at this system of claims as if a single social science field worker were making all of them in one short book or brief oral report, we would have to recognize that his concluding statement, "Therefore we know . . ." is a report at the level of knowledge which rests upon at least three closely interrelated sets of complex activities:

1. Observing.—Collecting information-in-society firsthand by maintaining alert attention, with maximum use of the observer's complement of perceptual abilities and sensitivities, to all the accessible and relevant interpersonal and intrapersonal events going on in the immediate field situation through a period of time.

2. Recording.—Writing an account of the observations that clearly discriminates between (a) what the field worker believes to be a full and fair account of his observations in the situation (including full quotations verbatim as they occurred in interviews or other interactions), and (b) what he now finds, at the moment of recording (preferably as soon as possible after making the observations), worth adding in the way of personal reflections and research interpretations (such things as comments on his own and others' feelings and behavior and comments on how the recorded observations, as "frozen percepts," may relate to the sought-for knowledge about society: the "fluid concepts" that accompany learning a social science or developing it on its frontiers).

3. Analyzing.—Reviewing, indexing, reorganizing, classifying, collating, and otherwise reducing items of information in order to turn them into data, and then submitting the data to further analysis (statistical analysis, if the data are numerical; comparative analysis, if the data are not numbers, but meanings).

The interdependence of these steps, culminating in the fourth one of reporting, is unmistakably important to everyone concerned in the social science enterprise. The fate of the latter, so far as it requires intellectual participation on the part of readers or auditors and writers or lecturers, clearly turns upon correct and adequate communications regarding each step and its interrelations with the others.

It stands to reason that a social scientist's statement at the level of knowledge ought to make sense not simply because it "sounds good" but because it can be demonstrated to have its roots in what persons in society talk about and do. The demonstration that reason calls for consists in showing the interconnections between statements that take the forms: "We

know . . . ," "The analyzed data show . . . ," "The data are items systematically translated from items of information that can be reproduced by entering this kind of situation of observation and performing these operations. . . ." Most of this book is concerned with illustrating the range and
variety of the situations and experiences that characterize the processes
of getting at the roots of knowledge in the social sciences.

A dimension like this one is itself a bit of knowledge about the makings
of a science of society. It suggests that there are at least two viewpoints
that may be opposed, or merged (or, sadly enough, confused), in the pursuit
of social science knowledge: (1) that which emphasizes knowledge, treating
it as a kind of intellectual artifact that exists only in print (as in an encyclopedia) but giving it at least the virtue of such clarity of statement that it
can be analyzed into hypotheses to be tested; (2) that which emphasizes information, treating it as the "inside dope," or the interesting news about
what people are doing and saying, the bits and pieces of what Robert E.
Park called "the Big News" (and thought might be written by the editors of
Fortune), the small voices that may make history in the long run.

The dimension thus suggests alternatives to be chosen or to be bridged,
as in some merger of the two emphases. I advise no final choice, and simply hope that pointing out this variety of tastes will help the reader to sample the fare from one end of the table to the other.

This chapter includes four excerpts from the work of professional social scientists: W. Lloyd Warner, A. R. Radcliffe-Brown, Everett C.
Hughes, and Bronislaw Malinowski.

The first excerpt briefly states the ideal of reporting not merely "results" of social research but also the facts about the research operations
which make the findings meaningful. Since reporting (in a publication, lecture, or otherwise) follows upon the field worker's recording of his observations, and many intervening steps of analysis, this ideal requires continuous observation and careful recording of all the research operations which
succeeded (or failed) in obtaining the information sought in each interview
or other episode in the situation of observation. Unless they are standardized, as in some kinds of interviewing for surveys or opinion polls, the
field worker's operations in each new situation of observation will require
his attention, observation, and recording concurrent with the attention, observation, and recording which he devotes to the more central objects of
study. In this sense, the first excerpt implies that "everything" should be
recorded, so that all the facts about operations that are relevant to making
the results meaningful can ultimately be reported.[1]

1. See Conrad M. Arensberg, "The Community-Study Method," American Journal of Sociology, LX (September, 1954), 109-24, especially the

When we examine possible contributions to knowledge resulting from social science field work, this ideal helps us to establish some guides to critical and independent thinking. "Everything" descriptive of the writer's or speaker's operations is admitted to question, for example:

"Who" was the field worker in the eyes of the people he observed?

What theoretical preoccupations did he take with him into the situation?

What happened throughout the course of the study, both to him and the others, intellectually as well as personally?

"Who" was and is the field worker in his self-conception as well as in the eyes of his present audience?

What analytical operations did he use to turn information into data and to synthesize his data in order to translate them into statements having their proper places in a matrix of knowledge about society?

Questions of this kind help to make more specific and concrete the very general and all too short question, "How do you know?" They do so by dividing the question into particular queries in the form, "How did you learn?"

It is clear that this ideal is logically no different from the rule for rigorous scientific inquiry in any field. Its application in the social sciences, however, discovers complexities that do not so severely hamper the development of knowledge in the physical and biological sciences. For one thing, observers in the latter fields can more easily adopt the role of instruments (as a standard observer, for example) in relations with other instruments and material objects. Even if the latter are living animals, including samples of mankind, they become laboratory specimens in such a situation of observation. But observers in the social sciences must openly play roles as persons who are, only incidentally and more or less covertly, also playing roles as instruments. Since knowledge in the social sciences is relative to the amount and quality of field work done by individuals, "who they are" as persons and "how they work" as instruments will always be questions of critical importance.

Our first excerpt, having set the ideal of recording "everything," is followed by one which recognizes that records are never enough—that the field worker as a human being has the faculty of memory and that even the subliminal sensation may later play its part in what is ultimately represented in full and rich reporting and, what may be more important, in the development of hypotheses that were not carried into the field as part of

---

statement, p. 112, that "...the nature of exploration in vivo is just that one does not prejudice the discovery of relevant factors by premature isolation of particular causes. The job is to establish the priorities of relevance."

the scientist's theoretical apperceptions. The late A. R. Radcliffe-Brown, author of the second excerpt, mentions the field worker's accumulation of "multitudinous impressions" over and beyond what he records which may well, on reflection, serve as his surest guides in his interpretation of the meanings of customs and beliefs that, alien to his audience, remain impenetrably strange and inexplicable even to those who may be experts but who have not encountered the phenomena in question firsthand.

The second excerpt therefore points to the problems of the field worker, and his audience, in evaluating his abilities and perhaps his compensations for disabilities. Memory, especially visual and auditory—and hence the individual's sensory equipment, particularly hearing and eyesight—and his general capacity for controlling himself in concentrating upon the tasks of field work, all these potentialities of the human organism, modified by training and conditioned by experience, go to make up what the field worker can be as an "instrument."

The third excerpt, from a field diary kept by Everett C. Hughes, further corrects the ideal of recording "everything." It is a realistic example that illustrates the value of a field diary which includes recorded observations which may never be reported as results or findings but which are significant details in a "conversation with one's self" in the course of exploring and mapping a new social terrain. Some of these details may be highly important to the field worker in giving an account of his operations later on. The field diary as distinct from the more formal records of interviews and observations which the field worker also makes has a subtle potential advantage in helping to maintain the observer's self-awareness, particularly about phenomena for observation which are either sensitive (matters of fact which the people concerned classify as secret or confidential or otherwise as not public information) or are least likely to be sensed (matters of fact for which the observer may have "blind spots" or a "deaf ear" in his habitual mode of interacting socially). The diary thus permits a private conversation, as if with a scientific and sympathetic colleague, that enables the field worker to bring back from the field a record of his efforts to be responsive, overtly or covertly as was proper, to every stimulus, and it may help him, while in the field, to maintain his poise between being a participant (a person) and an observer (a social scientist with suitable detachment).

The fourth and final excerpt in this chapter is a classic statement of the relevance of discipline in semantics to the conduct of field work and therefore the development of social sciences. From informal notes, as in a field diary, to careful records and final reports, the field worker is dealing chiefly with his and others' attempts to represent reality with words.

Scientific communications are composed of interactions between concept and percept, in endless reciprocation, and there is nothing like first-hand observation to bring this to vivid awareness, especially in one's earliest encounters with knowledge in any field. This may be peculiarly true of the social sciences, for the expert as well as the student, because on their respective frontiers of knowledge, or of knowing, data do not exist at all: there is only what I have called information about phenomena. The latter are to be found in the verbal behavior, the describable conduct, and the material artifacts of human beings in immediate and evanescent social situations. When we begin to classify the latter as contexts, and have otherwise conceptualized the observations we are recording, we are turning information into data. In a sense, we are translating every step of the way, and of all the operations of a science, this is one set on which to keep the sharpest eye. For this, an essential bit of optical equipment is training in semantics.

And this is yet another correction to avoid unlimited acceptance of the ideal of recording "everything": namely, that it is impossible. Malinowski shows that it is necessary, in order to understand a single utterance (a single bit of all the information sought by a field worker), to have or acquire the fullest possible knowledge of its context. The converse of this, in the form of a suggestion for balance in field work between recording "everything" and recording "nothing," would be: Whatever is observed and selected for recording should be clearly described in rich detail, with all statements verbatim and with all conceivable aspects of the context adequately and accurately specified.

Since context is a creature of concept and therefore provides a framework within which to observe phenomena, it should in each instance be subject to careful examination for its conformation and effect as a set of "blinders" defining the observer's field of view. Here too, the discipline of semantics can provide useful ways of thinking about social science at the higher levels of generalization which are called theory and which aim to articulate information, gained through recording observations, data, compiled from information and analyzed to produce classifications and meaningful relations, and knowledge, achieved through comprehension of all the levels of generalization and of their precise interconnections.

The Ideal of Recording "Everything" and "Reasons
for a Report on Research Operations"

W. Lloyd Warner once said in a lecture:

The conceptual schemes the individual social anthropologist ideates, the methods he uses, the materials he collects, depend largely upon his interests, but as a field man he knows he cannot ordinarily confine his attention to but one aspect of the primitive social world he is viewing. Ideally speaking, he must study every variety of social behavior found in the group. He must report, not only on the economic practices of the group, but must describe and interpret the religious behavior, the family life, the system of law, et cetera, and, in all, see the social behavior as an entirety. Students of special fields may later examine the cumulated results to their special ends, or the society may be viewed with attention focussed on a particular institution, but the field man's first duty is to gather material which covers the entire behavior of the group and the individuals in it.[2]

In the following excerpt,[3] Professor Warner prefaces an extensive description of the "Yankee City" research with some reflections on the special requirements of social science reporting. Like the other excerpts from studies based upon field work which are included in this book, it is intended to make a point or two and by no means to represent the entire work.

Research reports of social scientists usually present no more than brief summaries of their methods and even less of the theoretical assumptions and postulates which governed (1) the selection of their specific field of investigation, (2) the choice of facts collected, and (3) the ordering and classification of data during analysis and synthesis. Most reports tend to emphasize what are called results which, on the whole, are made up of facts, ordered and classified with no mention of how they were gathered. These "facts" and their classifications are but the momentary end result of a long sequence of activity. That is to say, they are but expressions of what the researcher was doing, thinking, and observing when he constructed his report. Thus had he presented it earlier, the "results" would have been what he was observing, thinking, and doing at that moment in time; or had he postponed it until later and continued his labors, they would have been, in general terms, much the same, except for his knowing that implicit within his last report was the state of his knowledge at a previous date.

The research which presents "facts" and "results" alone is too frequently based on the assumption that what is being said is only an explicit statement of the more exact movements of the world outside the operator. Actually, such an account is also an implicit statement of the changes taking place in the thinking and other activities of the researcher. Results ideally not only give a more exact measurement of a piece of reality under examination (and sometimes a firmer conviction that we know more about what we are looking at) but also tell how all or part of the conceptual framework, which was a fundamental part of the original research apparatus, has undergone modification during subsequent activities.

Many scientific social researches are notoriously guilty of beginning as if no other work had been done in the field. Other weaknesses in the methods of the social researcher are due to his not stating (1) what fundamental assumptions he started with, (2) what techniques he used, and (3) what changes his ideas and methods underwent as he learned more about his subject. Research is fundamentally a learning process for the scientist who does it; if what he learns is to be successfully transmitted to others, he must be able to communicate how and why he did it. Those who understand are then able to test his methods and conclusions by repeating what he did.

---

2. W. Lloyd Warner, "Contemporary Social Anthropology," a lecture given before the Division of Social Sciences, University of Chicago, December 8, 1936.

3. W. Lloyd Warner and Paul S. Lunt, The Social Life of a Modern Community (New Haven: Yale University Press, 1941), pp. 5-7. Volume I of the "Yankee City Series."

Criticisms of the conclusions arrived at by different techniques and methods have often resulted in confusion rather than in clarifying our knowledge of society. Results are meaningful only when operations are known, and to know the operations the critic must be acquainted with not only what was being done at the end of a research but also what took place from the beginning to the end. Hence our report will not only embody what we found out about Yankee City, but also attempt to describe what we were thinking and doing during various stages of our work.

To perform the task before us, we will briefly present the outlines of the community investigated, give the general theoretical point of view which guided the field operations, present the field and later analytical operations, and, finally, state the ideas and methods which were used when we began writing and closed the present research. Although the other volumes will present our results and conclusions, it will at times be necessary to review here certain of our findings in order that we may trace for the reader the development of our ideas.

The Importance of "Multitudinous Impressions"

The main point of the following brief excerpt[4] from a famous monograph on a very simple society is to call attention to the impossibility of obtaining an "exact and detailed" description of "everything" that goes on, even in the relatively uncomplicated social life of the Andamanese in the days before World War I; hence the importance of "multitudinous impressions" obtained by the field worker in his firsthand observations and especially their relevance to interpretation (theoretical formulation).

It is often urged that in ethnology description and interpretation should be most carefully separated. So far as this means that the facts observed by the ethnologist should be recorded free from all bias of interpretation, the necessity cannot be too often or too strongly urged. If, however, it is meant to imply that efforts at interpretation are to be excluded from works of descriptive ethnology, there is much to be said against such an opinion. In trying to interpret the institutions of a primitive society the field ethnologist has a great advantage over those who know the facts only at secondhand. However exact and detailed the description of a primitive people may be, there remains much that cannot be put into such a description. Living, as he must, in daily contact with the people he is studying, the field ethnologist comes gradually to "understand" them, if we may use the term. He acquires a series of multitudinous impressions, each slight and often vague, that guide him in his dealings with them. The better the observer the more accurate will be his general impression of the mental peculiarities of the race. This general impression it is impossible to analyse, and so to record and convey to others. Yet it may be of the greatest service when it comes to interpreting the beliefs and practices of a primitive society. If it does not give any positive aid towards a correct interpretation, it at least prevents errors into which it is only too easy for those to fall who have not the same immediate knowledge of the people and their ways. Indeed it may be urged, with some reason, that attempts to interpret the beliefs of savages without any first-hand knowledge of the people whose beliefs are in question, are at the best unsatisfactory and open to many possibilities of error.

The present position of ethnological studies may well be regarded as

---

4. A. R. Radcliffe-Brown, The Andaman Islanders (Glencoe, Ill.: Free Press, 1948), pp. 230-32 in chapter v, "The Interpretation of Andamanese Customs and Beliefs: Ceremonial."

anomalous. Many of the observers engaged in recording the customs of primitive people are very imperfectly acquainted with modern theories of sociology. One result of this is that they often neglect to record anything concerning the matters that are of fundamental importance for the theorist.* On the other hand those engaged in elaborating hypotheses do not, as a rule, observe for themselves the facts to be explained, but have to rely on what are in many cases imperfect documents, being thus unwittingly led into errors that might have been avoided. In this science, as in others, if progress is to be made, the elaboration of hypotheses and the observation and classification of facts must be carried on as interdependent parts of one process, and no advantage, but rather great disadvantage, results from the false division of labour whereby theorists and observers work independently and without systematic cooperation. The most urgent need of ethnology at the present time is a series of investigations of the kind here attempted, in which the observation and the analysis and interpretation of the institutions of some one primitive people are carried on together by the ethnologist working in the field.

It is clear that such studies need to be based on a scientific and carefully elaborated method. Unfortunately ethnologists are not yet agreed as to the methods of their science. The question of method is therefore, at the present time, of the greatest importance, and for this reason I have tried, in the present chapter, to present the argument in such a way that the various steps of the analysis shall be immediately apparent, so that the reader may be able not only to judge the value of the conclusions, but also to form a clear idea of the psychological methods by which they are reached.

Radcliffe-Brown explains his "working hypothesis" in connection with his problem of interpreting Andamanese ceremonial customs and beliefs[5] as follows:

Stated as briefly as possible the working hypothesis here adopted is as follows: (1) A society depends for its existence on the presence in the minds of its members of a certain system of sentiments† by which the conduct of the individual is regulated in conformity with the needs of the society. (2) Every feature of the social system itself and every event or object that in any way affects the well-being or the cohesion of the society becomes an object of this system of sentiments. (3) In human society the sentiments in question are not innate but are developed in the individual by the action of the society upon him. (4) The ceremonial customs of a society are a means by which the sentiments in question are given collective expression on appropriate occasions. (5) The ceremonial (i.e., collective) expression of any sentiment serves both to maintain it at the requisite degree of intensity in the mind of the individual and to transmit it from one generation to another. Without such expression the sentiments involved could not exist.

Using the term "social function" to denote the effects of an institution

---

*It may be worth while to mention that the interpretation of Andamanese customs given in this chapter was not worked out until after I had left the islands. Had it been otherwise I should have made careful enquiries into subjects which, as it was, escaped my notice.

5. Ibid., pp. 233-34. See also pp. 234-35 for "a few rules of method," the first of which points to a field work "must": "In explaining any given custom it is necessary to take into account the explanation given by the natives themselves." Also, of course, the student of field work will want to read all of chapters v and vi for the further development and application of this method.

†Sentiment,—an organized system of emotional tendencies centered about some subject.

(custom or belief) in so far as they concern the society and its solidarity or cohesion, the hypothesis of this chapter may be more briefly resumed in the statement that the social function of the ceremonial customs of the Andaman Islanders is to maintain and to transmit from one generation to another the emotional disposition on which the society (as it is constituted) depends for its existence.

The Uses of a Field Diary

In the phase of field work called "getting in," especially obtaining those first bits of information-in-society so important to learning more, a scientific rationale calls for keeping a field diary, "in the mood of an ethnologist," as Everett C. Hughes put it in recommending this procedure to beginning students in his field work courses.

A field diary might well be the field worker's repository for "all" his observations. Or it might be a journal of his attempts to "observe everything," a kind of record to prove to himself that it is impossible "to record everything observed." Perhaps its main value is to the field worker himself—as a way of reporting to himself his efforts to maintain a balance between systematic observation (recording data selected in advance, according to logical controls) and flexible observation (maintaining sensitivity to record observations of both "the obvious" and "the unexpected"; phenomena of any sort whatever which turn out to be significant, though not so conceived in advance).

The following extract from Professor Hughes's field diary is called a "Reconnaissance," and it points to the importance of beginning the field diary at the very outset of field work—even the stages preceding the selection of the site and especially the stages of getting oriented at the site: locating sources of information and making the initial contacts. This selection should be read in connection with Professor Hughes's book, French Canada in Transition.

Saturday, July 11, 1936 (first trip to Cantonville)
Emma drove us to Cantonville. St. Bernard we merely passed through. It is an old-looking town with well-kept houses and gardens along the river, and many religious establishments, some of red brick and others, newer, of stone, without much care to make the architecture match. Even from the outskirts Cantonville looks quite different. There are more lots for sale and more cheap new houses. Going through the town up toward the XYZ Plant, one can see a small new stone United Church. The whole end of town near the XYZ Plant and south along the river is new. Save for a couple of streets of "Staff Houses" owned by the company, nothing is planned or ordered. These two streets have good brick houses, trees and shrubbery, and there is a company recreation house and tennis courts. A sign at the end of the streets says "Private Property—Staff Houses" and threatens trespassers with a fine of ten dollars. I learned from Norton, an engineer, that the company has agreed with the town to build no more houses of its own. Also that the company property is, by agreement, free of taxes until next year.

The other streets are built up with houses and tenements of all sorts. Near the river and in some of the adjoining streets are rather nice houses in which members of the staff live. But nearby and sometimes in the same streets are three-story tenements of concrete blocks, brick, or wood, and houses of wood, square as boxes. Some lots even have an extra house in the back yard. There are apparently no building restrictions. Houses seem to be scarce and rents high, relatively.

There are many of these new cheap tenements between the plant and the older part of town, and new work is being done on sidewalks and streets. Water, electricity, and sewers have been extended to the newer districts only recently.

On the main street near the river, leading down into town are many beauty shops, etc., of a cheap sort. On one house was a sign, "Tireuse heureuse des cartes," and "Horoscopes à la main." It would be interesting to know the origin of the people who run these new small businesses, evidently established for the mill-worker trade, and their relation to the older business people of the town.

At the brow of the hill, below which lies the old business district, stands the old Protestant Church with a graveyard full of old-fashioned stones. The names are all English—Perkins was prominent, also Stuart. These were probably the original settlers' families. (The town was founded by English about 1812.) The fate of the old families ought to be looked into; they are not much in evidence now.

The business district lies below the little hill and seems small for a town of the size. The buildings do not look particularly old. One of them is a three-story building with flats on the upper floors, dated 1928.

At a barber shop I inquired for the mayor. He is M. Millet, who runs a hardware store. Since it was Saturday, he was rather busy, but he talked to me for a little while. He figures that there are 17,000 people in the district —including Cantonville and suburban parishes. The latter are adjoining villages, one at least having been only recently formed. I understood that each of these was a new Catholic parish. There are, he said, too many people coming to look for work. The city and district are now larger than St. Bernard. Before the mill came, there were but two hardware stores; one run by him and another in the upper town run by his cousin. Now there are seven: too many. There is, as before, but one movie.

There are practically no English farmers in the district; some about ten miles south in another community. The old English names in the town were Burns, Perkins, Stuart, etc. The city engineer is Lussier.

The secretary is Tremblay, a lawyer, who is running for the legislature on the Union Nationale ticket. He would have all the information about licenses for business, the number of building permits, etc.

The curé is M. Lachance. He makes an annual house-to-house census of the town and can therefore give the best information about the population.

In looking for a camp, we visited the police station and saw the Chief, who is a champion weight lifter. He was said to own a summer camp, but he had got rid of it. We went to it anyway, on the river about two miles south of the town. It was a colony of cottages in the woods, rented to the French people of the town by the week or month. There was none available for the week end. The man in charge said he had a son working in the XYZ Plant; he made no progress and, after four years, was earning $18 a week for day work and $22 in the weeks when he worked nights. The girls, he said, get the better pay, from $20 to $30 a week (sic). The whole town depends on the XYZ now, as the other factories are not working much. People are coming in from all over to look for work, so that there are now 4,000 unemployed (sic). Families come in trucks with their furniture, from the U.S. and from all over Quebec.

We camped on the other side of the river north of the town on the land of M. Beauchamp, who owns a hotel, the biggest garage, and this camp. His daughter runs a florist's shop. The camp is a wooded strip along the river with cottages for rent. They were all full, but M. Beauchamp gave us permission to camp under the pines at the lower end of his land. The Beauchamp family live, apparently for the summer only, in a very nice cottage

with screened porch, fireplace, etc. M. Beauchamp is a well-dressed busi-
nessman with a gracious manner (a hotel keeper) and speaks English well.
His wife speaks scarcely any English. She is a well-bred French lady.
There were a number of young people about the house. Beauchamp is apparently one of the leading businessmen of the town.

Sunday, July 12, 1936

On Sunday morning three small boys came walking by our camp and
stopped to talk and see our air mattresses. They were ten, twelve, and
thirteen. The two younger were brothers, born in New England, and brought
back here six years ago; they spoke no English. The younger one goes to
school to the "sisters"; the older, proudly, to the "brothers." He, the older,
learns singing at school and sings in the choir at the eight o'clock mass for
children. No, there are no men or women in the choir; only the boys and
the "brothers." There is, they said, a mass at 9:45 for the English. And a
"grandemesse" at eleven for the men. The thirteen-year-old's father was
blinded by "rougeole" some years ago; he now sells bluing from door to
door. An older brother is married and lives in the states. There are nine
children at home, of whom only one, aged ten, works. He works at Burnet's
and gets $6, $7, or if "chanceux" even $8 a week (five days).

Afternoon on Sunday quite a crowd of town people came swimming and
picnicking near us although the water was only about three feet deep below
the dam. Later on we visited the Nortons and were taken for a drive up the
river on the side opposite the town. At various places there were crowds
of French people swimming and picnicking. The French picnic does not
seem to be quite the same thing as the English or American. There is less
of cooking food on the beach and more pop. It is apparent that the Cantonville mill people have changed the general character of the country a good
deal. Norton took us to the golf course, the old Duff Estate; he says both
English and French people belong to the club. When French and English are
together, French is spoken.

Norton said there is an agreement that the XYZ Company will not hire
a person who has not a card from the city showing he is a resident, unless
it be for some special trained work, in which case someone would be
brought in. The wages are higher than in other mills in the province—but
this rule keeps down the number of people who would flood the town otherwise and increase the relief rolls.

As near as I can see there are the following categories of people in the
town:

1. The remnants of the old English families. I understand there is a
Perkins running a garage, but most of the businesses are French.

2. The French "town"—business people and others of pre-mill days.
The town administration seems to be of this group.

3. The mill "staff," English and Canadian engineers, white-collar people, etc. I gather the old-country and Canadians are socially rather separate.

4. The French mill workers.

The relations between these groups constitute a main part of the problem for study of community morale, social organization, etc.

Tuesday, July 21, 1936

Came to Cantonville by the train from Montreal, arriving at 2:45 P.M.
Took a taxi to Manoir Canton and got a room at $1.50. Walked around the
town, down MacDonald Street to its end, then over to Tussaud Street, and
back to post office. This is the older part of the town. On MacDonald Street
just below the church are a few big houses of doctors, etc., all French.
Then some small businesses, and poorer houses with rooms for rent. The
end of the street is again better, as is the lower end of Tussaud Street
abutting on the Duff Estate (now the golf club). Then walked up Tussaud
Street through the business district. Noted Perlman's store, apparently a
new Jewish business, a Woolworth Store, and other businesses. Walked on

up the street across the CNR tracks. Some distance beyond that are a number of old-style French houses, some small businesses, and many children. The women are well-dressed in summer clothes. In the park and on the corners are a good many men loafing. They are not so well-dressed. They are mostly in shirt sleeves and wear no neckties. Walked over a block or two from the river to Cleary Street, which has a number of new buildings and businesses. It is clear that the town, save for the few old houses mentioned, used to stop at the CNR.

Inquired the way to the office of La Semaine, the weekly newspaper. Found that it is no longer run by M. Jean, but by a M. Trudeau and a M. La Rue. Met M. Trudeau and told him something of what I am about. He gave me a directory of the city, put out by La Semaine. He also offered to run an ad for a family with whom I might take a pension. Like most of the businessmen in a small town, he thought I could get all the pertinent information just by a few parish statistics and reading the directory.

Then went to the office of M. Lussier, city engineer. He gave me a map of the city and the population as taken by the parish for a number of years. There are but two municipalities in the Canton de Burke: Cantonville and St. Lucien. There are other settlements not yet incorporated separately. There is a movement to create a municipality of Burke West to include the settlements not in the town or in St. Lucien thus to separate these settlements from the rural part of the township. St. Lucien has about 4,000 people, but no sewers or water. People from there smell, and St. Lucien smells, said M. Lussier. The land on which the XYZ Plant is built was incorporated with Cantonville when the company came here.

In regard to businesses, M. Tremblay would have the records. Anyone who has been here more than ten years is an old-timer. A few have been in business longer, but not many. The old business street was Tussaud, but now business is going to Cleary Street, on the other side of the CNR tracks toward the XYZ Plant. St. Lucien has only a few grocery stores and the like.

M. Lussier is a graduate of L'Université Laval, the polytechnical school. He suggested that I see the curé, M. Lachance, for population details. He says everything is full of politics just now. After a while he reverted to French and was apologetic about not having an hôtel de ville in the town. M. Millet, the mayor, mentioned this too, when I first met him. M. Lussier told a story of a boy here who was asked where to find the hôtel de ville. The boy answered, "L'hôtel de ville. Qu'est-ce que ça, l'hôtel de ville? Voila l'hôtel Manoir."

M. Lussier said that a new parish has just been established for St. Lucien.

Wednesday, July 22, 1936

About 10 A.M. I called on M. Lachance, curé of the parish. After the first passage at arms, he maintained that his English was worse than my French, so the conversation proceeded in French. I explained my mission, and he was very cordial. He suggested that M. Tremblay and M. Beauchamp knew a great deal more about the part of the town than did he and that I see them. He also suggested seeing the head of the labor department of the XYZ Plant.

"There are no classes in Cantonville. To be sure the better families do not descend into the taudis, but there are no aristocrats. For instance, M. Mercier's daughters [?] work in the office of one of the factories." (Not quite sure here of the families concerned in each case. Hence be careful of quoting.) "M. Mercier himself had an English mother. One of his daughters married an English Protestant, another an English Catholic. Same is true of other families. One of M. Beauchamp's daughters sells flowers in a little kiosque; one goes to the Marguerite Bourgeois College at Montreal. Two are réligieuse. Every year I have four or five marriages of daughters of French people to English men, especially in the white-collar class. The daughters of local businessmen work in the offices of the factories. [How do you account for these marriages?] There is a feeling, and with some reason, among the French that they must use English to get any advancement in the industries. Hence, the ambitious families send their sons to convent in Sherbrooke and Coaticook, etc., where there is a great deal of English spoken. Naturally, in such families, especially if there is a mixed marriage, the language tends to become English.

"They have been making silk in Cantonville only about ten years. Naturally the companies brought in English or American help to start the work, because they knew the processes. Also, the capital was foreign, and it was but natural that the owners should hire for the better jobs their own relatives and friends. That will no doubt continue for a generation.

"When the shirt company came here, they looked for a bilingual manager and hired a young man, but it soon became evident that he did not suit the job. So they brought in an English manager. Perfect bilinguals are bien rare. They found that most of the French people spoke some English but not enough to deal with department heads and with the outside officials and customers of the company. Besides, the local people did not know the silk business. Hence, the office and managerial positions were in the hands of English. But when this shirt company moved to Toronto some years later, the staff was entirely French, even the manager. [?] They took the French staff with them, and when later they started a factory in Australia, they took a French-Canadian staff way out there to start it.

"In the silk factories primarily young people are hired. It is not a question of métier. Many came directly from the land. The oldest son stays on the land, and the second son must go to the industrial centers to find work. I had 120 [?] marriages last year and 500 [?] baptisms. There are about equal numbers of garçons and filles. Some arrive here after having been in other industrial centers, say Shawinigan, Three Rivers, etc. The records show the place of baptism and marriage.

"You can take a record of these movements here whenever you like. There are about 1,800 families and a card for each.

"One reason why the French gradually replace the English in various positions is that they can pay the French about half the salary. They are new to industry and do not expect so much. So maybe in a generation the French will be in all the positions.

"The XYZ Plant brought in a considerable staff from England, and they are a very good class of people. They mix with the French families somewhat. [?]

"There have been two new parishes established just now, St. Lucien and St. Mathieu, with about 5,000 people altogether.

"Bouvard also has two daughters who work in the offices of the factories." [Note: My guess is that these girls of the better families work in the factories as stenographers, etc., and there meet the only young men whose future looks rosy enough to make them good marriage prospects, and they are English. M. Lachance's statement that there are no classes does not then mean that there are no social distinctions, but simply that the social distinctions have quickly adapted themselves to the new conditions under which position is determined by one's place in industry. This means that temporarily the upper-class French girl and the English white-collar men are on the same level and therefore thrown together. It may not be so in a generation or even less.]

M. Lachance also mentioned that the crise has brought a lot of people here to look for jobs. He is a very interesting and intelligent man, and apparently sees clearly what is going on.

Thursday, July 23, 1936
After copying some notes, I went to the presbytere and spent the morning copying data from the recensement of the parish as read to me by a boy priest. We did something more than a third of the cards. Data noted: age and birthplace of husband and wife, place of marriage, number and ages of children living at home and their places of birth, other members of the

household. M. Lachance suggested that I persuade the people who make the city directory to ask a few questions regarding origins, etc., when they are making their rounds to get their material. A good idea, and I shall try it. After talking with the people here, and sitting for hours copying data about families which are practically all French, it seems natural that they should lump all outsiders together in the phrase "strangers." The young priest speaks very little English and says there is but little opportunity or occasion to do so. I return tomorrow to continue the copying.

The only interlude came after lunch. In front of the post office a crowd of boys and young bucks, led by a handsome Pit'noire were kidding what looked like the village idiot. The latter was a sorry but good-natured looking specimen in overalls, old coat, and felt hat. All his back teeth were gone, and his front teeth were unduly long. He grinned a grin like Fernandel in Le Rosier de Mme. Husson. The chief kidder kept up a line, "Come on, sing and yodel a little for us. We'll take up a collection for you, and maybe I'll get you a job. I'll see President Roosevelt and the King of Spain tonight about it. Hey you, over there, stop laughing or I'll string you up to that tree." Finally the Dorftrottel sang and yodeled and cut a few capers. The collection was taken up and delivered; perhaps fifteen cents. Then the chief kidder tried to get a good-bye song out of him. The Trottel replied that if he did "just one more" then they would want "just one more" again and again. But after while he did "just one more." The conversation for some reason went on in English, but the songs were French. The chief kidder was one of the husky, dark ones, with open shirt, sleek hair, but a two-day growth of black whiskers. I begin to think the whiskers are cultivated a little as a sign of something. Shaving is only for keeping company with the girls.

Semantics and Field Work

A knowledge of semantics can be so broadly useful to the scientist and can be so richly applied to social science field work that it may be assumed that every field worker acquires it, either in formal instruction or in his own self-educating enterprise. As Pauline V. Young has noted, "Continued emphasis on semantics (the study of meanings of words and their effects upon the human system) may in due time sensitize writers and social scientists to careful use of words, but at present 'the tragedy of words' is well-nigh universal."[6] For an elementary discussion of the misuses of the English language, Miss Young suggests Stuart Chase, Tyranny of Words, for a particularly excellent treatment of the uses of language, S. I. Hayakawa, Language in Action, and for more fundamental discussions of semantics, C. K. Ogden and I. A. Richards, The Meaning of Meaning, and Alfred Korzybski, Science and Sanity.

On the chance, however, that semantics may come to be regarded as "out of fashion" or that acquaintance with semantics may become taken for granted, the following extract,[7] in which Bronislaw Malinowski deals with

6. Scientific Social Surveys and Research (2d ed.; New York: Prentice-Hall, Inc.), p. 234.

7. Bronislaw Malinowski, in Ogden and Richards, The Meaning of Meaning (3d rev. ed.; New York: Harcourt, Brace & Co., 1930), pp. 300-305.

a situation involving primitive language, is given. The rest of his article, and the entire book in which it appears, points to the necessities of using a knowledge of semantics in any field situation, especially those of greater social complexity such as the field worker encounters in his own society. For an American in a North American community, the language may be English, but he will surely be dealing with a variety of social rhetorics (manners of speech that vary according to the roles played by a speaker).

This general statement of the linguistic difficulties which beset an Ethnographer in his field-work, must be illustrated by a concrete example. Imagine yourself suddenly transported on to a coral atoll in the Pacific, sitting in a circle of natives and listening to their conversation. Let us assume further that there is an ideal interpreter at hand, who, as far as possible, can convey the meaning of each utterance, word for word, so that the listener is in possession of all the linguistic data available. Would that make you understand the conversation or even a single utterance? Certainly not.

Let us have a look at such a text, an actual utterance taken down from a conversation of natives in the Trobriand Islands, N. E. New Guinea. In analyzing it, we shall see quite plainly how helpless one is in attempting to open up the meaning of a statement by mere linguistic means; and we shall also be able to realize what sort of additional knowledge, besides verbal equivalence, is necessary in order to make the utterance significant.

I adduce a statement in native, giving under each word its nearest English equivalent:

Tasakaulo		kaymatana			yakida;
We run		front-wood			ourselves;
tawoulo		ovanu;		tasivila	tagine
we paddle		in place;		we turn	we see
soda;		isakaulo			ka'u'uya
companion ours;		he runs			rear-wood
oluvieki		similaveta			Pilolu
behind		their sea-arm			Pilolu

The verbatim English translation of this utterance sounds at first like a riddle or a meaningless jumble of words; certainly not like a significant, unambiguous statement. Now if the listener, whom we suppose acquainted with the language, but unacquainted with the culture of the natives, were to understand even the general trend of this statement, he would have first to be informed about the situation in which these words were spoken. He would need to have them placed in their proper setting of native culture. In this case, the utterance refers to an episode in an overseas trading expedition of these natives, in which several canoes take part in a competitive spirit. This last-mentioned feature explains also the emotional nature of the utterance: it is not a mere statement of fact, but a boast, a piece of self-glorification, extremely characteristic of the Trobrianders' culture in general and of their ceremonial barter in particular.

Only after a preliminary instruction is it possible to gain some idea of such technical terms of boasting and emulation as kaymatana (front-wood) and ka'u'uya (rear-wood). The metaphorical use of wood for canoe would lead us into another field of language psychology, but for the present it is enough to emphasize that "front" or "leading canoe" and "rear canoe" are important terms for a people whose attention is so highly occupied with competitive activities for their own sake. To the meaning of such words is added a specific emotional tinge, comprehensible only against the background of their tribal psychology in ceremonial life, commerce and enterprise.

Again, the sentence where the leading sailors are described as looking back and perceiving their companions lagging behind on the sea-arm of Pilolu, would require a special discussion of the geographical feeling of the natives, of their use of imagery as a linguistic instrument and of a special use of the possessive pronoun (their sea-arm Pilolu).

All this shows the wide and complex considerations into which we are led by an attempt to give an adequate analysis of meaning. Instead of translating, of inserting simply an English word for a native one, we are faced by a long and not altogether simple process of describing wide fields of custom, of social psychology and of tribal organization which correspond to one term or another. We see that linguistic analysis inevitably leads us into the study of all the subjects covered by Ethnographic field-work.

Of course the above given comments on the specific terms (front-wood, rear-wood, their sea-arm Pilolu) are necessarily short and sketchy. But I have on purpose chosen an utterance which corresponds to a set of customs, already described quite fully.* The reader of that description will be able to understand thoroughly the adduced text, as well as appreciate the present argument.

Besides the difficulties encountered in the translation of single words, difficulties which lead directly into descriptive Ethnography, there are others, associated with more exclusively linguistic problems, which however can be solved only on the basis of psychological analysis. Thus it has been suggested that characteristically Oceanic distinction of inclusive and exclusive pronouns requires a deeper explanation than any which would confine itself to merely grammatical relations.† Again, the puzzling manner in which some of the obviously correlated sentences are joined in our text by mere juxtaposition would require much more than a simple reference, if all its importance and significance had to be brought out. Those two features are well known and have been often discussed, though according to my ideas not quite exhaustively.

There are, however, certain peculiarities of primitive languages, almost entirely neglected by grammarians, yet opening up very interesting questions of savage psychology. I shall illustrate this by a point, lying on the borderland between grammar and lexicography and well exemplified in the utterance quoted.

In the highly developed Indo-European languages, a sharp distinction can be drawn between the grammatical and lexical function of words. The meaning of a root of a word can be isolated from the modification of meaning due to accidence or some other grammatical means of determination. Thus in the word run we distinguish between the meaning of the root—rapid personal displacement—and the modification as to time, tense, definiteness, etc., expressed by the grammatical form, in which the word is found in the given context. But in native languages the distinction is by no means so clear and the functions of grammar and radical meaning respectively are often confused in a remarkable manner.

In the Melanesian languages there exist certain grammatical instruments, used in the flection of verbs, which express somewhat vaguely relations of time, definiteness and sequence. The most obvious and easy thing to do for a European who wishes to use roughly such a language for practical purposes, is to find out what is the nearest approach to those Melanesian forms in our languages and then to use the savage form in the European manner. In the Trobriand language, for instance, from which we have taken our above example, there is an adverbial particle boge, which, put

*See Argonauts of the Western Pacific—An account of Native Enterprise and Adventure in the Archipelagoes of Melanesian New Guinea, 1922.

†See the important Presidential Address by the late Dr. W. H. R. Rivers in the Journal of the Royal Anthropological Institute, III (January-June, 1922), 21, and his History of Melanesian Society, II, 486.

before a modified verb, gives it, in a somewhat vague manner, the meaning either of a past or of a definite happening. The verb is moreover modified by a change in the prefixed personal pronoun. Thus the root ma (come, move hither) if used with the prefixed pronoun of the third singular i—has the form ima and means (roughly), he comes. With the modified pronoun ay —or, more emphatical, lay—it means (roughly) he came or he has come. The expression boge ayna or boge layma can be approximately translated by he has already come, the participle boge making it more definite.

But this equivalence is only approximate, suitable for some practical purposes, such as trading with the natives, missionary preaching and translation of Christian literature into native languages. This last cannot, in my opinion, be carried out with any degree of accuracy. In the grammars and interpretations of Melanesian languages, almost all of which have been written by missionaries for practical purposes, the grammatical modifications of verbs have been simply set down as equivalent to Indo-European tenses. When I first began to use the Trobriand language in my field-work, I was quite unaware that there might be some snares in taking savage grammar at its face value and followed the missionary way of using native inflection.

I had soon to learn, however, that this was not correct and I learnt it by means of a practical mistake, which interfered slightly with my fieldwork and forced me to grasp native flection at the cost of my personal comfort. At one time I was engaged in making observations on a very interesting transaction which took place in a lagoon village of the Trobriands between the coastal fishermen and the inland gardeners.* I had to follow some important preparations in the village and yet I did not want to miss the arrival of the canoes on the beach. I was busy registering and photographing the proceedings among the huts when word went round, "they have come already"—boge laymayse. I left my work in the village unfinished to rush some quarter of a mile to the shore, in order to find, to my disappointment and mortification, the canoes far away, punting slowly towards the beach! Thus I came some ten minutes too soon, just enough to make me lose my opportunities in the village!

It required some time and a much better general grasp of the language before I came to understand the nature of my mistake and the proper use of words and forms to express the subtleties of temporal sequence. Thus the root ma which means come, move hither, does not contain the meaning, covered by our word arrive. The form boge laymayse, which I heard that memorable morning in the lagoon village, means to a native "they have already been moving hither" and not "they have already come."

In order to achieve the spatial and temporal definition which we obtain by using the past definite tense, the natives have recourse to certain concrete and specific expressions. Thus in the case quoted, the villagers, in order to convey the fact that the canoes had arrived, would have used the word to anchor, to moor. "They have already moored their canoes," boge aykotasi, would have meant, what I assumed they had expressed by boge laymayse. That is, in this case the natives use a different root instead of a mere grammatical modification.

Returning to our text, we have another telling example of the characteristics under discussion. The quaint expression "we paddle in place" can only be properly understood by realizing that the word paddle has here the function, not of describing what the crew are doing, but of indicating their immediate proximity to the village of their destination. Exactly as in the previous example the past tense of the word to come ("they have come") which we would have used in our language to convey the fact of arrival, has another meaning in native and has to be replaced by another root which ex-

---

*It was a ceremony of the Wasi, a form of exchange of vegetable food for fish. See Argonauts of the Western Pacific, pp. 187-89 and Plate XXXVI.

presses the idea; so here the native root wa, to move thither, could not have been used in (approximately) past definite tense to convey the meaning of "arrive there" but a special root expressing the concrete act of paddling is used to mark the spatial and temporal relations of the leading canoe to the others. The origin of this imagery is obvious. Whenever the natives arrive near the shore of one of the overseas villages, they have to fold the sail and to use the paddles, since there the water is deep, even quite close to the shore, and punting impossible. So "to paddle" means "to arrive at the overseas village." It may be added that in this expression "we paddle in place," the two remaining words in and place would have to be retranslated in a free English interpretation by near the village.

With the help of such an analysis as the one just given, this or any other savage utterance can be made comprehensible. In this case we may sum up our results and embody them in a free commentary or paraphrase of the statement:

A number of natives sit together. One of them, who has just come back from an overseas expedition, gives an account of the sailing and boasts about the superiority of his canoe. He tells his audience how, in crossing the sea-arm of Pilolu (between the Trobriands and the Amphletts), his canoe sailed ahead of all others. When nearing their destination, the leading sailors looked back and saw their comrades far behind, still on the sea-arm of Pilolu.

Put in these terms, the utterance can at least be understood broadly, though for an exact appreciation of the shades and details of meaning a full knowledge of the native customs and psychology, as well as of the general structure of their language, is indispensable.

It is hardly necessary perhaps to point out that all I have said in this section is only an illustration on a concrete example of the general principles so brilliantly set forth by Ogden and Richards in Chapters I, III and IV of their work. What I have tried to make clear by analysis of a primitive linguistic text is that language is essentially rooted in the reality of the culture, the tribal life and customs of a people, and that it cannot be explained without constant reference to these broader contexts of verbal utterance. The theories embodied in Ogden's and Richard's diagram of Chapter I, in their treatment of the "sign-situation" (Chapter III) and in their analysis of perception (Chapter IV) cover and generalize all the details of any example.

III

THE FIELD WORK SITUATION: SOCIAL
ROLES FOR OBSERVATION

Field workers have not published very much regarding the basic processes of field work as they have experienced them, not even much about the dimension which relates the observer to the situation through the social role he plays, whatever it may be from episode to episode in his inquiry. Despite their apparent reticence, or perhaps their bowing to space limitations in publications emphasizing "results," what is available in print and what can be learned in "shop talk" with field workers strongly suggests that a few major themes run through the field experiences of all social scientists, beginners as well as experts.[1] When viewed as a social process, the single interview, especially if it continues for more than a few minutes (is more than a traffic survey stopping motorists to ask starting points, destinations, etc.), reveals many analogies to the full-scale community or organization study.

For example, one of the more common and provocative of these themes is that sometimes called "achieving rapport" (not to mention the problem of "over-rapport"[2]). This term is a useful shorthand, taken from the French by psychology, for a very complex social process in which the field worker enters into relationships with those he observes—relationships he discovers, selects, or creates in order to get the information he seeks. How that information is socially evaluated by the person or persons in the particular

---

1. See, for example, the fictionalized account of a social anthropologist's field work in West Africa, Return to Laughter by Elenore Smith Bowen (pseudonym) (London: Victor Gollancz Ltd., 1954). In a note (p. 5) Miss Bowen explains: "When I write as a social anthropologist and within the canons of that discipline, I write under another name. Here I have written simply as a human being, and the truth I have tried to tell concerns the sea change in one's self that comes from immersion in another and alien world." The book itself is most entertaining and rich in illustrations of the process of "change in one's self."

2. The phrase comes from S. M. Miller, "The Participant Observer and 'Over-Rapport,'" American Sociological Review, XVII (February, 1952), 97-99. For a critique of the widespread faith in "the rapport interview," see David Riesman and Mark Benney, "The Sociology of the Interview," Midwest Sociologist, XVIII (Winter, 1956), 3-15. Also see the entire issue of American Journal of Sociology of September, 1956, devoted to "The Interview in Social Research" and edited by David Riesman and Mark Benney.

situation and how it is evaluated, reciprocally, by the field worker, has a determining effect upon the form and content of the relationships which are found, chosen, or created by the field worker in order to enable his information-gathering to go on. The local or immediate social evaluations of the kinds of information the field worker seeks are the proper subject of his first information-gathering activities, both because he must learn these in order to learn more later and because they are clues to the fundamental nature of the social situation in which he is interested. They enable him to make explicit to himself some working hypotheses regarding the character of the total situation, in a manner analogous to the way an interpreter of projective test protocols seeks, in the cues so provided, patterns from which to construct working hypotheses as to the personality dynamics of the individual tested (or even the psychodynamics of a particular social role). In field work, there is a clear and important reason why this process goes on: the very information sought may be, at one level, what any "initiate" has to learn in order to be inducted into the group, or even, at a deeper level, what the child must learn as he becomes oriented and socialized in his particular culture. The field worker begins, straightway, tapping the fundamental common understandings that permit the socialized members of the group to carry on their social life.

If there is ever to be a scientific (that is, tested) rationale for building a science of living societies or human organizations, it may be well to begin with questioning "everything" the field worker has to do to gather information for such a science. For example, it will be necessary for the field worker to provide, for himself and the people in each situation, communicable answers to the questions, "Who am I?" and "Why am I doing these things?" There ought at least to be, for the situation of the particular "Me" having to do field work in a given setting, some general principles of action and reflection derived from the experiences of others in like situations. There can be no simple set of do's and don't's for field workers generally, but there ought to be some useful ways of thinking about a particular situation such that the field worker can choose "the right approach"—the one that best fits both the situation and him, knowing "who he is."

The search for these "useful ways of thinking" for social science field work leads one into the sociology of such an occupation, and if we look at it as a matter of understanding field work only for sociology, we can see that this leads eventually to a sociology of sociology. What this implies can be suggested by the contrast to the field of medicine: there could be no medical study of medical work, but there can be a sociological study of sociological work.

This is because the field worker, in order to initiate his observations, first goes about learning how to enter the social situation and get along with the persons he intends to observe. He may receive some guidance from a more experienced field worker or some help from the literature on his kind of situation, or perhaps he simply generalizes from his earlier experiences in responding to everyday social cues. And then, if all goes well, he engages in a rather curious task. In effect, he learns all the fundamentals of the social situation as he enters and survives in it—he "learns the social organization" before he completely and explicitly knows what he has learned.

Since the field worker deals primarily in communications (interactions in which all kinds of information are exchanged, by voice, social gesture, conveyance of feelings, or even by artifact, such as a document), his first concern is with the kinds of distinctions people make in selecting what to communicate and to whom to communicate it. He therefore pays attention to the two dimensions that are simultaneously in use: (1) that which categorizes information-in-society and (2) that which categorizes the social roles of communicants (especially his own social role).

Since information-in-society is evaluated in ways that vary from one situation to another, the field worker develops sensitivity to the many kinds of distinctions people may make over a range from public to private. (Insensitivity, or inability to take the role of the other and sufficiently accept his values to facilitate communication, will not be rewarded in the situation of observation and may even be punished, just as rudeness is in everyday life.) Even though parts of the range may not find explicit or detailed representation in the data-about-society he publishes, all these distinctions are latent in every social situation and hence affect what can be communicated to him. This range may be indicated by the general labels and descriptions which follow:

Public.—"What everybody knows and can talk about." One form of this is "the news," either as it appears in a newspaper or other public record or as it turns up in whatever people are interested in and "talk about openly." Field workers sometimes call the information received at this level the "community norms," the "logics" or "ideologies," the "apologia," etc. (Even children may recognize it, as in satirizing "teacher-talk.") But what may appear to be evaluated as "public" within a situation may also be regarded as "confidential" or "secret" vis-à-vis outsiders, and in that event the field worker's sensitivity to such a basic fact about the social organization under study will help him avoid blunders.

Confidential.—What is "told in confidence." One form of this is the statement made "not for attribution," which means that if it is ever used in a field worker's published report, it is to be so presented as to protect the giver's anonymity.

Secret.—What is known to members of an in-group who avoid letting it be known to any outsider, since its exclusive possession is important to the in-group's solidarity and continued existence. As such it cannot be reported by a social science field worker, but it can be imparted in a scientific communication as information received and reported, like information at the confidential level, in such a manner as to protect the anonymity not only of the giver but of the in-group itself. One form of this is information obtained in a secret society, or in the "inner fraternity" of a profession, or in a suppressed group presenting some opposition to authority (slaves, convicts, adolescents, etc.).

Private.—What is personal to an individual and can be told only with certain kinds of help from others (such as a psychotherapist, who receives private information in accounts of dreams, free associations, and other kinds of private symbolic behavior). One or another form of this is presented to the field worker continuously, instant by instant, as he goes about his field work—the unconscious gesture, the "Freudian slip," the style of dress or room furnishing, the multitude of personal choices people make in everything they do. How these phenomena are to be recorded or ignored and what account of them is to be given in a social science publication are questions whose solution from scientific and ethical value positions must also take account of the possible consequences of current and later evaluations made by the persons concerned. In that regard, private information must be treated by the field worker with the same respect he owes to secret, confidential, and even public information, if he wants to survive in the field and also wants his social science to thrive.

In this and succeeding chapters the reader will encounter illustrations of these categories of information-in-society and what appear to be some of their consequences for the field worker's choice, selection, or creation of the social roles which enable him to gather such information by making observations of what people do and say. Here, referring to Chart 2, I shall set forth my own conceptions of four theoretical social roles for field work. These range from the polar ideal type of complete participant to that of complete observer, and I shall now summarize what I believe is known from field work on field work, about the social positions (vis-à-vis the people observed) and activities of field workers taking these roles.

I. Complete Participant.—In this role, the observer's activities as such are wholly concealed. The field worker is or becomes a complete member of an in-group, thus sharing secret information guarded from outsiders. The field worker's freedom to observe outside the in-group system of relationships may be severely limited, and such a role tends to block perception of the workings of the reciprocal relations between the in-group and

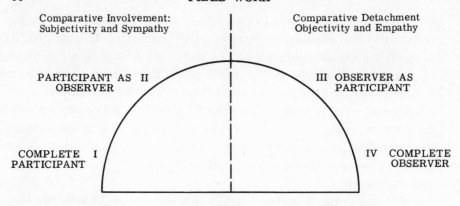

Chart 2. Theoretical Social Roles for Field Work

the larger social system, nor is it easy to switch from this to another role permitting observation of the details of the larger system. When the complete participant emerges, so to speak, to report as a social scientist, he may expect to be evaluated by some persons as something of a spy and he must also be prepared to cope with difficult problems of ethics and professional responsibility, not to mention problems of identity and self-conception.

This role may be suitable, and scientifically even absolutely necessary, in those social situations in which the people make sharp and clear evaluations about the information a field worker might seek: that is, they try to maintain a maximum of categorical difference between what is public, confidential, secret, and private, and one might expect that just as the in-group severely limits what may be made public to those in the larger system, so they would also set up barriers to the field worker's penetration into the secret level if he were an outsider to begin with. If the in-group is the kind that takes in converts, a rather prolonged period of indoctrination and testing may have been instituted, and this may be the mode by which the field worker chooses or is led to become a complete participant. Alternatively, if the field worker has always been a member of the in-group, at least until he left it physically or intellectually long enough to become indoctrinated either as a social scientist or as one serving social science purposes, his problems may be less those of getting in and staying in and more those of getting out. Such problems are likely to include maintaining sufficient detachment intellectually and reporting with the objectivity and empathy his scientific audience will demand. If he escapes the problems of a spy, he takes on those of a traitor.

II. <u>Participant as Observer</u>.—In this role, the field worker's observer activities are <u>not</u> wholly concealed, but are "kept under wraps" as it were, or subordinated to activities as participant, activities which give the people in the situation their main bases for evaluating the field worker in his role. This role may limit access to some kinds of information, perhaps especially at the secret level: precisely how he "rates" as a pseudo-"Member of the Wedding" will affect the field worker's ability to communicate below the level of public information. In his reporting, the social scientist who uses this position finds he must gear his responsibilities to the degree of secrecy (or confidentiality) of the information he was allowed by the people to obtain, under the implicit bargain which won him acceptance more as participant ("good friend") than as an observer ("snooping stranger").

III. <u>Observer as Participant</u>.—This is the role in which the observer activities as such are made publicly known at the outset, are more or less publicly sponsored by people in the situation studied, and are intentionally <u>not</u> "kept under wraps." The role may provide access to a wide range of information, and even secrets may be given to the field worker when he becomes known for keeping them, as well as for guarding confidential information. In this role the social scientist might conceivably achieve maximum freedom to gather information but only at the price of accepting maximum constraints upon his reporting. In a given situation, this combination of freedom and responsibility is likely to hinge upon the previous behavior of social scientists who have conditioned the people in it. Hence the question of professional ethics may be more critical for this position than for other roles. If the people find it possible to accept the field worker as a person with a scientific mandate and a publicly accorded right to receive information at all four levels from public to private, they are very likely to expect that the "contract" as it developed during the field inquiry will be honored at the time of reporting. One constraint, for example, will require the scientific reporter to maintain the people's distinctions between public, confidential, and so on. The consequences of this for the necessary publication of a scientific contribution to knowledge may well deserve some thought in advance of conducting field work in and through this role. The latter may have advantages for some scientific problems and not for others.

IV. <u>Complete Observer</u>.—This describes a range of roles in which, at one extreme, the observer hides behind a one-way mirror, perhaps equipped with sound film facilities, and at the other extreme, his activities are completely public in a special kind of theoretical group where there are, by consensus, "no secrets" and "nothing sacred." Such a group is not found naturally in society, so far as I know, but its form and functioning may be approximated in small experimental groups in which the observer has a formal role, as in situations created in a group dynamics laboratory. At the latter kind of extreme, all levels of information are theoretically equally accessible to all participants and hence an observer would become instead

a kind of complete participant—though different from what is implied by
such full participation in a natural group.

In less extreme form, this role may be thought of as taken by the field
worker at rest or reflecting or as taken in a similar sort of vicarious activity by a learner who may usefully think of himself as there but not involved, as a participant but not really participating, etc. Of course, in these
forms it is strictly an imaginary role, not evaluated by the people in the situation being studied, but of some use to the development of the beginner's
self-concept as a social scientist, perhaps.

The role of complete observer is more imaginary than real or possible,
although, as noted, it may be approximated in a laboratory or simulated in
reflection, and its actualization would require the existence in society of a
group, with provision for such a person, and with such a state of perfect
communication, such a void of secrets, that is so rare as to have escaped
observation. It might be argued that such a group is present when one is in
a colleague group of psychiatrists or field workers which accepts a member
playing this role, but it seems highly likely that this would soon reform itself into a proper in-group and such would change the role of the observer
to that of complete participant with all that it implies.

In Chart 2, and in these definitions, it is made to appear that the four
roles can be sharply distinguished and that the field worker will find himself cast in one and only one position, with its opportunities and limitations
as indicated. But the practicing field worker may well find his position and
activities shifting through time from one to another of these theoretical
points, even as he continues observing the same human organization. Indeed,
as hinted in the foregoing, imaginary role-taking is part of the process by
which the field worker, in periods of reflection, can estimate where events
have taken him and can speculate upon whether a change in his tactics has
a chance of success or whether the cues being received indicate that the
wisest course is consistency in the same role. In some studies of communities or other large organizations that require field work over a relatively
long period of time, and in the early stages of reconnaissance, the first activities of the field worker may be in the role of complete observer, but after a while, as he interacts with more and more people, he moves into the
observer-as-participant role and later still, perhaps, into the participant-
as-observer role. Looking at events from the field worker's point of view,
he finds himself oscillating along this range, day by day or even moment to
moment, and, from the viewpoints of individuals with whom he interacts,
for some he is more participant than observer, for others he remains more
observer than participant, and there may even be many individuals in complex situations who are not at all aware of him as in any way extraordinary

but who might regard him as queer or threatening if they saw him as an observer. In not interacting with these, the field worker may retain some activities of the complete observer role, but in his relations with others his activities inevitably take on some of the variable meanings attached to participating both by him and by the others.[3]

It is not possible to specify the combinations of conditions and thence to write prescriptions for role choices to match social science problems, if only because field workers vary so greatly in respect to identity and self that each must learn to solve these problems as they crop up. Moreover, the ability to find such solutions, and to reject impossible field work tasks, doubtless develops as each field worker learns more about self and about the repertory of roles possible and even most congenial for him, given who he is.

There are at least four groups of variables which interact to define or subtly affect the social roles of observers: (1) conditions inherent in the situation of observation prior to the field worker's entry (a community, tribe, or any human organization never before studied by a social science field worker imposes requirements on his getting in, staying in, and easing out that would be very different from those presented by a business organization whose members, long accustomed to surveys of many kinds, feel no threat at all in the appearance of merely one more interviewer); (2) conditions arising from the abilities, identity, self-understanding, reference-group attachments (such as colleagues or anticipated audiences), theoretical orientation, and other characteristics of the field worker entering the situation; (3) modifications through time that occur in the situation itself, as an on-going social process, including the effects of the field worker's activities; (4) changes in the observer himself, as an organic item, as a

---

3. For an insightful discussion of the role and self problems of field workers and informants, see Raymond L. Gold, "Roles in Sociological Field Observations," Social Forces, XXXVI (March, 1958), 217-23. Dr. Gold describes our four field work roles "as 'master roles' for developing lesser role-relationships with informants" and in the article cited, analyzes them with "the aid of certain conceptions of role and self." Incidentally, he distinguishes the observer-as-participant role as limited to "studies involving one-visit interviews" in which formality and brief contact make for mutual misunderstandings and frustration of the field worker's human need for self-expression. Consistent with this limitation by definition, Dr. Gold sees the participant-as-observer role as most frequently used in community studies, "where an observer develops relationships with informants through time, and where he is apt to spend more time and energy participating than observing." His complete paper should be read to complement, by his closer attention to the individual observer's problems, our own emphasis upon the manifest content and the ethical and scientific implications of the observer's activities. I shall, however, return to the individual field worker and his problems in chapter v, in connection with the learning experiences of students.

person, a role-player, social scientist, and so on.

To these variables, planned for or uncontrollable but at least capable of being perceived during the field inquiry, may be added those latent factors which, in retrospect as the observer prepares his contribution to social science knowledge, acquire significance as having had unrecognized effects upon his field worker position and activities, and hence his necessarily selective recording of information. Such a process of visual and auditory recalling of the sequence of events in the particular field situation could not have affected those earlier events in fact, but it may well affect the observer's present reporting of them or his taking account of them in analyzing and publishing his results. A problem of balancing scientific aims and ethical considerations may be discovered, along with delayed insights and recall of subliminal cues that may shatter the observer's original theoretical framework and present him with a task not only of reconstruction but of reporting how this became necessary and was accomplished.

In view of this complex mix of factors, how are we to arrive at a tested rationale for field work? The answer now seems to be only pari passu with our approach to the ultimate goal of a science of society. Meanwhile it is useful to have some categories for classifying statements about field work activities, results, and their varied meanings—personal, social, and scientific. The working outline below suggests categories for these in a chronological model for an entire research enterprise, as if the four stages of planning, doing, analyzing results and publishing, and reappraising succeeded each other with no overlapping. Reflection will show the reader how the six categories given in the first stage might well be repeated in the other three.[4]

Working Outline for Developing a Rationale for Field Work

I. Planning: Statements regarding what the field worker plans or planned to do; statements indicating conscious directed thought and purposeful selection and application of techniques; in general, the observer and participant aspects of field work intellectually conceived.

    A. Theoretical Orientation.—research aims and objectives (e.g., complete ethnographic description, study of a particular institution or culture complex, testing of a theoretical hypothesis); general theoretical approach (e.g., historical, functional, psychological); formulation of research program; reasons for choice of particular field site; etc.

---

4. The six categories A through F under Planning and their definitions are quoted by permission from the section on "Methodology" in Outline of Cultural Materials, by George P. Murdock, et al. (3d ed.; New Haven, Conn.: Human Relations Area Files, Inc., 1950), I, 2-3, secs. 121-26.

B. Practical Preparations.—source of financial support; selection and assembly of equipment; arranging problems of transportation and bureaucratic red tape; familiarization with previous descriptive literature; etc.

C. Observational Role.—techniques for establishing rapport; assumption or ascription of a status in the community; methods of altering observer's status; adoption of the technique of participant-observation; degree of participation in community life actually achieved; effect of the observer's presence on the life of the community; limitations imposed by sex of observer; etc.

D. Interviewing.—methods of selecting informants or subjects (e.g., sampling); use and selection of interpreters; methods of checking and rewarding informants and interpreters; group interviewing; methods of interviewing (e.g., question and answer, non-directive, use of topical outlines); special techniques (e.g., life history, genealogical, event centered); use of documents prepared by informants; etc.

E. Tests and Schedules.—description of tests used (e.g., intelligence, projective); schedules and questionnaires employed (e.g., preparation, pretesting); administration of tests, schedules, and questionnaires; sampling techniques; methods of scoring; use of control groups; special experiments; etc.

F. Recording.—methods of note-taking (e.g., verbatim, post-interview, summaries); taking of native texts; use of diaries and journals; utilization of sound and photographic equipment; preparation of sketches, charts, maps; etc.

II. Doing: Statements about what the field worker actually does in his particular field situation; activities and experience in observing, recording, and reflecting; the unplanned adaptive activity in the field work situation; the more or less conscious generalization of learned behavior to new social situations (e.g., "she treated me like a guest" in order to control the observer and limit freedom to observe); the problems around the questions, "Being who I am, what can I learn from these people?" etc.; in general, the participant and observer aspects of field work as emotionally experienced and more or less completely rationalized.

A. The Field Work Situation.—information-in-society and the field worker's role:

1. Kinds of information sought from people; learning how these people evaluate such information (as public, confidential, secret, or private); roles of informants (as defined by the people, e.g., informer; as defined by the field worker, e.g., "opinion

leader," "windbag," "silent one," etc.); and the field worker's development of a role or roles in terms of these considerations (his selections from, or adaptations of, the four major types of field worker role: complete participant, participant as observer, observer as participant, complete observer).

2. The field worker as a person (social or sociological aspects, as distinguished from psychological aspects), as a personality (his psyche, or what is known about it), as an observer (capacities and limitations of sensory apparatus, etc.), and his role and self problems in learning and doing field work.

B. Stages of Field Work in a Given Situation.—sensing, improvising, and timing activities with respect to getting in, staying in, and easing out.

III. Analyzing Results and Publishing: Statements about what the field worker does in dealing with problems of translating information-in-society into data-about-society that may be published, whether in print or in other communications such as lectures.

IV. Reappraising: Considering the interdependence of planning-doing-analyzing-publishing phases of field work and the advance of knowledge in the social sciences; statements about the dependence of social science knowledge upon a tested rationale for field work, and this as a fundamental assumption in modern science; statements about a sociology of the occupation, social science field worker; statements about sociology of knowledge in the social sciences.

The rest of this chapter presents eight selections from publications of thoughtful field workers, each of whom illuminates social processes personally experienced in field situations that were, for them, apparently loose-knit or easily accessible. These stand in some contrast to the close-knit or tight situations described in chapter iv, in which the field workers emphasize their varying adaptive approaches.

Modified Participant Observation

We begin with a selection from a paper by Emilio Willems,[5] now of Vanderbilt University and of German origin and training, who spent many

---

5. "Neuere Tendenzen sozialanthropologischer Feldforschung," in Soziologische Forschung in unserer Zeit, ed. K. G. Specht (Westdeutscher Verlag, Köln und Opladen, 1951), pp. 76-77. The translation is by Everett C. Hughes.

years in São Paulo, Brazil, where he studied assimilation of immigrants and other problems in that country. In the present paper he notes first of all the extension of the anthropological field to include communities not considered primitive, and thus a necessary approach to sociology in problem and method. This tendency has created new problems in methods of observation.

The field work approach described by Willems might be labeled "the techniques of modified participant observation" and seen as an illustration of _movement_ from what we have called observer as participant to participant as observer. Willems is careful to distinguish this from "participant observation" which he defines in a way that describes our complete participant, and he indicates the comparative advantages of the participant-as-observer role for community studies of the kind he and his students undertook.

To the traditional anthropologist social structure meant predominantly the structure of familism and of kin groups. In modern communities the structure of the family is generally less complex, but other structural elements, such as social classes, political, economic and religious associations come to the fore. The study especially of strata got a strong impetus from the Yankee City series of W. Lloyd Warner.

. . . What effects did this extension of the anthropological field have upon the practice of field observation? It is undoubtedly true that in many non-primitive groups the course of numerous institutional processes can be observed without any disturbance of the proceedings being caused by the presence of the observer. But still one continually runs into this same difficulty: How can the investigator remain in the field without setting in motion limiting or disruptive reactions of the normal manner of conduct of the group? Only in the rarest cases will a truthful explanation of his activity have the desired effect. Generally he will simply not be understood; in other cases (and this holds especially in Latin America) his explanation would be met with great skepticism. The magical suspicions of the primitive are replaced in many rural communities and small cities by conscious opposition of many individuals against investigation of all those elements of their culture of which they are ashamed, or knowledge of which could in any case injure certain persons or groups. Here belong, for example, the study of magical practices, sexual life and local politics. These, like many other aspects of culture, cannot be ignored if one has in mind something more than superficial reportage.

On the basis of such experiences one has given increasing attention to the so-called "participant observation." "Participant observation means conscious and systematic participation, so far as circumstances allow, in the life activities and even in the interests and movements of mood of the group. Its purpose is the accumulation of data about ways of behaving through direct contact and under special conditions which reduce to a minimum the distortion which arises from the fact that the observer is an outsider." (Florence Kluckhohn, 1940.) Participant observation is only possible (1) when the group to be studied is left in the dark as to the intentions of the observer; (2) when the observer succeeds in taking a position in the community which so explains his presence that it appears above suspicion and natural to all. In other words, life goes on without anyone knowing the real intent and activity of the investigator. He is thus in the position of taking part in all events which lie in the field of his temporarily assumed role. This naturally does not mean that he has access without further ado to all spheres of the culture.

It is further beyond dispute that participant observation, in the full sense of the above definition, is applicable only in exceptional cases. It is never possible among primitive tribes, and in peasant or small town communities it requires a considerable talent for detective work. There are, however, techniques which are close to participant observation without corresponding to it in all particulars. In our field investigations in Brazil, which we generally carried out with the help of advanced students, the following typical ways of conduct of the local population were exploited so far as possible:

1. Competitive hospitality. Usually the first superficial contact was followed by an invitation to a meal. This having got around, other invitations followed, and the leading families sought to outbid one another for our company.

2. A special pattern of friendship, peculiar to Latin American culture. After a few weeks of easy contacts, common eating and drinking, in which the investigator must show a genuine interest in local events and relationships, he is usually on intimate footing with a series of people (of the same sex, mark well), who willingly give him the wished-for information, often quite spontaneously. The chief condition is, however, that the investigator possesses a warm, human sympathy with his subjects.

Most communities have a strong interest in progress. People want new streets, electrical power, hospitals, schools, etc., projects which can be realized only with financial help from the state or national government. The presence of the investigator is usually associated with these strivings for progress and people hope that his report and personal participation will favorably influence local developments. This often leads to a certain willingness to help him, but it can also hinder his work insofar as it leads people to conceal certain aspects of the local culture.

Full use of these patterns of culture brought us so close to many persons that we could penetrate into the hidden spheres of culture. But this would not have been possible except for the fact that at least one member of our group was a woman. After a few weeks our situation was so far cleared, that a great part of the population was favorably disposed toward us. To be sure, not all of our assistants were successful in personal contacts. Even a long field experience is usually no substitute for personal readiness to enter into comradely relations with people.*

The Individual Participant as Observer

Field work as an individual enterprise often permits the field worker to give an intimate account of the social processes and personal experiences involved. Such accounts have advantages, for our purposes, over the more formal statements that may accompany reports of field work as a group enterprise.

The Preface to the first edition of William F. Whyte's Street Corner Society[6] provides us with a relatively compact but rich statement of the important features common to field work of this kind which I seek to point up by inserting a brief summary of content before each paragraph of the

---

*This does not mean to say that comradeship is always the right attitude. This depends completely upon the patterns of conduct of the culture being studied.

6. William Foote Whyte, Street Corner Society: The Social Structure of an Italian Slum (Chicago: University of Chicago Press, 1943; 2d ed., 1955). Preface to first edition, pp. v-xii.

original. The "Introduction: Cornerville and Its People" and the Appendix "On the Evolution of Street Corner Society" (both of which appear in the second edition) should also be read, the first for its explanation of why the role of "participant as observer" was chosen and maintained as "the only way . . . to gain the most intimate knowledge of local life." The book as a whole, of course, amplifies the context of the field work experiences summarized here, and the more the reader knows about that context, the richer should be his appreciation of the field worker's experience. The student might ask himself: "If, after reading this book, I could interview the author, what more would I want to learn about his field work?" and also, "What would I do to gather this kind of information in this kind of situation?"

1. Becoming a participant, "learning the language" as a useful activity with important by-products in winning acceptance.

This book is a report upon a three-and-a-half year study of "Cornerville." My aim was to gain an intimate view of Cornerville life. My first problem, therefore, was to establish myself as a participant in the society so that I would have a position from which to observe. I began by going to live in Cornerville, finding a room with an Italian family. Since the mother and father of the family spoke no English, I began studying Italian. Conversations with them and practice with the Linguaphone enabled me to learn enough to talk fairly fluently with the older generation. As I became largely concerned with the second-generation men, who conducted their activities in English, Italian was not essential to me; but the fact that I made the effort to learn the language was important, since it gave the impression that I had a sincere and sympathetic interest in Cornerville people.

2. Living with a family and making contacts through them and their kin.

Staying with an Italian family gave me a view of family life and also provided important contacts with the community. Through the family I met a cousin of State Senator George Ravello's secretary. Through the cousin I met the secretary, and through the secretary I met Ravello. In this way I was able to establish myself in the politician's office at a time when he was running for Congress. He had no opposition from within Cornerville in this campaign, which made it possible for me to work for him without losing standing with other local groups. During the campaign, I did various odd jobs which were of no particular significance for the organization but which gave me an excuse for being around when things were happening. It was in this way that I found most of my material on politics.

3. Sponsorship by a settlement house—disadvantages and advantages.

I made my first contacts with the "corner boys" known as the Nortons through the Norton Street Settlement House. I subsequently learned that too close identification with the settlement would prevent me from becoming intimate with the rank and file of the people, but at this time I was fortunate in meeting corner boys who, while they had some contact with the settlement, also had a recognized position outside of it. Through the Nortons I came to know the college men of the Italian Community Club.

4. Field Worker changes his social identity—in this case, in the larger society by marriage—and this enlarges the number, range, and variety of social relations accessible to him in the immediate field situation.

After I had lived eighteen months with the Italian family, I married, and my wife and I moved into a flat on Shelby Street. This opened for me a new field of contacts. One evening I went with the son of my Italian family to a banquet in honor of the local police lieutenant. There were three main groups of people present; policemen, politicians, and racketeers. My companion had met Tony Cataldo, a prominent local racketeer, and Tony had seen me around his district. We became acquainted in this way, and shortly thereafter Tony invited me and my wife to dinner at his house. We spent a number of evenings with the Cataldos and also came to know other members of the family. In order to study the influence of the racketeer upon a specific group of people, I joined the Cornerville Social and Athletic Club. Since the organization was located on Shelby Street, my contacts made it quite natural for me to join.

5. Dealing with "suspicion" regarding any stranger by winning acceptance from leaders of informal groups who thenceforth sponsored the field worker among their friends and followers.

It was not enough simply to make the acquaintance of various groups of people. The sort of information that I sought required that I establish intimate social relations, and that presented special problems. Since illegal activities are prevalent in Cornerville, every newcomer is under suspicion. So that I would not be taken for a "G-man," I had to have some way of explaining my presence. I began by telling people that I was studying the history of Cornerville since the beginning of the Italian immigration, but I used this story only a few times. I found that in each group I met there was one man who directed the activities of his fellows and whose word carried authority. Without his support, I was excluded from the group; with his support, I was accepted. Since he had to take the responsibility of vouching for me, I made a practice of talking with him quite frankly about the questions in which I was interested. When his friends questioned him, he knew much more about me than they did, and he was therefore in a position to reassure them. In the course of my stay in Cornerville, several of these men came to have a very clear and detailed idea of the nature of my research, and this knowledge made it possible for them to help me by observing and discussing with me the sort of situations in which I was interested.

6. The "halo effect" of acceptance by group members: they evaluate the field worker as "writing a book" but show little or no interest in the details (that is, the field worker was seen as carrying on an activity apparently regarded by the people as mildly mysterious, of rather high prestige value, but not threatening to anyone in "Cornerville").

When I became accepted into a group, it was no longer necessary for me to explain what I was doing. Being accepted meant that whatever I was doing was all right. It became generally understood that I was writing a book about the old Italian customs in Cornerville, and occasionally I was asked, "How is your book coming:" I always replied that I was making progress but that there was still a lot for me to learn. No further answer was necessary, although I tried to give the impression that I was prepared to tell much more about my work than my questioner wanted to know.

7. Extension of participation through time and the gradual development

of more intimate familiarity with a group: changing the field worker's "mandate" from a right to inquire as a somewhat distant associate to a right to inquire as a somewhat closer friend.

The first few weeks of my association with any group brought in little information of value. Although my right to associate with the men was unquestioned, they could not feel at ease in my presence until they became familiar with me. Therefore, I put in a great deal of time simply hanging around with them and participating in their various activities. I bowled, played baseball and softball, shot a little pool, played cards, and ate and drank with my Cornerville friends. This active participation gave me something in common with them so that we had other things to talk about besides the weather. It broke down the social barriers and made it possible for me to be taken into the intimate life of the group.

8. Discovering the local social definitions of "a friend" but also taking care to set limits on participation on this basis in order to avoid influencing the situation unduly. Avoiding "moral admonitions" (which would have reaffirmed the original social distances based on ethnic and social class grounds). (See also paragraphs 14 and 15.)

My aim was to be a friend to the people whom I was with, and I tried to act as a friend was supposed to act in that society. My friends helped me with my work, and I helped my friends as individuals in whatever way I could. I found it even more important to my social position to ask them to help me. I made it a rule that I should try to avoid influencing the actions of the group. I wanted to observe what the men did under ordinary circumstances; I did not want to lead them into different activities. I violated this rule several times and did so particularly flagrantly during the political crisis in the Cornerville S. and A. Club, but on the whole, I held to it. Of course, my presence changed the situation for the group. I tried to minimize that change because it was much easier for me to study group activities if I could assume that my own influence had not been a significant factor in bringing about the actions I observed. Above all, I avoided making moral admonitions. I did not tell people that they were behaving improperly or suggest to them the way in which they should act. I was there to learn about Cornerville life, not to pass judgment upon it.

9. Field worker subordinates interest in broad theoretical orientations to the task of gathering detailed information on social relations: informal interviews as a participant in group activities, supplemented by individual interviews in the privacy of field worker's own home. (See also paragraphs 10 and 17.)

I was not immediately interested in broad generalizations upon the nature of Cornerville life. It seemed to me that any sound generalizations must be based upon detailed knowledge of social relations. Therefore, I concentrated my attention upon the interaction of individuals in their groups. I was concerned not only with the "important events," because at the outset I had no basis for determining what was important except to my own preconceived notions. I tried to keep my eyes and ears open to everything that went on between people in my presence. Frequently, I asked people to explain to me what had happened. Most of my interviewing was conducted informally while I was participating in group activities. I found that what people told me helped to explain what had happened and that what I observed helped to explain what people told me, so that it was helpful to observe and interview at the same time. In order to fill in the background in the history of the individual and of the group and to take up things which could best be discussed in private, I invited men to come separately and talk with me at my home. Much of the background of the Norton and the Italian Community Club was gathered in this way.

10. Theoretical orientation of the sociologist in the study of slums is customarily in terms of "social disorganization," but this field worker stressed "social organization"—particularly the hierarchies within each group and the hierarchical organization of the groups themselves within Cornerville.

It is customary for the sociologist to study the slum district in terms of "social disorganization" and to neglect to see that an area such as Cornerville has a complex and well-established organization of its own. I was interested in that organization. I found that in every group there was a hierarchical structure of social relations binding the individuals to one another and that the groups were also related hierarchically to one another. Where the group was formally organized into a political club, this was immediately apparent, but for informal groups it was no less true. While the relations in such groups were not formally prescribed, they could be clearly observed in the interactions of individuals. To determine the relative standing of members of this group, I paid particular attention to the origination of action. When the group or several of its members engaged in some common activity, I wanted to know who suggested what was to be done and whose agreement was necessary before the action could be carried out. Observation of this sort provided the basis for the charts of hierarchical organization which are presented in the stories of the Nortons and the Cornerville S. and A. Club and for the discussion of "The Gang and the Individual" in my conclusions.

11. "Maps" showing day-to-day spatial positions of men in groupings within the Cornerville S. and A. Club, and their use as evidence of cliques and subdivisions within each clique.

The study of the Cornerville S. and A. Club presented some special problems. Since at times there were as many as fifty members, it was necessary to study the club through observing the groupings into which the men naturally divided themselves. Every afternoon or evening when I went into the club I looked around to see which members were grouped together, playing cards, listening to the radio, or talking. When the men were moving around, I could not retain all the movements; but, when they settled down, I counted the men present and fixed in my mind the spatial position of each individual in relation to the others. When I went home, I mapped the spatial positions of the members and indicated which ones were participating together. These maps showed quite clearly the main division between the two cliques and the subdivisions within each clique.

12. Records of events of interaction, "too detailed to be included in a book of this nature," helped to determine "the relative positions of minor members" of the Club. Major members' positions are indicated in the events described in the book.

The events to be described will provide the evidence for assigning positions to the most prominent members of the Cornerville S. and A. Club. The relative positions of the minor members were discovered by observing which men took the initiative in group action when one of the top men was not present. The evidence for fixing the positions of all minor members is too detailed to be included in a book of this nature.

13. Development of skill in making permanent records of observations of interactions and spatial positions; also development of skill in recording interviews verbatim.

My observations of interactions and of spatial positions would have been of no use to me if I had not made a permanent record of them. When I went to political rallies and campaign committee meetings, I was able to take notes on the spot; but on all other occasions I had to rely on my memory until I could write in private. When I recorded conversations, I tried to put down in so far as possible the exact words that were said. Frequently, the phrase used carries a meaning which escapes my paraphrase, and therefore I felt that it was important to try for verbatim recordings. This is a skill which develops with practice. At first I found that I could remember only a few phrases used and give an impressionistic picture of the rest of the conversation; but, as I went on, I was able to record in greater and greater detail, so that I feel confident that the quotations I cite represent substantially what was actually said. I had the same experience in mapping spatial positions.

14. Use of volunteer assistants among leaders of other corner gangs to extend observations and discuss tentative conclusions with these natural observers in the situation.

The stories of the Nortons and of the Cornerville S. and A. Club provide a body of information upon corner gangs, but they constitute only the smallest fraction of the total number of such groups to be found in Cornerville. So that I might be able to generalize upon the nature of the corner gang, I solicited the aid of several corner-boy leaders who discussed with me their own experiences and became interested in making the same sort of detailed observations that are found in my corner-boy stories. One of these men, Sam Franco, leader of the Millers, made a remarkably intensive study of his own group and of groups that hung near his corner. With all these volunteer assistants I discussed my tentative conclusions to make sure that they accorded with the observations of men who were in the best possible positions for observing what went on in the corner gang.*

15. The "easing out" stage of the field work: discussing gang structure with informants and the effects of this in making them "conscious of the nature of their unreflective behavior." Changing the situation "to that extent" was justified by its contribution "toward building up a systematic picture of the corner gang." [The study went on for three and a half years. The problems of deepening involvement through time are not further discussed.]

The corner boys do not explicitly recognize the structure of the gang, but it is implicit in all their actions. When, toward the end of my study, I discussed these matters with my informants, I made them conscious of the

---

*Methods for studying the informal group are discussed in much greater detail in my article, "Corner Boys: A Study of Clique Behavior," American Journal of Sociology, XLVI (March, 1941), 647-64.

nature of their unreflective behavior. To that extent I changed the situation; the men talked to me about things that they had never formulated before. This did not mean that they were enabled to act more effectively. Doc, my chief informant, once told me:

> You've slowed me up plenty since you've been down here. Now when I do something, I have to think what Bill Whyte would want to know about it and how I can explain it. . . . Before I used to do these things by instinct.

This awareness, however, contributed toward building up a systematic picture of the corner gang.

16. Practical aspects of field work: acknowledgements of financial support.

This study is the product of many hands besides my own. A Junior Fellowship from Harvard University made the research possible by supporting me for a period of four years. Without the complete freedom afforded me by the Society of Fellows, I should never have been able to undertake the study of Cornerville. The University and Marshall Field fellowships at the University of Chicago supported me while I was writing up my results.

17. Theoretical orientation and field-work techniques: acknowledgments.

I owe a great personal debt to Professor Conrad M. Arensberg of Brooklyn College, from whom I learned my field-work techniques. I discussed my plans with him before I began my study and had the benefit of his advice and criticism every step of the way. Dr. Eliot D. Chapple, in collaboration with Dr. Arensberg, worked out the conceptual scheme for the study of interactions which I have used throughout this book.

I am indebted both indirectly and directly to Professor W. Lloyd Warner of the University of Chicago, who conducted the Yankee City Study. The techniques and the conceptual scheme of Drs. Arensberg and Chapple developed out of field-work experience beginning in Yankee City. Professor Warner has also offered invaluable advice and criticism in the final preparation of the manuscript.

18. Theoretical orientation and crystallization of ideas in the field: acknowledgment to another field worker in Cornerville, especially for suggesting the "analysis of leadership."

John Howard spent two years of field work in Cornerville. In this book I have found it wise to concentrate upon my own material, which I know best, but discussions of our separate observations were exceedingly valuable in clarifying my ideas. Mr. Howard was the first to suggest that an analysis of leadership would provide a means of integrating the study.

19. Other acknowledgments, for help in developing "powers of self-criticism" (Henderson) and in learning "techniques of interviewing" (Mayo), etc.

The late Professor Lawrence J. Henderson, chairman of the Society of Fellows, helped me to develop powers of self-criticism. Professor Elton Mayo of the Harvard Business School guided me in learning the techniques of interviewing used in my research. Professor Everett C. Hughes of the University of Chicago and Professor E. B. Wilson and James Ford of Harvard gave me some valuable criticisms and suggestions.

20. Acknowledgments to author's wife for collaboration in field work and in preparation of the manuscript.

Throughout the last two years of my research I was aided by Kathleen King Whyte. She also did the charts and criticized the manuscript in every step of its preparation, thus simplifying my job immeasurably.

21. Theoretical orientation, acknowledgment to Lincoln Steffens for his Autobiography as an influence in the study.

I cannot leave off without acknowledging the debt that I, in common with so many other students of my generation, owe to Lincoln Steffens. His Autobiography first suggested to me that it would be possible to find out some of the things that are discussed in this book.

22. Further phase of "easing out" stage of field work, expression of appreciation to the anonymous people of Cornerville who "made the research possible" and gave "very active assistance."

Since fictitious names are given to all characters in the book, I cannot acknowledge directly the help of local informants. The people of Cornerville had a greater part in making this book than most of them will ever realize. Their hospitality made the research possible and made my stay in Cornerville a thoroughly enjoyable experience. I count some of the people of the district among my closest friends. They gave me very active assistance in my study. They helped me, in part, because they thought my book might help Cornerville. That is perhaps too much to expect, but at least I hope that it will not bring harm to them or to any of the people of Cornerville.

It is in the Preface, too, that Whyte accepts responsibility for defects and acknowledges permission to use material which has already appeared elsewhere.

Proper Conditions for Ethnographic Work

In Argonauts of the Western Pacific, Bronislaw Malinowski gives the reader not only a detailed account of the Kula, a very elaborate trading system among native enterprisers of the archipelagoes of Melanesian New Guinea, but one of the first works of modern social science to provide an adequate account of the personal experiences and social processes of field work when performed by an ethnographer—particularly one possessing Malinowski's consistently "functionalist" approach to an esoteric culture. Some of the requirements of this approach are recognized in Sir James G. Frazer's prefatory remarks:[7]

In regard to method, Dr. Malinowski has done his work, as it appears to me, under the best conditions and in the manner calculated to secure the best possible results. Both by theoretical training and by practical experi-

---

7. From the Preface to Bronislaw Malinowski, Argonauts of the Western Pacific (New York: E. P. Dutton & Co., Inc., 1950), pp. vii-viii.

ence he was well equipped for the task which he undertook. . . . In the Trobriand Islands . . . Dr. Malinowski lived as a native among the natives for
many months together, watching them daily at work and at play, conversing
with them in their own tongue, and deriving all his information from the
surest sources—personal observation and statements made to him directly
by the natives in their own language without the intervention of an interpreter. In this way he has accumulated a large mass of materials, of high
scientific value, bearing on the social, religious, and economic or industrial life of the Trobriand Islanders.

While the modern field worker is not likely nowadays to be the first
non-indigenous person to learn the language and seek scientific understanding of the whole life and labor of a simpler society, his own training and
field operations will recapitulate, in a sense, what Malinowski lived through,
". . . in the laborious years between the moment when he sets foot on a native beach, and makes his first attempt to get into touch with the natives,
and the time when he writes down the final version of his results."[8] Indeed,
the contemporary scientist faces a shortage of unstudied esoteric cultures
—at least, away from the "jungles" of the modern metropolis—and a considerable likelihood that the indigenous population he seeks out will be growing in literacy and producing not only politicians but their own anthropologists. A preface to understanding this aspect of the great world changes
under way, and its possible consequences for social science, may be sought
in the contrasting difficulties and opportunities encountered in the era of
Malinowski's lonely field work, when "his people" could still be seen by the
ethnographer as in a state of nature not yet seriously contaminated by modern culture contacts, and as very unlikely to read his reports, at least in
his lifetime.

The following excerpts[9] from Malinowski's Introduction will, we hope,
lead the reader to review the complete account. The student may find it instructive to analyze this and other publications by or about the same author
in order to arrive at his own formulation of how completely this ethnographer "lived as a native among the natives." In terms of our own formulation
of field work roles, it seems very clear that Malinowski did not act, sociologically, as complete participant, however much he sought to do so, psychologically. Instead, he seems to have come as close as he could, by acting as participant as observer—thus exploiting an opportunity, not to "go
native" but to adopt the role in which the unlettered "natives" were enabled
to become relatively indifferent to him as a participant because, at the outset and all through, they had so little understanding of his mission as an

---

8. Ibid., p. 4.

9. Ibid., pp. 6-24.

observer. (Their lack of understanding did not, of course, prevent them from teaching him a very great deal.)

. . . These [proper conditions for ethnographic work], as said, consist mainly in cutting oneself off from the company of other white men, and remaining in as close contact with the natives as possible, which really can only be achieved by camping right in their villages. . . . It is very nice to have a base in a white man's compound for the stores, and to know there is a refuge there in times of sickness and surfeit of native. But it must be far enough away not to become a permanent milieu in which you live and from which you emerge at fixed hours only to "do the village." It should not even be near enough to fly to at any moment for recreation. For the native is not the natural companion for a white man, and after you have been working with him for several hours, seeing how he does his gardens, or letting him tell you items of folk-lore, or discussing his customs, you will naturally hanker after the company of your own kind. But if you are alone in a village beyond reach of this, you go for a solitary walk for an hour or so, return again and then quite naturally seek out the natives' society, this time as a relief from loneliness just as you would any other companionship. And by means of this natural intercourse, you learn to know him, and you become familiar with his customs and beliefs far better than when he is a paid, and often bored, informant.

There is all the difference between a sporadic plunging into the company of natives, and being really in contact with them. What does this latter mean? On the Ethnographer's side, it means that his life in the village, which at first is a strange, sometimes unpleasant, sometimes intensely interesting adventure, soon adopts quite a natural course very much in harmony with his surroundings.

Soon after I had established myself in Omarakana (Trobriand Islands), I began to take part, in a way, in the village life, to look forward to the important or festive events, to take personal interest in the gossip and the developments of the small village occurrences; to wake up every morning to a day, presenting itself to me more or less as it does to the native. I would get out from under my mosquito net, to find around me the village life beginning to stir, or the people well advanced in their working day according to the hour and also to the season, for they get up and begin their labours early or late, as work presses. As I went on my morning walk through the village, I could see intimate details of family life, of toilet, cooking, taking meals: I could see the arrangements for the day's work, people starting on their errands, or groups of men and women busy at some manufacturing tasks. Quarrels, jokes, family scenes, events usually trivial, sometimes dramatic but always significant, formed the atmosphere of my daily life, as well as of theirs. It must be remembered that as the natives saw me constantly every day, they ceased to be interested or alarmed or made self-conscious by my presence, and I ceased to be a disturbing element in the tribal life which I was to study, altering it by my very approach, as always happens with a new-comer to every savage community. In fact, as they knew that I would thrust my nose into everything, even where a well-mannered native would not dream of intruding, they finished by regarding me as part and parcel of their life, a necessary evil or nuisance, mitigated by donations of tobacco.

Later on in the day, whatever happened was within easy reach, and there was no possibility of its escaping my notice. Alarms about the sorcerer's approach in the evening, one or two big, really important quarrels and rifts within the community, cases of illness, attempted cures and deaths, magical rites which had to be performed, all these I had not to pursue, fearful of missing them, but they took place under my very eyes, at my own doorstep, so to speak. And it must be emphasized whenever anything dramatic or important occurs it is essential to investigate it at the very moment of happening because the natives cannot but talk about it, are too excited to be reticent, and too interested to be mentally lazy in supplying details. Also, over and over again, I committed breaches of etiquette, which the natives, familiar enough with me, were not slow in pointing out. I had to learn how to behave, and to a certain extent, I acquired "the feeling" for native good and bad manners. With this, and with the capacity of enjoying their company and sharing some of their games and amusements, I began to feel that I was indeed in touch with the natives, and this is certainly the preliminary condition of being able to carry on successful field work. . . .

. . . let us descend to more detailed consideration of method. The Ethnographer has in the field, according to what has just been said, the duty before him of drawing up all the rules and regularities of tribal life; all that is permanent and fixed; of giving an anatomy of their culture, of depicting the constitution of their society. But these things, though crystallized and set, are nowhere formulated. There is no written or explicitly expressed code of laws, and their whole tribal tradition, the whole structure of their society, are embodied in the most elusive of all materials, the human being. But not even in human mind or memory are these laws to be found definitely formulated. The natives obey the forces and commands of the tribal code, but they do not comprehend them; exactly as they obey their instincts and their impulses, but could not lay down a single law of psychology. The regularities in native institutions are an automatic result of the interaction of the mental forces of tradition, and of the material conditions of environment. Exactly as a humble member of any modern institution, whether it be the state, or the church, or the army, is of it and in it, but has no vision of the resulting integral action of the whole, still less could furnish any account of its organization, so it would be futile to attempt questioning a native in abstract, sociological terms. The difference is that, in our society, every institution has its intelligent members, its historians, and its archives and documents, whereas in a native society there are none of these. After this is realized an expedient has to be found to overcome this difficulty. This expedient for an Ethnographer consists in collecting concrete data of evidence, and drawing the general inferences for himself. This seems obvious on the face of it, but was not found out or at least practiced in Ethnography till field work was taken up by men of science. Moreover, in giving it practical effect, it is neither easy to devise the concrete applications of this method nor to carry them out systematically and consistently.

Though we cannot ask a native about abstract, general rules, we can always enquire how a given case would be treated. Thus for instance, in asking how they would treat crime, or punish it, it would be vain to put to a native a sweeping question such as "How do you treat and punish a criminal?" for even words could not be found to express it in native, or in pidgin. But an imaginary case, or still better, a real occurrence, will stimulate a native to express his opinion and to supply plentiful information. A real case indeed will start the natives on a wave of discussion, evoke expressions of indignation, show them taking sides—all of which talk will probably contain a wealth of definite views, of moral censures, as well as reveal the social mechanism set in motion by the crime committed. From there, it will be easy to lead them on to speak of other similar cases, to remember other actual occurrences or to discuss them in all their implications and aspects. From this material, which ought to cover the widest possible range of facts, the inference is obtained by simple induction. The scientific treatment differs from that of good common sense, first in that a student will extend the completeness and minuteness of survey much further and in a pedantically systematic and methodical manner; and secondly, in that the scientifically trained mind, will push the inquiry along really relevant lines, and towards aims possessing real importance. Indeed, the object of scientific training is to provide the empirical investigator with a mental chart, in accordance with which he can take his bearings and lay his course.

To return to our example, a number of definite cases discussed will reveal to the Ethnographer the social machinery for punishment. This is one part, one aspect of tribal authority. Imagine further that by a similar method of inference from definite data, he arrives at understanding leadership in war, in economic enterprises, in tribal festivities—there he has at once all the data necessary to answer the questions about tribal government and social authority. In actual field work, the comparison of such data, the attempt to piece them together, will often reveal rifts and gaps in the information which lead on to further investigations.

From my own experience, I can say that, very often, a problem seemed settled, everything fixed and clear, till I began to write down a short preliminary sketch of my results. And only then, did I see the enormous deficiencies, which would show me where lay new problems, and lead me on to new work. In fact, I spent a few months between my first and second expeditions, and over a year between that and the subsequent one, in going over all my materials, and making parts of it almost ready for publication each time I knew I would have to re-write it. Such cross-fertilization of constructive work and observation, I found most valuable, and I do not think I could have made real headway without it. I give this bit of my own history merely to show that what has been said so far is not only an empty programme, but the result of personal experience. In this volume, the description is given of a big institution connected with ever so many associated activities, and presenting many aspects. To anyone who reflects on the subject, it will be clear that the information about a phenomenon of such high complexity and of so many ramifications, could not be obtained with any degree of exactitude and completeness, without a constant interplay of constructive attempts and empirical checking. In fact, I have written up an outline of the Kula institution at least half a dozen times while in the field and in the interval between my expeditions. Each time, new problems and difficulties presented themselves.

The collecting of concrete data over a wide range of facts is thus one of the main points of field method. The obligation is not to enumerate a few examples only, but to exhaust as far as possible all the cases within reach; and, on this search for cases, the investigator will score most whose mental chart is clearest. But, whenever the material of the search allows it, this mental chart ought to be transformed into a real one; it ought to materialize into a diagram, a plan, an exhaustive, synoptic table of cases. Long since, in all tolerably good modern books on natives, we expect to find a full list or table of kinship terms, which includes all the data relative to it, and does not just pick out a few strange and anomalous relationships or expressions. In the investigation of kinship, the following up of one relation after another in concrete cases leads naturally to the construction of genealogical tables. Practiced already by the best early writers, such as Munzinger, and, if I remember rightly, Kubary, this method has been developed to its fullest extent in the works of Dr. Rivers. Again, studying the concrete data of economic transactions, in order to trace the history of a valuable object, and to gauge the nature of its circulation, the principle of completeness and thoroughness would lead to construct tables of transactions, such as we find in the work of Professor Seligman. It is in following Professor Seligman's example in this matter that I was able to settle certain of the more difficult and detailed rules of the Kula. The method of reducing information, if possible, into charts or synoptic tables ought to be extended to the study of practically all aspects of native life. All types of economic transactions may be studied by following up connected, actual cases, and putting them into a synoptic chart; again, a table ought to be drawn up of all the gifts and presents customary in a given society, a table including the sociological, ceremonial, and economic definition of every item. Also, systems of magic, connected series of ceremonies, types of legal acts, all could be charted, allowing each entry to be synoptically defined under a number of headings. Besides this, of course, the genealogical census of every community, studied more in detail, extensive maps, plans and diagrams illustrating ownership in garden land, hunting and fishing privileges, etc., serve as the more fundamental documents of ethnographic research.

A genealogy is nothing else but a synoptic chart of a number of connected relations of kinship. Its value as an instrument of research consists
in that it allows the investigator to put questions which he formulates to
himself in abstracto, but can put concretely to the native informant. As a
document, its value consists in that it gives a number of authenticated data,
presented in their natural grouping. A synoptic chart of magic fulfills the
same function. As an instrument of research, I have used it in order to ascertain, for instance, the ideas about the nature of magical power. With a
chart before me, I could easily and conveniently go over one item after the
other, and note down the relevant practices and beliefs contained in each
of them. The answer to my abstract problem could then be obtained by
drawing a general inference from all the cases. . . .

Living in the village with no other business but to follow native life,
one sees the customs, ceremonies and transactions over and over again,
one has examples of their beliefs as they are actually lived through, and
the full body and blood of actual native life fills out soon the skeleton of abstract constructions. That is the reason why, working under such conditions
as previously described, the Ethnographer is enabled to add something essential to the bare outline of tribal constitution, and to supplement it by all
the details of behavior, setting and small incident. He is able in each case
to state whether an act is public or private; how a public assembly behaves,
and what it looks like; he can judge whether an event is ordinary or an exciting and singular one; whether natives bring to it a great deal of sincere
and earnest spirit, or perform it in fun; whether they do it in a perfunctory
manner, or with zeal and deliberation.

In other words, there is a series of phenomena of great importance
which cannot possibly be recorded by questioning or computing documents,
but have to be observed in their full actuality. Let us call them the imponderabilia of actual life. Here belong such things as the routine of a man's
working day, the details of his care of the body, of the manner of taking
food and preparing it; the tone of conversational and social life around the
village fires, the existence of strong friendships or hostilities, and of passing sympathies and dislikes between people; the subtle yet unmistakable
manner in which personal vanities and ambitions are reflected in the behaviour of the individual and in the emotional reactions of those who surround
him. All these facts can and ought to be scientifically formulated and recorded, but it is necessary that this be done, not by a superficial registra-
tion of details, as is usually done by untrained observers, but with an effort
at penetrating the mental attitude expressed in them. And that is the reason
why the work of scientifically trained observers, once seriously applied to
the study of this aspect, will, I believe, yield results of surpassing value....

As to the actual method of observing-and recording in field work these
imponderabilia of actual life and of typical behaviour, there is no doubt that
the personal equation of the observer comes in here more prominently,
than in the collections of crystallised, ethnographic data. But here also the
main endeavour must be to let facts speak for themselves. If in making a
daily round of the village, certain small incidents, characteristic forms of
taking food, of conversing, of doing work are found occurring over and over
again, they should be noted down at once. It is also important that this work
of collecting and fixing impressions should begin early in the course of
working out a district. Because certain subtle peculiarities, which make an
impression as long as they are novel, cease to be noticed as soon as they
become familiar. Others again can only be perceived with a better knowledge of the local conditions. An ethnographic diary, carried on systematically throughout the course of one's work in a district would be the ideal
instrument for this sort of study. And if, side by side with the normal and
typical, the Ethnographer carefully notes the slight, or the more pronounced
deviations from it, he will be able to indicate the two extremes within which
the normal moves.

In observing ceremonies or other tribal events, such, for instance, as the scene depicted in Plate IV [a scene of a ceremonial distribution], it is necessary, not only to note down those occurrences and details which are prescribed by tradition and custom to be the essential course of the act, but also the Ethnographer ought to record carefully and precisely, one after the other, the actions of the actors and of the spectators. Forgetting for a moment that he knows about and understands the structure of this ceremony, the main dogmatic ideas underlying it, he might try to find himself only in the midst of an assembly of human beings, who behave seriously or jocularly, with earnest concentration or with bored frivolity, who are either in the same mood as he finds them every day, or else are screwed up to a high pitch of excitement, and so on and so on. With his attention constantly directed to this aspect of tribal life, with the constant endeavour to fix it, to express it in terms of actual fact, a good deal of reliable and expressive material finds its way into his notes. He will be able to "set" the act into its proper place in tribal life, that is to show whether it is exceptional or commonplace, one in which the natives behave ordinarily, or one in which their whole behaviour is transformed. And he will also be able to bring all this home to his readers in a clear, convincing manner.

Again, in this type of work, it is good for the Ethnographer sometimes to put aside camera, note book and pencil, and to join in himself in what is going on. He can take part in the natives' games, he can follow them on their visits and walks, sit down and listen and share in their conversation. . . . Out of such plunges into the life of the natives—and I made them frequently not only for study's sake but because everyone needs human company—I have carried away a distinct feeling that their behaviour, their manner of being, in all sorts of tribal transactions, became more transparent and easily understandable than it had been before. . . .

Besides the firm outline of tribal constitution and crystallised cultural items which form the skeleton, besides the data of daily life and ordinary behaviour, which are, so to speak, its flesh and blood, there is still to be recorded the spirit—the natives' views and opinions and utterances. For, in every act of tribal life, there is, first, the routine prescribed by custom and tradition, then there is the manner in which it is carried out, and lastly there is the commentary to it, contained in the natives' mind. A man who submits to various customary obligations, who follows a traditional course of action, does it impelled by certain motives, to the accompaniment of certain feelings, guided by certain ideas. These ideas, feelings, and impulses are moulded and conditioned by the culture in which we find them, and are therefore an ethnic peculiarity of the given society. An attempt must be made therefore, to study and record them.

But is this possible? Are these subjective states not too elusive and shapeless? And, even granted that people usually do feel or think or experience certain psychological states in association with the performance of customary acts, the majority of them surely are not able to formulate these states, to put them into words. This latter point must certainly be granted, and it is perhaps the real Gordian knot in the study of the facts of social psychology. Without trying to cut or untie this knot, that is to solve the problem theoretically, or to enter further into the field of general methodology, I shall make directly for the question of practical means to overcome some of the difficulties involved.

First of all, it has to be laid down that we have to study here stereotyped manners of thinking and feeling. As sociologists, we are not interested in what A or B may feel qua individuals, in the accidental course of their own personal experiences—we are interested only in what they feel and think qua members of a given community. Now in this capacity, their mental states receive a certain stamp, become stereotyped by the institutions in which they live, by the influence of tradition and folk-lore, by the very vehicle of thought, that is by language. The social and cultural environment in which they move forces them to think and feel in a definite manner. Thus, a man who lives in a polyandrous community cannot experience the same feelings of jealousy, as a strict monogynist, though he might have the elements of them. A man who lives within the sphere of the Kula cannot become permanently and sentimentally attached to certain of his possessions, in spite of the fact that he values them most of all. These examples are crude, but better ones will be found in the text of this book.

So, the third commandment of field-work runs: Find out the typical ways of thinking and feeling, corresponding to the institutions and culture of a given community, and formulate the results in the most convincing manner. What will be the method of procedure? The best ethnographical writers—here again the Cambridge school with Haddon, Rivers, and Seligman rank first among English Ethnographers—have always tried to quote verbatim statements of crucial importance. They also adduce terms of native classification; sociological, psychological and industrial termini technici, and have rendered the verbal contour of native thought as precisely as possible. One step further in this line can be made by the Ethnographer, who acquires a knowledge of the native language and can use it as an instrument of inquiry. In working in the Kiriwinian language, I found still some difficulty in writing down the statement directly in translation which at first I used to do in the act of taking notes. The translation often robbed the text of all its significant characteristics—rubbed off all its points—so that gradually I was led to note down certain important phrases just as they were spoken in the native tongue. As my knowledge of the language progressed, I put down more and more in Kiriwinian, till at last I found myself writing exclusively in that language, rapidly taking notes, word for word of each statement. . . .

Our considerations thus indicate that the goal of ethnographic field-work must be approached through three avenues:

1. The organisation of the tribe, and the anatomy of its culture must be recorded in firm, clear outline. The method of concrete, statistical documentation is the means through which such an outline has to be given.

2. Within this frame, the imponderabilia of actual life, and the type of behaviour have to be filled in. They have to be collected through minute, detailed observations, in the form of some sort of ethnographic diary, made possible by close contact with native life.

3. A collection of ethnographic statements, characteristic narratives, typical utterances, items of folk-lore and magical formulae has to be given as a corpus inscriptionum, as documents of native mentality.

Protecting One's Informants

Margaret Mead has contributed so much, both to scientific knowledge and method and to the effective communication of results and of the field work necessary to achieve them, that it is not easy to select one or a few excerpts to represent the great range of her thinking and practice with regard to field work.

The excerpt presented here was selected because it calls attention to one of Dr. Mead's earliest and least-known publications, and because it deals with the problems of "protecting one's informants"—an aspect of the field worker's perennial problem in reporting. Since her other writings are widely available, this item is included as a reminder to the reader to review them as well.

The student, in particular, will want to read her Male and Female[10]—

10. Margaret Mead, Male and Female: A Study of the Sexes in a Changing World (New York: William Morrow & Co., 1949).

especially chapter ii, "How an Anthropologist Writes," appendix ii, "The Ethics of Insight-Giving," and appendix iii, "Sources and Experience in Our American Culture," which latter includes a bit of autobiography as well as a bibliography listing her writings on American culture.[11]

The following excerpts are not intended to represent the study as a whole or even the problems of studying culture contact that are dealt with. A few lines from the Foreword by Clark Wissler are given first, to help place this study—really an early approach to applied anthropology—in relation to previous knowledge of the American Indian.[12]

This is a pioneer study in a neglected field. Many years of patient research have been given to recording and understanding what aboriginal cultures were before and during the early period of contact between Indian and white, with scarcely a thought as to what has happened since then. Naturally such studies were undertaken to satisfy curiosity rather than to be useful, but even so they were the first necessary steps to a study of culture change as presented in this book. Further, it is because this initial task has been so well done for the Indian tribes of the United States that the way is now clear to study the Indian in our midst instead of the Indian living a free life in forest and plains. Thus the author of this volume could approach her chosen problem well equipped with an intimate knowledge of white culture on the one hand and on the other a well-organized body of data respecting the old tribal culture which ultimately came into collision with white culture, the result being the situation in which the tribe now finds itself. No one seems to be satisfied with the outcome, Indian or white. According to popular belief, the Indian has met with little short of disaster at the hands of the whites. . . . Such statements may be too sweeping, in that attention is fixed upon the most tragic phase of the adjustment instead of upon the whole cycle of contact. . . .

A complete study of the Antlers would entail a searching inquiry in each of these successive periods of white contact, a program now under way among some neighboring tribes. Dr. Mead, however, undertook a more restricted examination of the tribal woman as she reacts in this present period of white contact. . . .

From the book itself, the excerpt below[13] illustrates activities in the particular instance of the role of participant as observer developed by Dr. Mead in this situation:

In selecting an Indian community in which to study the American Indian woman in transition, I was guided by several considerations: the tribe chosen must still preserve its group integrity, so that it could be studied

---

11. Ibid., pp. 22-47, 431-50, 451-63. On the problems of anthropological training, see also her article "The Training of the Cultural Anthropologist," American Anthropologist, LIV (July-September, 1952), 343-46; and its companion-piece by Eliot D. Chapple, "The Training of the Professional Anthropologist: Social Anthropology and Applied Anthropology," pp. 340-42.

12. Margaret Mead, The Changing Culture of an Indian Tribe (New York: Columbia University Press, 1932). Foreword by Clark Wissler, pp. vii-ix.

13. Ibid., pp. 15-18.

as a community; contact must have been sufficiently prolonged so that English could be used in the investigation; it was desirable to have some good ethnographic data on the aboriginal condition of the tribe in question; the group had to be large enough to present variety and perspective and small enough so that the total situation could be envisaged and analyzed. The group chosen had these desiderata. It is presented anonymously here, under the pseudonym of the Antler Tribe, to shield the feelings of individuals and to give no affront to the tribal pride. This study should be regarded as a statement of conditions on an American Indian Reservation in 1930, conditions which are by no means typical of all reservations, but which have, nevertheless, much in common with past conditions on some reservations, with conditions into which other groups of allotted Indians may, under similar circumstances, be expected to drift.

The investigation was conducted during the months of June to October in the summer of 1930. English was used throughout, as there is not sufficient unrecorded cultural material to warrant the necessary expenditure of two or three months' time in learning the language. The Indians were not cognizant of the fact that any such investigation was being conducted but believed that I was merely killing time in idle conversation or attendance at ceremonies. For the most part, no notes were taken in the informants' presence but conversations were written up immediately afterwards. The one exception to this was detailed reorganization of census material which the informant believed I was doing for another investigator. Such unawareness was essential to the successful prosecution of a study involving intimate details of contemporary life. I took into the house with me a young Indian girl from one of the more conservative families. As these Indians do not work habitually as servants, and as most contact between white and Indian on the reservation is superficial and extradomestic, this was a sufficiently aberrant situation to set up more intimate relations with all her kin than would otherwise have been possible. As I became responsible for her chaperonage, I gained a most vivid insight into the mother and daughter situation on the reservation. At the same time, as I accompanied her in a less official capacity to many festivities, I also became well acquainted with her age group. From among the many women with whom I became acquainted, I selected a few as capable spokeswomen of different general and selected points of view. So I had one special informant from the first generation who went away to school, and one of that generation who did not go away; a wife who had clung hard to the older customs, and a wife who had married an Indian from another tribe and therefore had to make a different adjustment; a woman from another tribe who had married an Antler, a white woman who had married an Antler, a half-breed woman who had married a full-blood, etc. These special informants, with whom I grew more intimate than with the majority of the Antler women of my acquaintance, I used to illuminate the problems which were especially relevant to their position in the tribe. In the limited time at my disposal this was the only possible method to pursue. I spent a great deal of time acquiring, with apparent casualness, the personal histories of people whom I had not yet met—so that when I met them, I could divert the conversation along revealing lines. In this way, chance contacts at dances, in a store, at someone else's house, could be utilized. I was able to give less attention to the children than I have ever given before, partly through pressure of time and partly because of the scattered residence conditions. I knew well two small girls of nine and twelve, and knew enough of their friends so that I could use them in some measure as informants. I also knew a few men, selected because they were typical of some group in the tribe. Work of this sort and participation in group activities such as dances and funeral ceremonies were supplemented by various types of tabular treatment of the regular census lists. Conditions or tendencies revealed by such analysis were then re-examined with individual informants.

It is my plan to present first a general picture of tribal conditions among the Antler, and to follow this with studies of individuals. Any historical statement, it will be understood, must necessarily be of so general a character as to give background without the precise details which would be too revealing. The whole investigation is presented tentatively as a first step in this kind of analysis of primitive societies in the throes of transition.

The Observer as Participant and the Problem of Bias

In their Methods of Social Study, Sidney and Beatrice Webb carefully describe and illustrate their entire rationale for research and include many bits of wisdom regarding field work. Perhaps the few selections given here will be provocative enough to interest the reader in the entire volume.

The Webbs provide a case for a rationale for research which, especially with respect to its long-run political purposes and its scientific theoretical orientation, predisposed them to the field worker role we call observer as participant. That is, they became publicly known, and even famous, primarily as observers. As they became public figures, they also developed their roles as participants (or even partisans), and they may even have, on occasion, stepped over into the field worker role we call participant as observer. But in gathering information for their social studies, they seem to have subordinated participation to observation. As for the role we call complete participant, the Webbs clearly state both its advantages and the extreme rarity of its use in the social sciences.[14]

In their Preface, the Webbs define the scope of their book in terms of what their speciality is as well as what it is not.[15]

In this short book we have done little more than give in detail the methods of investigation used by us in our successive studies of British Trade Unionism, Consumers' Co-operation, and Local Government. It is true that, in our first chapter and in the last, we have attempted to define the scope and necessary limitations of the science of society. But these pages do not claim to be anything of the nature of a treatise on methodology, or even on the place of social science or sociology in the classification of the sciences. They merely explain our own approach to an understanding of the department of sociology dealing with the upgrowth, the modification and the dwindling, sometimes even to insignificance—of particular kinds of social institutions. Hence the reader must not look for any discussion of the relation of political science to ethics, or whether or not there can usefully be a "pure" science of economics, proceeding by logical deduction from theoretical assumptions or postulates as to the universality or predominance of particular human motives. . . . Moreover, in the department on which our studies have been concentrated, we have been unable, through lack of qualification, to use, and perhaps even adequately to appreciate, the Statistical Method. Our speciality has been a comparative study of the working of particular social institutions in a single country, made by observation and analysis, through personal participation or watch-

---

14. Sidney and Beatrice Webb, Methods of Social Study (London: Longmans, Green & Co., 1932), chapter viii, "Watching the Institution at Work," especially pp. 158-60 and p. 159 n.

15. Ibid., Preface, pp. v-vi.

ing the organization at work, the taking of evidence from other persons, the scrutiny of all accessible documents, and the consultation of general literature. . . .

The Webbs begin the first chapter with an exposition of their working theoretical orientation:[16]

If this were a book on the methods of chemical study it would not be necessary to begin with a chapter on the province of the science of chemistry. But social science or sociology is neither so clearly marked off as chemistry from other branches of knowledge, nor is its scope so uniformly understood by all sorts and conditions of men. A loose and indefinite impression as to the exact sphere of social science may not interfere with our learning all that the citizen needs to know about the constitution and functions of the various social institutions amid which we live. If, however, our object is to make new discoveries in social science, that is, to extend in this sphere, the boundaries of knowledge—if, moreover, we desire to make the best use of the instruments of investigation and research that are open to us—it is important, at the outset, to clear up our ideas as to the province of the science on which our attention is to be concentrated.

There follows a discussion of "The Subject-Matter of Sociology," "The Facts with Which Sociology Deals," and "Classification of Social Facts"—a fourfold classification of social institutions "for which we claim no higher value than that of practical convenience in handling the subject."[17] They mention other possible classifications, but conclude: "None of these classifications seems to us to have any bearing on the methods by which the subject can be best studied" and add, "How best to undertake this task will be the subject of the following chapters."[18]

In chapter ii, "The Mental Equipment of the Social Investigator," we find the following:[19]

What is the mental equipment, what is the ideal state of mind, with which the student should start on the exploration of any specific piece of social organization? First, he must be able to focus his attention on what he sees or hears or reads. Secondly, he must be prepared to set himself deliberately and patiently to ascertain all the accessible facts about the social institution that he is studying; and not imagine that he can, until he has mastered these facts, discover the solution of any problem, or obtain any useful answer to any general question, that may have been in his mind. Finally, he must realize that he is biassed, and somehow or other he must manage to discount this bias. We deal separately with these three warnings. . . .

The Need for Trained Attention

The first indispensable factor in successful investigation or fruitful observation, and one which is often overlooked, is an efficient attention. It

16. Ibid., p. 1.

17. Ibid., pp. 29-30.

18. Ibid., p. 30.

19. Ibid., pp. 31-33.

is quite easy to read books or hear lectures without apprehending one half of what they contain—a carelessness amounting almost to blindness or deafness. . . . This common failure of attention is not due merely to intellectual dullness or slowness. Many intelligent and even quick-witted people make a like failure owing to a sort of kink in their minds, which, unless corrected by mental training, will always destroy most of their efficiency as discoverers, and even reduce enormously their capacity as learners. . . .

 . . . To be a good listener you need genuinely to desire to hear what others have to say, rather than to utter what you have yourself to say. There is, in fact, a "moral" defect at the root of the failure of most beginners to achieve discoveries. They fail, it has been said, "because they set out to prove something rather than to arrive at the truth, whatever it may be. They do not realize that a good half of most research work consists in an attempt to prove yourself wrong. Intellectual honesty is discouraged by politics, religion, and even courtesy. It is the hardest and most essential of the habits which the scientist, whether professional or amateur, must form."

What the Webbs call "The False Start of a Question To Be Answered" should be read in its entirety for the full development of their argument, and for the bit of autobiography contributed by Mrs. Webb, "the daughter of a successful business entrepreneur in Victorian England," who personally experienced the contradictory results of inquiries by "individualists" and "socialists." The central point is concisely put in the following:[20]

The False Start of a Question To Be Answered

And this brings us to a danger point at the very outset of social study. The false start which pseudo-investigation usually takes is the plausible one of asking a question. We are all apt to begin by referring to the arbitrament of "the facts" some question in which we happen to be particularly interested, a question which has all the appearance of strict impartiality, but which is almost invariably what the lawyers call a "leading question," if only because it is necessarily put in a phraseology involving a particular environment or set of conditions.

In our terms, the role of complete observer is rejected by the Webbs[21] as "inhuman" and impossible:

An Objective Study of Facts

Hence the only right way in which to approach the subject matter of sociology is not to focus the enquiry upon discovering the answer to some particular question in which you may be interested. On the contrary, you should choose a particular section of the social environment, or, more precisely, a particular social institution, and sit down patiently in front of it, exactly as if it were a form of energy or a kind of matter, the type-specimen of a plant or some species of animal, and go on working steadfastly to acquire all possible information about it, with the sole purpose of discovering every fact concerning its constitution and its activities, together with every ascertainable action and reaction between it and its environment.

The Inevitable Presence of Bias

"Know thyself" is the maxim uniquely imperative on the investigator of

---

20. Ibid., p. 34.

21. Ibid., pp. 41, 44, 46-47.

social institutions. For the greatest obstacle to the advancement of knowledge—an obstacle blocking up the very gateway of the enquiry—is an obstacle in the mind of the student, the presence of bias. He must take it as certain that he will not approach his subject-matter with complete intellectual
disinterestedness. Nor can such an inhuman detachment be asked of him....
. . . The practical suggestion is that we must, if we are to arrive at
correct conclusions—that is, if we are to succeed in making "our order of
thought" correspond with "the order of things"—seek to choose methods of
approaching the subject-matter and of conducting our investigations that
will, for the time being, throw our bias out of gear.

Having accepted it as inevitable that the social researcher will always

be personally biased as a participant, they state it as a task to learn how

to "throw our bias out of gear," and in the following[22] they discuss the oth-

er face of this same coin:

The Need for Sympathetic Understanding

Here we touch on a possible obstacle to investigation and a hindrance
to discovery which is the very opposite of personal bias, and for which due
allowance is seldom made. It has been suggested that, at any rate in the
sphere of psychology and in that of sociology, no one can adequately appreciate in other persons—perhaps no one can even recognize in them—feelings, emotions, or intellectual experiences which the investigator has not
himself in some degree felt or endured. Can a seeing person ever understand what life means to one blind from birth? . . . And, to put the issue
more generally, can the investigator, coming from one social class, ever
accurately analyze the dynamic force and the specific direction of the feelings of another social class?
It is clear that a sensitive mind and broad human sympathies, coupled
with width and variety of experience, form part of the equipment of the
ideal investigator, as they do that of the greatest novelist or dramatist.
. . . We cannot expect our social investigators to be Shakespeares or
Goethes. We may, however, warn them of the specific hindrance, in their
vocation, of imperfect sympathies. They can be on the watch for the com-
moner sorts of social blindness or deafness, which makes us fail to appreciate whatever we have not ourselves known. They can remember to take
precautions against omissions and inattentions. They can arrange to supplement their own investigations by those of persons having different temperaments or different experiences. Above all, they can always keep in
mind that, not even for the sake of extirpating their own personal bias,
must they for a moment lose their abiding sense of human fellowship.

In our own terms, the Webbs here suggest that while the role of com-

plete participant may not be feasible for gathering all the information field

workers seek, the range and variety of personal experiences as a natural

(non-scientific) complete participant in many different social groupings

may be increased desirably in the life careers of social investigators, ei-

ther before they come to work as such or during their work, especially in

the field, in their vocation as social scientists. In the latter case (as in the

model of the complete participant who penetrates the in-group from the out-

side), the role for the field worker is one in which his being conscious of

his duties as an observer puts him under considerable stress to maintain

_____

22. Ibid., pp. 47-49.

all the pretenses that the expected behavior requires of him. The Webbs
are not arguing for this model, so much as they are recognizing that in the
individual's entire life career he may have a whole series of experiences
as a natural complete participant in a number of groupings and situations
and that the depth or quality and range or variety of these experiences contribute to his personal equipment for the vocation of social investigator.
The Webbs also speak from the point of view one may call "the management
of research" when they advise, as above, supplementing one's own investigations "by those of persons having different temperaments or different experiences" and when they urge the "positive advantage in 'group work' over
individual effort"[23] in sociological inquiries. But in this book they give
more attention to "individual effort" than to the design and direction of
group enterprise.

In concluding their consideration of "The Mental Equipment of the Social Investigator," the Webbs offer some bits of wisdom[24] which should
serve the student who wishes to appraise his own capacities for, and commitment to, a professional career in the kind of social investigation which
interested the Webbs:

Preliminary Education

Is there any particular education that will fit the student to carry out
from start to finish a big and complicated investigation? As soon as the
public becomes aware of the importance of deciding policy on political and
industrial activities upon the basis of a genuinely scientific knowledge of
the structure and functions of society, this question will require to be answered.

The present authors cannot claim sufficient knowledge or experience
of alternative methods of training the intellect and the character to be able
to answer this question. What may be useful will be for them to indicate
the kind of faculties that they have found to be required by the sociological
investigator, and to add their own very loose observations as to the results
of particular kinds of education and of social antecedents upon the amateur
scientist.

First, let us note the distinction between the faculties required in the
technique of social investigation presently to be described, and the intellectual qualities called for both in the initiation of the enquiry, and in the successful application—which has to be both scientifically productive and effectively rendered from a literary standpoint—of what is discovered. For
the daily routine of social investigation—which we shall presently explain
in detail as the art of note-taking, the methods of personal observation and
the interview, the use of documents and literary sources, and the collection
and manipulation of statistics—the predominant requirements are patience
and persistence in work; precision in the use of words and figures; prompt-
ness of decision in picking out new facts and ignoring what is only "common
form"; a genuine satisfaction in continuing to progress along a previously
determined course; above all, that particular form of intellectual curiosity
that delights in unravelling complicated details irrespective of their immediate relevance to the main lines of the enquiry—the impulse in fact of

23. Ibid., p. 43.

24. Ibid., pp. 49-53.

Browning's "Grammarian." "All the scholars of any distinction have pos-
sessed the instincts of the collector and puzzle-solver," remark MM. Lang-
lois and Seignobos. And last, but by no means least, there is a great advantage of a handwriting sufficiently neat and legible, to render the subsequent
reading of the notes by yourself and other people an easy, or at least, a not
too repellent task. Now, all these capacities seem to us to be within the
reach of almost every intelligent person who has been properly educated.
It is unfortunate that they seem more generally developed in the England of
today in men and women who have enjoyed some such training as that of the
elementary school teacher, or that of the newer types of professionals (such
as the auditor and the actuary), or that of the second division clerk in the
civil service, than in all but the ablest of those who have had the advantage
of what is usually called the Public School and University education in the
humanities. Whatever may be the particular accomplishments or graces of
the successful graduate in Arts, especially when he comes from a well-to-
do home, it is disappointing to record that such students are, when they
leave the university, often lacking in certain characteristics required for
the daily task of sociological investigation. So many of them have a high
standard of leisure and holidays; an impatience with what they feel to be
mere drudgery; an objection to the uncomfortable conditions of life that are
often called for in the methods of personal observation and the interview; a
distaste for the boredom involved in intimate association with uninteresting
or positively disagreeable people; an attitude of aloofness from the life and
labour of the ruck of men and women who constitute the very object of the
study in question; and the usual craving for "quick returns," especially in
the form of attractive generalizations with political or other topical applications—all characteristics which, for the purpose of sociological enquiry,
need to be corrected if it is desired to start without a grave handicap in the
race for the advancement of knowledge as distinguished from that for the
popularization of ideas. On the other hand the wide reading in philosophy
and history; the personal intercourse with politicians and journalists that
may have been enjoyed; the intimate contact with leading men of business
and highly placed civil servants; foreign travel; and a working acquaintance
with foreign languages, literature, and institutions will give such graduates
a great advantage in the work of initiating and organizing an enquiry and in
the literary expression of its results, over those investigators who have
had a more intensive and more narrowly specialized training; and especially over those who have had to begin their working lives whilst still non-
adult. Moreover, the predominantly mathematical training obtained by some
students, especially if this has included a real application to statistics,
gives such graduates advantages of their own in the use of statistical method, even if they find it necessary to learn that the mathematician is in danger of paying for the superiority of his instrument by a tendency to under-
value the qualitative estimate of his data, leading even to unsoundness in
his logical inferences. To the impatience with whatever cannot be discovered in a comfortable study and quantitatively expressed in a formula or
an equation we shall subsequently recur. How best to combine in the education of a single individual, the training which produces the most effective
daily work of the sociological investigator with that which enables the investigation to be most skillfully chosen and initiated, and ensures the most
fruitful presentation and application of the result, is a practical problem
of which we can offer no solution.

Field Work Roles in Applied Anthropology

The field work which concerns us in this book emphasizes obtaining
information-in-society through some role permitting a kind and degree of
"participation" in an on-going situation that is geared to both scientific and
ethical considerations in the long as well as the short run. These consider-

ations become important, and raise the most difficult problems, when the field work is done on those frontiers of knowledge where certainty of the exact nature of the data needed is not great, and the urge of "curiosity" is not only strong but favorably encouraged to cast the net as wide as possible. In this case the search is not for data but for information from which, it is hoped, new constructs in knowledge-about-society will be derived that may point to correspondingly new kinds of data that then need to be more sharply specified for widely repeated researches to secure verification of the new hypotheses.

In applied social science studies, it is necessary to pursue different goals which call for a different combination of field work activities. There is accordingly a much greater emphasis upon direct collection of data—the recording of instances or occurrences of what has been agreed upon, in advance, as meaningful to a number of skilled observers including the one reporting. One prototype of the skilled observer is the psychiatrist, a possibly derivative type is the survey interviewer (or social laboratory observer) who, after prescribed training, gathers data under supervision or other controls. Thus, the skilled (or controlled) observer, by virtue of his competence (due to supervision or instruments) selects and records only what is significant. Knowledge of the data is built into the observation processes, so to speak, and "curiosity" may be intentionally fettered, out of regard for limited resources to accomplish the applied task and with the intent of reducing "noise" (information which, like radio static, obscures the desired signals or data "bits").

How this problem was viewed in a remarkable study accomplished during World War II in the Poston (Arizona) Japanese Relocation Camp is summarized in the following excerpt:[25]

Methods of collecting data through staff activities and through our own field work were developed rather gropingly, but eventually took the form of five general approaches applied more or less simultaneously.[*]
1. General observation of what was happening and what was being said in all the parts of the community we could reach. Casual conversations were included in these recordings, but special emphasis was placed on meetings that were held concerning community problems, politics, religion and recreation.
2. Intensive interviews which consisted in prolonged and repeated discussion with certain representative individuals on topics relevant to ascertaining information about sentiments and social organization.
3. Records were collected, in whole or in part, from all available

25. Alexander H. Leighton, The Governing of Men: General Principles and Recommendations Based on Experience at a Japanese Relocation Camp (Princeton, N.J.: Princeton University Press, 1945), pp. 388-90.

*A. H. Leighton and associates, "Assessing Public Opinion in a Dislocated Community," Public Opinion Quarterly, VII (Winter, 1943), 652.

sources such as the census office, the employment division, welfare and
schools.

4. Public opinion polls according to standard techniques were conducted during the latter part of our field work. (We are greatly indebted to
Harry H. Field, director of the National Opinion Research Center and to
the members of his staff for training two of our field workers, Toshio Yat-
sushiro and Iwao Ishino, in public opinion polling methods and for supervis-
ing their subsequent surveys.)

5. Personality studies of a limited number of individuals with emphasis on life-stories, interpersonal relationships, mental and emotional make-
up, and deeper patterns of sentiment were secured through interviews and
a few psychological tests.

Our view of the data-gathering problem in the community may be represented schematically in the accompanying diagram.

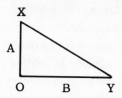

A indicates the amount of data gathered per individual, increasing toward the top, while B indicates the number of persons concerning whom it
is possible to gather data, increasing toward the right. Thus there is a con-
tinuum from studies of one individual to studies of the entire community,
with the amount of materials that it is possible to gather inversely related
to the number of individuals. Personality studies would come at the upper
apex of the triangle (X) representing considerable material about a few individuals while census records, containing as they did some facts on everybody, would be at the bottom (Y). Between these two extremes come the
other forms of data gathering.

What the diagram helps to make clear is that any type of material is
rendered much more valuable by correlation with other types than when
condensed by itself. For example, a personality study might reveal sentiments of considerable significance in understanding a particular Japanese
American tuna fisherman, but whether or not these were important among
tuna fishermen generally could be found only by some sort of sampling
through interview or observation; and whether or not tuna fishermen are
significant in the total community would involve some reference to census
records. Conversely, the "deeper" meanings of sentiments discovered
through polling techniques might very well be much illuminated by personality studies on a few individuals.

Consequently, we determined to obtain as much material as possible
from the total area represented in the triangular figure and to avoid viewing the community through one technique limited to one level of data sampling.

With the realization of the importance of breadth, there was at the
same time the need to avoid becoming so all-inclusive as to be inconclu-
sive. The aims of the research which have been mentioned limited the
manner in which the total area in the triangle would be used. We were not
trying to acquire all the facts about everything but to approach our particular problems in such a way that we would gather all the facts pertinent to
our problems from all sources. Of course, we did not succeed in this, but
it was a goal, the striving for which sharpened rather than muddled our
work.

In the full report from which this excerpt is taken, it becomes clear
that a wide repertory of field work roles was developed, ranging from those

close to our complete participant type (e.g., the training of aides among the Japanese evacuees), through participant as observer (e.g., the author, and others, were staff members in the administration at Poston, as well as observers), and observer as participant (e.g., the author and others, again, in winning the confidence of the evacuees as persons who were "all right," partly through playing "a role somewhat analogous to the 'counselors' in the Western Electric Company"[26]). Even the complete observer type of role received some use: for example, in addition to recording data as assigned, the field workers each kept "a journal that was absolutely private and personal" which enabled him "to put things down as he saw and felt them and then decide later about how and when to contribute them," and these "private notes on things that had high emotional significance" could make valuable additions to the general file "months afterward, when the matter had cooled off."[27] While in one phase this activity of a staff member was in the complete participant type of role, the delay in reporting permitted him to regain his detachment by imaginatively taking on the complete observer role (not letting it be known what he had recorded) but then eventually to resume his staff member role as a contributor of valued observations, with the objectivity permitted by acting in the observer as participant position.

In this last excerpt we have hinted at the great variety of adaptations made by field workers in practice. In the next chapter we shall take a closer look at some adaptations made by researchers in "tight" situations or in dealing with "delicate" information and the like.

---

26. Ibid., p. 382.

27. Ibid., p. 392.

IV

THE FIELD WORKER'S ADAPTATIONS

Certain situations of observation for social science, such as that for the ethnographer who must start from scratch by learning the language of his esoteric people, present something like a darkened labyrinth, a social maze through which the field worker must "feel his way." His general adaptation, or his adoption of a role that suits most occasions, grows from a multitude of trial-and-error attempts to improve his opportunities to learn more. He undergoes a more or less profound "sea change" in himself, and whether for better or worse becomes unlike other men, for he has lived in at least two worlds.

Other situations of observation, more often encountered by sociologists in some part of an otherwise already familiar cultural milieu, differ from this ethnographer model. The field worker studying an institution in his own society must also thread his way through a maze of relationships, but he will often be able to anticipate specific adaptations in what he may call his methodology and hence to design and even schedule his field activities so as to limit the unexpected. This is partly because he already has access to knowledge about the kind of organization to be studied and even about the major kinds of relationships and persons he will encounter. His own experiences and those of others before him facilitate his tailoring of adaptations in advance of each stage, at least, of his research enterprise, and he may even be able to formulate a general approach to be maintained throughout.

The selections which follow emphasize the adaptive approach of the field worker to situations which, while familiar to him as a member of the same larger society, are "tight" (or otherwise not easy of access for direct observation) and which require him to secure "delicate" information and solve special problems in social science reporting. The excerpts are given in an order that illustrates such situations for research into: the family, the person, the business enterprise, the medical profession, the public school, and the urban parish.

In making these selections I have not emphasized, though I include mention of, adaptations that go to the extreme of what is commonly called "the participant-observer method," namely, that which we label the complete participant role. It is possible that some attempts to do research

from this position are based upon confusion between this role and that of
complete observer. That is, the disengagement and objectivity that scientific observation seems to require are sought by adopting, intellectually, a
stance like that of complete observer, but, in practice, the field worker
finds himself entering the situation with a burden of many pretenses and a
commitment to complete participant activities.

Two recent books, by authors far from so naïve as to be guilty of the
confusion mentioned, do however illustrate the hazards, as well as the advantages, of the approach in question. The first is a study[1] of a small
group called the "Seekers," who claimed to be receiving messages from beings in outer space who warned them of the impending end of the world on a
specified date. A few of the researchers joined the group and observed reactions when the prophecy failed. The second briefly summarizes William
Caudill's experience as "a concealed observer"[2]—that is, one in the role
of complete participant as a patient in a psychiatric hospital, receiving
"psychotherapy," etc.—and the body of the book consists of his report on a
later study of the same hospital which he carried out openly in the role of
"research anthropologist"—that is, one which allowed him to act in the observer-as-participant position most of the time, with occasional activities
in relations with patients and nurses in "a minor functional role" as a staff
member, one who, however, "avoided being drawn into decision-making situations." Both Dr. Redlich, the psychiatrist who initiated both studies as
the head of the hospital, and Dr. Caudill, the anthropologist, agree that
they do not recommend "a repetition of the first type of study" and the
many reasons include ethical considerations as well as serious doubts
about the scientific value of results so obtained.

The Family

In the following, Professor Bossard points to the social evaluations
people make regarding the information sought by the field worker interested in personal and intimate affairs, and the consequences of those evaluations for his operations and hence for his role. He makes us realize that,
in using the questionnaire or other methods which manifestly guarantee the
anonymity of the respondent, even to the observer, the latter can identify

---

1. Leon Festinger, Henry W. Riecken, and Stanley Schacter, When
Prophecy Fails (Minneapolis: University of Minnesota Press, 1956). Also
see, for a discussion of the role as perceived by one of the observers and
co-authors, Henry W. Riecken, "The Unidentified Observer," American
Journal of Sociology, LXII (1956), 210-12.

2. The Psychiatric Hospital as a Small Society, with a Foreword by
F. C. Redlich, M. D. (Cambridge: Commonwealth Fund, Harvard University Press, 1958).

himself as a social scientist in a role somewhere between that of complete observer and that of observer-as-participant. Insofar as the scientist can elicit meaningful responses with minimal participation on his part, he remains somewhat removed from the observer-as-participant position.

Mutual and total anonymity of subjects and field workers would, of course, put the scientist in the complete observer position, but if, in order to induce the desired responses, he uses his rank or general position in his respected institution of learning, he reduces by so much his own anonymity and would at least be acting as an institutional representative.

Actually, in this case,[3] the field workers were quite openly taking the role of observer as participant and Professor Bossard can thus publicly discuss the confidential, secret, or even private kinds of information on which data for his scientific purposes depend, because he can protect the anonymity of respondents.

One of the curious omissions in the literature on methodology in the study of human behavior is the relative failure to recognize the adaptations which need to be made (a) on the basis of the nature of the subject studied, and (b) of the differentials which exist among the people from whom the information is obtained. The common assumption seems to be that sound methodology is sound methodology, wherever and on whomever it is applied. Our experience in the study of the family is quite the reverse, emphasizing the fact that methodology is rather a relative matter which needs to be adapted, and re-adapted, constantly on the basis of circumstances encountered. One is reminded here of the experience of many novices when they turn to the game of golf. Instruction from golf mentors is apt to overwhelm the learner so completely with admonitions and rules on the "form" to be maintained that he forgets the main object of the game, which is to sink a golf ball in the next hole in the fewest possible number of strokes. It is not unlikely that many students of behavior are so overwhelmed with the emphasis on the technical forms and procedures in research that they forget the main object, which is to obtain new insight into a problem. All this, of course, is not said to depreciate the value of sound instruction and training in research: it is rather meant as a note of warning concerning a too slavish devotion to the relative emptiness of mere rule of thumb.

The first factor necessitating adaptations of methodology is the nature of the subject to be investigated. Consider, for example, such a difficult problem as sex behavior. What method or methods are of the greatest value in such a study? Kinsey and his associates* place their reliance on the personal interview, with much emphasis upon the methods of establishing contacts with cases; securing the interest, and self-interest, of those interviewed; the establishment of rapport between the interviewee and the interviewer; and various technical devices in interviewing. By way of contrast, Lewis M. Terman, of no mean experience as an investigator of human behavior, suggests that some of the information sought by Kinsey and his associates "would have been more accurately reported had a method been

————————
3. James H. S. Bossard, "The Study of Family Life: A Methodological Postscript," chapter x in Ritual and Family Living: A Contemporary Study by James H. S. Bossard and Eleanor S. Boll (Philadelphia: University of Pennsylvania Press, 1950), pp. 217-23.

*Alfred C. Kinsey, W. B. Pomeroy, and C. E. Martin, Sexual Behavior in the Human Male (Philadelphia: W. B. Saunders Co., 1948), chap. ii.

used which prevented the investigator from learning the identity of any of his respondents."[*] Obviously, Terman has in mind the questionnaire method.

An example from our own experience might also be cited. For some years we have been seeking primary information on the child's discovery of the sex life of his parents. For many reasons, this is a painful and difficult subject on which to obtain data. Trial of various methods had led us to rely mainly on written accounts anonymously submitted. By explaining fully the nature of our quest to various groups of persons, we have sought, with limited success, to interest individuals in writing out a personal document in this field, with some accompanying but not specifically identifying information.

The study of family ritual has, by its very nature, been a relatively easy subject to study. There is nothing embarrassing about such a subject of investigation. Most families observe a few rituals, at least; most of them are quite willing, and often eager, to tell or to write out accounts of them. The very sense or feeling of rightness which accompanies the observance of family rituals makes the informant willing to describe them ordinarily to the interested and sympathetic student. Our distinctive approach in this particular study, then, has been to assume with our cases that families ordinarily developed some rituals as a matter of course, that they were of all kinds and varieties, and that our main interest was in discovering their range and relative frequency. Other aspects and applications of the study were made known subsequently. This seemed on the whole a satisfactory mode of operation.

The second factor necessitating adaptations in the methodology of research into family behavior is to be found in the differences which prevail among the persons from whom information is obtained. Some persons are outgoing in their responses: frank, objective often, uninhibited to some degree at least. It is easy for them to look at their own behavior and to help you do so. There are others who are "tight-eared" or "tight-lipped," i.e., they have difficulty in understanding what it is that one wants to know, or in telling one if they do know. Differences of this kind are partly a matter of individual variation, but one comes also to wonder if there are not group differentials of this kind, as for instance between cultural groups. Do Jews as a group frequently combine introspective tendencies with willingness to verbalize to a relatively high degree? Is it true, as one has been told repeatedly, that the Pennsylvania German would rather "part with his right arm than tell his marital problems to anyone?" Does the reticence of the Vermonter carry over when he is a subject in a scientific investigation? Here is an intriguing problem in research methodology: to discover if, and to what extent, there are group differentials of this kind in responsiveness to social investigation, especially to questions and problems of a more personal and intimate kind.

Another striking difference between individuals and groups, is to be found in their varying capacities to understand and use words. We have written elsewhere of the different levels of language at which families express themselves, and of the fact that social class marks the most striking line of cleavage in our language records of families.[†] These differences are of many kinds—words commonly used, use of imagery and figurative expressions, precision in word meaning, range of vocabulary and appreciation of verbal distinctions. One cannot consciously observe word usages among people without becoming aware of the fact that many persons do not verbalize readily, and hence have difficulty in understanding just what information is wanted, as well as in telling what they do know. These differ-

---

[*]Lewis M. Terman. "Kinsey's Sexual Behavior in the Human Male: Some Comments and Criticisms," Psychological Bulletin, XLV (September, 1948), 443.

[†]James H. S. Bossard, The Sociology of Child Development (New York, Harper & Bros., 1948), chap. ix.

ences often coincide with educational and class levels. Certainly the use of the questionnaire, interview, or life history document must be guided to a large extent by the ability to verbalize of the individual or group involved. Here again is a challenging problem in research methods: How do social-class differentials necessitate adaptions in research methodology?

Then there is the problem of class status of the researcher in relation to that of the person from whom information is being sought. It is amazing that this problem has not been recognized in the literature of methodology. Whatever its role in the rote-gathering of certain kinds of objective data, its importance in the study of the intimate aspects of family living must be considerable. Certain aspects of this are obvious, even if their manifestations may be somewhat subtle. For example, upper-class families will give information of certain kinds only to upper-class seekers of that information. Middle-class families tend to withdraw if the interrogator is identified as of lower-class status. On the whole, class recognizes class and will speak of intimate matters only to social equals, or superiors. A feeling of kinship on the class level makes for rapport between a questioner and questionee; awareness of class difference militates against it.

Similar to class differences is the role of ethnic differences. Feelings of discrimination on ethnic bases prevail widely among peoples the world over. Consciousness of kind, or lack of it, is a factor in research procedures, as well as in Giddings' interpretation of the social process. Lithuanians may hesitate to be frank about family matters with an Italian student; a Bulgarian family may "freeze up" against a Greek researcher; and an old New England family of Vermont persuasion may find it slightly difficult to speak freely of family matters to a Russian Jew. We are speaking here of psychological realities, not of emotional evangelism, in the field of ethnic group relations.

Finally, to be noted here, is the attitude of the individual toward the particular subject of the research project. In the study of family ritual we encountered a wide variation in personal attitude toward ritual. Some persons were frankly antagonistic, not necessarily to the study, but to the very idea of rituals in family living. The explanation of some of these cases inhered in the nature of their family situations and of the personalities involved, as for example when a dominating parent imposes ritual upon a resistant child. Here the rebellion against the parent expresses itself also in rebellion against family ritual. In a few cases we found that, where the dominating parent was the mother and the rituals were mostly feminine in character, the rebellion was against the "sissiness" of the rituals. In most cases, however, such rejection is not personal but cultural, that is, the child rejects the culture of parents and kinsfolk, as often happens in second generation immigrant families. In these cases, the child rejects the rituals in his family, and develops a skeptical or openly antagonistic attitude toward ceremonial aspects of his earlier life which are in any way associated with the family background which he rejects. One such case was Harold May. Harold is a Jew. His father is a scientist, who has no use for religion or anything smacking of the ceremonial. The son is a scientist, too, realistic and "tough-minded." He has changed his name and is married to a gentile woman. A part of his life pattern involves a breaking away from Jewish connections, and one phase of this has been a rejection of all ceremonials of the Jewish group in particular and of the rituals of life in general. In contrast to such cases are those families, with a long and proud past in the prevailing culture, whose members are pleased to recall the rituals in their family experience, and who treasure them in later life.

On the whole, we are inclined to conclude that the attitude of a person toward ritual is a fairly reliable index of his integration into his background. Rebellion against family, church, or even school background seems to express itself in attitudes toward ritual, ranging from open antagonism to sly skepticism; friendly pride in ritual seems to betoken the acceptance of the group personnel and culture in which the ritual obtains.

The study of family ritual is a comparatively easy matter. It is a phase of the life of a family of which its members ordinarily are proud. Because of its very nature, there is a sense of rightness about it which predisposes family members to recall readily and to describe easily its nature, operation, and implications. There is less a feeling of hesitation and shame about ritual than about most other phases of family life. One has the feeling, therefore, that family rituals, to which this volume is devoted, are as responsive to scientific analysis as they are important to an understanding of family life.

Summary

1. Family life is richly complex, and its study may be approached (a) as an aspect of the life of the larger society, (b) as a psychosocial group, (c) in terms of husband-wife relationship, (d) as the basic social relationship between successive generations, and (e) as a changing social institution.

2. The present study is an original one, based on some four hundred case records. These were obtained from six sources: authors of autobiographies, university students, residents surrounding a social settlement and participating in its activities, residents in a middle-class suburban area, members of the Junior League, and a group of unselected adults.

3. Three techniques were cultivated in the gathering of information through interactive interviews: inconspicuous listening, inconspicuous observation, and unsuspected recording.

4. Methodology in the scientific study of family behavior must be adapted on the basis of (a) the subject to be studied, (b) the nature of the persons dealt with, (c) their attitude toward the subject studied.

The Person

The following passages illustrate certain adaptations felt to be required for interviewing "older people" for a particular research project. That this study was carried out by graduate students gives the report of their experiences a freshness of viewpoint sometimes lacking in statements by experienced researchers. Viewed as a contribution toward a more tested rationale for field work, the author's "adjustive approach" turns out to have much wider applications than might at first be supposed.

There is some mention of "fatigue and failure" and an assertion of the importance of "sufficient rest and adequate time" to enable the field worker to perform up to par. Like certain other occupations, field work calls for a certain energy level or capacity to create and sustain social interactions which may be intensive, numerous, and prolonged as well as doubly-loaded for the field worker making efforts to observe "everything." Each field worker has to discover for himself what he can take along these lines and somehow work this into his career line and concept of self. It is not possible, of course, for any single observer to be sensitive to everything and yet the effort is often made due either to the inner drive of the beginner that makes him try, or to the scientific curiosity of the experienced field worker that impels him, in his realization of how very little is really known, not to miss anything that may prove illuminating. While the obvious remedy for fatigue is rest, the field worker may be compelled, in observing unique or rarely repeated situations, to take some chances with exhaustion on his part and to try so far as possible to make allowances for its effects on his sensory systems and whatever they enable him to record. Certainly there is honesty in the account which recognizes possibilities like these.[4]

Flexibility, adaptability and an adjustive approach are requisite in interviewing older people as with any other age group. The writer found it impossible to rely upon a stereotyped approach. The approach varied from situation to situation and was frequently changed on the spot. The older people who were sought and encountered and the younger people who often answered the door, must be "sized up" and accorded the right to be suspicious, too busy, and hesitant in giving information to a stranger. Older people, as well as younger people, are not acquiescent but in turn "size up" the interviewer.

The following approaches were largely ways of procuring attention, overcoming suspicion and gaining cooperation. They were techniques as facilitating the introductory phase of the interview and can be regarded as part of an adjustive approach in interviewing older people. These approaches emerged in the course of survey experience and were in part suggested by the background reading on interviewing and the literature in the field of later maturity.

Addressing Older People in Terms of Importance

Since we were concerned with older people in a working population, retired and in the labor force, we assumed that these men and women would have an interest in the problem being investigated. A further assumption was that they would have the experience and perspective which would help us define a problematic area in later maturity.

. . . A helpful approach to gain the cooperation of an informant was to address him, in the second person, as you possessing experience to help me. The question most readily suitable to this approach in our study was: IS THERE SOME AGE AT WHICH YOU THINK THAT PEOPLE SHOULD STOP WORKING? By immediately asking for an opinion and showing genuine interest in what the informant had to say, the approach facilitated interviewing on the conversational level with little conscious effort. Rapport developed as a matter of course since an opinion was requested about a problem so close to the respondent's immediate experience. The "common man" may have an opinion, but it may be a unique experience to have it regarded as being important. He is not as inarticulate or disinterested as may be presumed. An informant would say, "What difference does it make what I think? It won't do me much good to talk about it." An older retired man would answer, "I'm too old to be of much use to anyone." The sincerity and the genuine interest of the interviewer can overcome such a response. They aren't just old and unimportant people being questioned for the momentary present. They are live human beings with important ideas. If they are worth being called upon at all, the interviewer must respect such comments but not regard them as a final refusal. A sincere persistence can help them express their ideas. This isn't probing. The interviewer can, through his manner of expression, indicate his interest is sincere and not idle curiosity.

---

    4. Luise Krause, "Problems of Interviewing with Older People," chapter iv in "Personal Adjustment in Old Age" by John Hair, L. Krause, J. Singleton, and W. Smith (Joint Master's Thesis, Department of Sociology, University of Chicago, 1950), pp. 84-115.

Avoiding Specific Age Categories[5]

. . . The time and help of the informant are important. The interviewer's time is of secondary importance. The informant is cooperating and the interviewer must budget his time in accordance with the activities of the household. It may be necessary to come back at the convenience of the respondent. Frequently such a suggestion from the interviewer resulted in an immediate interview. Men and women have a right to say, "I've got no time, and can't you see I'm busy?" An interviewer must recognize that the respondent is giving his time and at the same time impart this recognition to the informant. These small considerations are significant aspects of interviewing older people. They can overcome refusals and enable the interviewer to proceed quite readily with the questions.

Setting a Male-Female Perspective

. . . During our exploratory study the comments of the housewife often indicated she was not accustomed to giving an opinion on an important issue. The man as the head of the household frequently speaks for his wife. . . .

Quite often the housewife answering the door would say, "I've got no ideas about such things and my man isn't home." The interviewer was able to overcome such a response in many situations by expressing the opinion that the ideas of both men and women are important. . . . As a matter of course the interviewer requested the "opportunity" to speak to the husband also. If a specific time was set it enabled the interviewer to budget time for recalls within the immediate vicinity.

If the initial interview was with a married man, a request for interviewing the wife followed. A typical response to such a request quite frequently was, "But my wife thinks the way I do. She doesn't know much about these things. Anything I said goes for her too." The interviewer in such situations would state his help was greatly appreciated but would add, "I want to talk to women too. I would like to talk to your wife if she can give me the time." By signifying that this wife should be represented rather than the wife of another man, the informant generally agreed to call his wife. The housewife was often quite pleased to be included.

Emphasizing 1000 Cases as the Goal of the Survey

The interviewer can expect to encounter skepticism on a number of occasions. This becomes a healthy challenge to test the ingenuity of the interviewer in endeavoring to cope with the doubt and to gain the help of informants. Although it was possible by using the introductory letter, a general letter does not tend to reassure. It often raises more questions than it answers.

The interviewer should endeavor to so state the importance of the survey that an appeal for cooperation is forceful but brief. Lengthy explanations can give rise to a series of questions which are more confusing to the interviewer than to the respondent. By a sudden shift, it becomes altogether possible for the interviewer to become interviewed instead of doing the interviewing. It is not unnatural for the informant to raise questions as to the significance of the canvassing. The interviewer would perhaps do the same thing if he were in like position. If necessary the interviewer can endeavor to set the perspective early in the interview. There is no rule to follow, but perhaps the best guide would be pure "hunch." A reasonable device that was helpful during the survey was setting 1000 as the goal. This

---

5. Ibid., pp. 88 ff. Under this heading the author discusses telling the informants that the age limits for the study were set at fifty-five to one hundred, with the emphasis put upon "the importance of talking to men and women who are at least fifty-five." The few lines quoted here are part of a discussion of the interviewers' typical approach, which evidently stressed a great deal of deference to "age."

approach enabled the interviewer to reassure the respondents that every confidence would be respected, since it would be impossible to use so many names. Attention was directed toward the size of the project and toward the informant as a possible participant. A variation of this approach was, "If we get to 999 and have one more we'll have 1000 good ideas. Each person that helps, gets us closer to 1000." A question raised a number of times was, "How do I know you won't get my name off the mail box and use what I say against me in the paper?" By re-emphasizing that names were not being taken and that 1000 was the goal the interviewer was generally able to reassure the informant regarding his anonymity. Often this resulted in the free suggestion, "You can use my name and say I said so." It would be inadvisable to promise publicity in newspapers, magazines, or a book. Promising results may create a dependent relationship. On the other hand it can arouse suspicion regarding the purpose underlying the project. If the informant has expanded rather freely he may wonder if he has said too much.

Identification with the Group

The population we interviewed was relatively stable. Many of the informants had lived in the area from fifteen to forty-seven years. They have a strong sense of identification with the community. The interviewer mentioned that many others in the area had already been interviewed. The use of names of streets was one aspect which helped overcome the natural tendency to be suspicious of strangers, particularly in an urban environment. As the names of streets were mentioned the interviewee might ask, "What did Mr. Brown over on Aberdeen say? He's seventy-seven, you know." This gave the interviewer the opportunity to state the number that had been interviewed and the chance to reassure the informant that interviews were confidential. The interviewer would say, "I never ask for names, and whatever the men and women tell me I don't tell to others because it wouldn't be right. Whatever you will be willing to help me with will be just as important." A brief, frank reassurance regarding the importance and the confidential nature of an interview can gain the cooperation of an informant.

Using a Vocabulary Appropriate to the Group

If a common world of discourse is to emerge it is in terms of simplicity and genuine interest. Words beyond the comprehension of an informant will not gain cooperation. In order to interview older people, the interviewer should be aware of the necessity of conversing with a "comfortable" vocabulary.

Older people are not educated in terms of high school diplomas, college degrees and graduate research. The predominant proportion of our study group has an elementary education, which is average for their own generation. Such comments as, "I had to quit school early," "I started to earn money when I was ten," and "In those days we didn't have the chance young people have now," revealed that these men and women entered employment at an early age. The older people interviewed used such words as good, right, kind, true, help, talk, and work. From the observations already suggested, it becomes apparent that the difference in the formal educational level between the informant and the interviewer should not be referred to in manner or speech. Such reference would diminish rapport. Older men and women have a perspective, wisdom, and experience that does not come from formal education and research. It is a perspective the interviewer should appreciate. It is a wisdom the interviewer can well profit from. Whether the informant is a housewife, who has scrubbed all her life or a worker in a factory, or an older man who has shoveled coal and hauled crates, it should be recognized that these older people have the experience which can help define and perhaps ultimately control a problematic area in later maturity. Through sincerity and genuine interest the interviewer can impart this recognition to the older people he is interviewing. Artificial devices and simulated interest are generally detected by the respondents. Sympathetic identification emerges when the interviewer understands that older men and women are live human beings with the same needs, hopes, wishes, and aspirations as any other people. The interviewer who recognized that older people need to feel important and worthwhile, just as any other men and women, is well on the way to finding a "common world of discourse."

The use of words such as study, questionnaire, project and schedule may increase the distance rather than facilitate the interview procedure. The reaction may be, "Who wants to be studied?" In addition, the questions should not be put in an inquisitorial manner. Older people will readily talk but become suspicious if the questions are stated too rapidly. These men and women in later years are more than "sets of answers" to "sets of questions." They are willing to give their opinions and express their ideas if they are not being "studied."

Recognition of Social Conventions

Older people are quick to recognize and appreciate the observation of social conventions and ordinary everyday ritual. This observation can overcome the feeling that the interviewer is intruding. The attitude of the interviewer can do much to procure interviews and ease the situation.

A woman who had been crying, answered the door with, "Oh, I thought it would be someone from the undertaker. I just came from my sister's funeral and we are waiting." In this situation the interviewer said, "I know I am a stranger, but may I extend my sympathy." The expression of sympathy served to procure several interviews. It was impossible to start with any questions immediately. However, the informant visited for a time and gave some of the details of her sister's death. Within a comparatively short time, the interviewer was "invited" to ask questions. Attentive interest, a willingness to listen, and a respect for silence and sorrow can help the interviewer cope with such a situation.

In interviewing older people it is to be expected that informants who have some serious physical handicaps will be encountered. Blindness, crippled arms and legs, heart conditions, and other serious physical defects are not unusual. In this particular example of interview situations, a younger woman answered the door. In response to the initial approach she replied, "My mother is blind and wouldn't have anything to say. She doesn't get out much and nobody calls." A request to "visit" served to gain an interview with a woman who had been blind for ten years. In this situation the modulation of the voice, a sympathy broad enough to appreciate the interviewee's life situation, a control of feelings, not absence of feelings, and an avoidance of emotional coloring are necessary in conducting an interview. The difference of possessing sight or not possessing sight must be recognized but not emphasized. How does an interviewer know what a world of darkness means or what adjustment has been made to the handicap on the basis of one brief interview? At the close of this interview the woman, age seventy-four, said, "May I touch you, you are just a soft voice to me, you know." The response given was, "May I shake your hand for helping me."

Interviewing on the Conversational Level

A discriminating sense of timing is needed in interviewing older people. Increased physical handicaps, visual and hearing difficulties, the tendency to glorify the past and the need for recognition are some of the aspects making it necessary for the interviewer to avoid "rushing in." It is essential to be a good listener, to have a respect for silence and a respect for the "deeds" they may relate. To go too slowly may introduce monotony. The interviewee may wonder why you were sent out to interview. To go too rapidly may result in many "no answer" categories being coded. Rapid interviewing may arouse suspicion regarding the purpose behind the canvassing. It denies the interviewer the experience of more fully appreciating the perspective of those in later years.

Problems Emerging in Interviewing

There are numerous problems which enter into the ordinary interview situation. Among these problems are requests for help and advice, questions the respondent may ask about the interviewee's background, the development of dependent relationships, and the problem of reassurances.

Frequently the informants would ask, "How old are you?" Women as well as men would ask, "Are you married?" A frank brief answer to such questions is preferable to ignoring the question or telling too much. Unwittingly more may be told than the informant is interested in knowing. It is not unusual for older people to wonder about the background of the interviewer. The interviewer is asking a number of questions regarding the living situation of the informant. In turn, the respondent may be curious about the living situation of the person calling. The interviewer should be continually aware of the purpose behind the interview. This can help him direct attention back to the informant and the data to be procured.

Dependent relationships may arise by giving advice, offering help, promising results such as publication, or appearing too friendly. It would be impossible to give a formula, "a set of rituals," or a definitive answer for the control of the development of excessive negative or positive feelings. The research students should remember the purpose of the interview and the significance of each question. A sympathetic attitude necessarily involve an appreciation of an informant's life situation.

Numerous writers point out that the attitude of the interviewer is of par amount significance. It follows that an interviewer should not be judgmental regardless of what remarks an informant may make. Although the interview er necessarily interprets for himself, this judgment should not become a part of the interview proper. The interviewer's judgment may be erroneous. Interpreting for the respondent may arouse suspicion and antagonism. . . .

In the interview situation presented by the exploratory study in which informants must be located by house-to-house canvassing, rigidity and compulsiveness, fatigue, and failure to allow adequate time, preclude the fruitfulness of the interviewing experience. The possibility of satisfactory results is diminished. For the writer refusals seemed to accompany fatigue and failure to choose a suitable time. It is difficult to observe social conventions, establish rapport, be mentally alert, and genuinely interested when sufficient rest and adequate time are not allowed.

The Business Enterprise

The two articles for this topic continue to be useful in explaining field work "inside the walls" of any human organization both to beginning students and to possible sponsors of such intramural explorations.

In the first article[6] the authors spell out the advantages and disadvantages of three of our four types of field worker roles for research in industry. These are, to use our own terminology, that of the complete participant, "the researcher obtains employment and enters the organization through the regular channels"; that of the participant as observer, "one who is doing more than just a job"; and that of observer as participant, the observer enters the factory "for the acknowledged purpose of research." Hav-

---

6. Burleigh B. Gardner and William F. Whyte, "Methods for the Study of Human Relations in Industry," American Sociological Review, XI (October, 1946), 506-12.

ing learned from experience the preponderance of advantages favoring the observer-as-participant role, the authors describe the continuing processes of getting in, and getting along, and they indicate their progress toward "a combination of research and experimentation."

The Committee on Human Relations in Industry* at the University of Chicago was organized early in 1943 to carry on research in the social organization of industry and of our industrial society. On the basis of our own earlier studies we have formulated certain ideas as to the research approach to this field, which will be discussed here.

We do not offer any fundamental innovations in methodology. Rather we are concerned with the application and adaptation of certain well recognized methods to this relatively new field.

Experience has shown that effective research on human relations in industry requires the fulfillment of certain conditions:

1. The researcher must be able to get into industry.

2. He must be able to establish and maintain relationships within the organization to be studied.

3. He must have tools for collecting the pertinent data without interfering with his relationships.

4. For anything more than superficial studies, there must be a continuity of research relationships with a given organization.

5. To permit such relationships to continue and to allow for the possibility of experimentation, management must understand the research and take an interest in its development. (Where unions are involved in the studies, this same condition applies to them.)

It must be remembered that factories are social organizations with walls around them. Management controls the admission of people within these walls, and there is no access without such permission. Furthermore, management tends to be touchy about exposing its personnel problems to outside scrutiny and fearful of the effects of permitting outsiders to enter the organization. There is a widespread belief that allowing a researcher to interview a worker on his problems will create in the worker's mind problems that he was not previously aware of and will therefore build up antagonism toward management. So we find that where management considers its human relations to be in good shape, it is inclined to "let well enough alone," and where it recognizes serious frictions it is inclined to bar access to the researcher on the grounds that he may touch off an explosion.

A position in a prestige institution such as a university may be of some help in overcoming these barriers, but identification with the social sciences is of dubious value. While executives may recognize that a real social science would be of value to them, they are inclined to look upon us as impractical dreamers who talk a language they do not understand and who are out of touch with the realities they face.

Nevertheless, it has been possible to gain access to industry—and in several ways. Here we talk primarily of our own experience, recognizing, of course, that we are not the only people who have carried on in-plant studies.

By one approach, the researcher obtains employment and enters the organization through the regular channels. When this is done without knowledge of the organization, he can function only as a participant-observer and

---

*The members of the Committee on Human Relations in Industry are: G. Brown, School of Business, A. Davis, Department of Education, B. Gardner, School of Business, F. Harbison, Department of Economics and Industrial Relations Center, R. Havighurst, Department of Education, E. Hughes, Department of Sociology, N. Jacoby, vice-president of the University, W. Lloyd Warner, Departments of Anthropology and Sociology, and W. Whyte, Department of Sociology. Warner is committee chairman.

is strictly limited by the job he is on. Thus he may have little freedom of
movement and may have contact with only a small segment of the organization.

In spite of the limitations this imposes on the observer, it does provide opportunity to study the situation without the behavior being affected
by the study itself. Some of the best descriptions of the daily experiences
of the worker and of the dynamics of the informal relations in work groups
have been obtained in this way.

Another limitation of this method is that after putting in a full day at
work the observer has little time or energy left to record his observations
and experiences or to think about them. If he is to get the most out of this
experience, he must keep his work diary faithfully and make a very detailed
report on his observations. In some cases a part time job has enabled the
observer to do a better job of recording and organizing his material.

Sometimes it has been possible to place the observer on a selected job
with the knowledge and permission of management and union. This permits
somewhat more freedom since the observer may be able to select the best
job for his purposes or can be transferred from job to job to get more extensive material. This has to be handled carefully lest the fellow workers
become antagonistic and the observer must conduct himself so that they do
not feel he is spying, yet will not be disturbed when they realize he is doing more than just the job. In some cases this has been handled by the observer letting it be known that he was a student interested in learning at
first hand about work situations.

Aside from its merits for research we regard this approach as excellent training for the student. Doing a job in industry and recording his observations gives the student a "feel" for the phenomena of human relations
in this field. While intuition is no substitute for scientific research, it can
serve to point out profitable areas of investigation.

When the observer attempts to enter the factory for the acknowledged
purpose of research, the way must be carefully paved for him. The purpose
of the research must make sense to management. The executive must see
possible benefits to the organization, must have confidence that the study
will not disturb the plant, and must be assured that the data will be confidential and not put to use in any way which will harm the organization.

How can these assurances be given? We have found that we cannot
count upon logical explanations of the purpose of the research plus the appropriate promises as to the methods to be used and to the confidential nature of the findings. Fundamentally, management must have confidence in
us and in our research assistants. This cannot be put across in a sales
talk. It must generally grow out of a more informal sort of relationship
maintained over a period of time.

Our experience here is instructive. We received our first financial
support from management on the basis of projected studies of the worker
in the community. Nothing was said of in-plant studies.

As the community research got under way, Gardner visited the plants
and offices of the sponsoring companies periodically and interviewed executives upon the problems they faced. We held dinner meetings for these executives about once every six weeks. While these were organized around
presentation of a paper of research findings, we undertook to make them
as informal as possible. Aside from promoting a closer relationship between executives and research directors, the meetings gave us the opportunity to learn how to translate our ideas into symbols that would make
sense to executives.

Several months of this process led to our first in-plant study. One of
the sponsor companies had some serious personnel problems in one of its
departments. In fact, the situation was so bad that it did not seem possible
for us to make it any worse. Therefore we were invited in and Gardner directed a study of the department. Fortunately, we were able to point the
way to a considerable improvement in that situation, and the practical application of the research was received with satisfaction by both manage-

ment and the union.

This demonstration that we had some knowledge of practical value opened up much broader possibilities for our studies. We developed our in-plant studies to a point where we are more limited by shortage of trained research assistants and directors than by inability to gain access to plants. In fact, we are approaching a position where we can pick and choose the types of studies we want to make and then carry through the necessary arrangements.

While no in-plant study can be undertaken without the approval of top-management, such sanction is not enough in itself to assure its general acceptance. The research must be explained to all levels of the organization which are involved in it. It must be explained by top-management, and it must also be explained and re-explained by the researchers as they go along making their contacts. A full and elaborate explanation is not necessary, but people must have some simple and clear definition of the researcher's role. Otherwise they will develop anxieties and work up their own definitions.

If the research is to include observations or interviews at the worker level, it will also be explained to the workers. Where the plant is organized the research must also be discussed with the union leaders and then presented to the rank and file, preferably at a general meeting.

We have undertaken a number of studies involving union acceptance of our work, and we are expanding our research in the area of union-management cooperation. This may seen a paradoxical situation since all of our non-university financial support has come from management. Nevertheless, we have experienced no difficulties on this score.

There seem to be several factors which allow us to proceed in this manner. Our university positions give us at least some claim to impartiality. We do not work with companies which are engaged in union busting campaigns. This does not mean that union-management relations are always harmonious where we operate. It does mean that management is committed to trying to get along with organized labor. Our position on this point is simple. Getting along with a union requires more than simple good will. Skill in human relations and an understanding of the social system of factory and union are also necessary. As we study union-management friction, we are in a position to provide the information which will make more cooperative relationships possible.

Apparently this approach makes sense to union leaders. We assure them that all individual confidences will be respected and that we will not become substitutes for the union in adjusting individual grievances with management. They recognize, however, that we can be a channel to transmit to management an analysis of problems at the work level which the union may be unable to get across. The union leadership may be looked upon by management as having an axe to grind. As long as we can maintain our position of having an unbiased interest in discovering how to make a cooperative system work, we can count on the support of both sides, even when there is considerable friction between them.

When the initial relationships with management and the union have been established, the researcher is free to enter the factory, but unless he can maintain good relationships at all the levels to be studied, he has difficulty in collecting data and runs the risk of creating so much disturbance that he may be forced to withdraw from the situation.

Certain guides should help in creating and maintaining proper relationships. The job cannot be done in a hurry, nor, once done, will it stay done. This must be a continuing process. The researcher must feel his way into the situation. He must try to size up the factory pattern of relationships and fit in unobtrusively. He must be friendly and interested in people, without forcing himself upon them. He must avoid taking sides in arguments and must be very careful not to subordinate people in word or manner. He must be considered trustworthy—and this especially takes time. He cannot expect that promises as to the confidential nature of the work will suffice. People

will only have full confidence in him as they get to know him and make up
their minds as to what kind of a person he is.

If the researcher needs to maintain a good relationship over a long period of time, it is necessary for him to maintain his interaction in the organization. Time and again we have met the following difficulty. The researcher spends considerable time in a factory and builds up friendly relations with the personnel, so that they talk freely of their problems. Then for
a period of a month or two he is unable to visit that plant. When he does return, he finds the people still friendly but somewhat cool and uneasy and
not talking so freely. From such experiences we conclude that frequency of
contact is important to maintaining close relations and that after any long
period of absence, the researcher has to spend some time in restoring his
former relationship.

Another factor which seriously affects the development of good relations is the general social tone of the situation. Where there is antagonism
between levels and apprehension of authority, it is always difficult to gain
acceptance. The tension in such situations makes everyone more wary of
what he does and says, especially before the outsider who is sanctioned by
management and might be a channel of communication to the top. Where
such apprehension of authority is at a minimum there is little difficulty in
gaining easy acceptance.

Significantly enough, in tense situations the lower supervisors are often the slowest to accept researcher. If the shop is organized the approval
of the union leaders is often all that is needed to gain the acceptance of the
workers. In such situations there is often strong antagonism to the interme-
diate levels and the workers feel that the research presents an opportunity
to communicate their feelings to top management in spite of their immediate supervisors.

Even where foremen or workers are very apprehensive of management,
it has been possible for interviewers to win their confidence so that they
discuss their problems freely. Aside from the skill and University ties of
the interviewer, there seems to be one other major factor which makes such
a relationship possible. Where we find such anxieties at the bottom levels,
we also find that upward communication in the organization has been blocked
off. The men at the bottom don't feel free to discuss their problems with
their superiors. They must keep their worries to themselves, no matter
how insistently the problems demand expression. If the interviewer comes
along and handles his role correctly, the opportunity to blow off steam cannot be indefinitely resisted.

In his efforts to build up rapport at the lower levels, the researcher
must take care lest he build anxieties and lose support at the top. We had
such an experience in one plant. The researcher came in with the support
of the plant manager. First interviews were with him, and he saw to it that
the researcher was properly introduced to the next lower levels. The interviewing was then carried on at successively lower levels until the researcher settled down and began intensive work with workers and first line supervisors.

In the beginning of the study, the researcher enjoyed frequent informal
contacts with the manager, but, as the study proceeded at the bottom levels,
these contacts dwindled away. At the end of about two months, the researcher noted a decided change in the manager's attitude toward him. The man
had only been on the job for five months when the study began, and he knew
that some supervisors and workers were strongly hostile to him. Subsequent
interviews showed that he felt the researcher was not interviewing the "right"
people, that he was not getting "the true picture" of the situation. His presence, therefore, was no longer welcome, so far as the manager was concerned.

By returning to interview the manager, the researcher was able to re-
pair some of the damage, and yet from this point on the manager always
talked with his guard up and never gave free expression to his feelings. Had
the manager been consulted regularly for advice on people to be interviewed

and for his statement of "the true picture," it seems unlikely that this es-
trangement would have developed.

In a large organization, it is obviously impossible for a single interviewer to maintain interaction at all levels. Where he is interviewing at
lower levels, it may therefore be necessary to have a research director
meet fairly regularly with management to allow the executives to tell their
story. Nor should this be considered simply as a sop thrown to management.
To understand human relations in industry, we need a knowledge of patterns
of thought, sentiment, and action at all levels of the organization.

To carry on such studies, the researcher needs skill in social adjustment and in gathering information. These skills must go together.

The nature of the social situation is such that certain techniques are
ruled out, at least in the early stages of the study. Management is generally reluctant to permit the questionnairing of its employees, and, in any case,
the effective use of the questionnaire depends, first, upon some knowledge
of the particular social area being studied, and, second, upon securing the
cooperation of key people in the informal organization. Without such cooperation, the questionnaire will be ignored or made fun of. The same holds
true of tests of various kinds. These methods may be applied successfully
providing we know the territory well and have built up good rapport in the
organization.

At present, our findings depend primarily upon observation and interviewing. The sort of observation required need not be discussed here, for
examples are set forth in the paper by Everett Hughes.*

Our interviewing is based upon the personnel counseling approach discussed in Management and the Worker† or the non-directive interview of
Carl Rogers.‡ Modifications have been introduced because our purpose is
not therapy but research. When a personnel counseling program is in operation, the worker has a general idea that it will do him some good to talk
his problems out, and the counsellor acts simply to stimulate this free expression, regardless of where it takes the informant.

We cannot count upon any such general understanding of our purposes,
and we cannot offer therapy—though the informant does find the good research interview a pleasing experience. We must begin by describing our
purposes in terms of research, but such explanations are not enough in
themselves to get people talking. We have had some experience in trying
to conduct the interview as non-directly as possible, and we find that unless the informant is given some leads as to the specific areas we are interested in, he feels lost and does not know how to proceed.

This does not mean that we go in with a preformulated set of questions.
Such an approach would make free expression impossible. Instead we
start with a few general questions that will put the informant at ease and
warm up the conversation. We don't, of course, begin by asking a worker
how he feels about his supervisor or about the Union; such questions arouse
immediate anxiety. Rather we ask him to explain to us the particular job he
is doing. We express an interest in how people happen to get into this line
of work and ask him to explain to us how he happened to take a job here,
and tell where he worked before. Sometimes the interview drifts naturally
from this point into a discussion of some parts of the informant's life history.

These first questions are all formulated in such a way that the informant can talk freely without exposing attitudes which might be subject to man-

---

*"The Knitting of Racial Groups in Industry," see also W. F. Whyte's
"Corner Boys: A Study of Clique Behavior." American Journal of Sociology,
XLVI (March, 1941), 647-64.

†Roethlisberger and Dickson (Cambridge, Mass.: Harvard University
Press, 1941).

‡Counselling and Psychotherapy (Boston: Houghton Mifflin, 1942).

agement censure. He may volunteer opinions about management and his supervisors, but he should not feel that he is expected to do so.

While we have gathered some highly revealing first interviews, the interviewer should not think of them in terms of the information they supply.
They should be used to establish rapport, to establish a relationship in
which the informant talks freely and the interviewer responds to him.

The interviewer should then continue to cultivate this relationship. As
he senses that anxieties have been allayed and a friendly tie established,
he can begin tentatively to move along into areas of actual or potential emotional conflict. He must map out for himself the areas he wishes to explore
and then set about developing interviews which will provide the required
information. Always he must be careful not to move too fast or to probe
too deeply, lest he damage the relationship he is building up.

The interviewer begins by assuming general direction of the conversation, but, as quickly as possible, he passes the reins over to the informant.
As the relationship develops, he assumes direction now and then to guide
the conversation into areas of his interest. However, he must always be
flexible in his approach and quick to encourage the informant to develop
quite unanticipated points.

The direction of the interview then depends in part upon what the interviewer is looking for and in part upon what the informant has to say. As interviewers, broadly speaking, we are interested in determining the structure of the social system studied and observing the place of the individual
in it. We want information upon the pattern of human relations which exists
at the present time and upon the changes that have taken place in this pattern. We are also interested in observing the impact of the technology upon
the social system. And we seek to explain the attitudes and behavior of the
individual in terms of his experience in the system of human relations. A
full explanation of what we are looking for would, of course, require a long
paper on our conceptual scheme.

This concludes the discussion of our field work procedures. However,
we do not stop simply at this point. Our work is now emphasizing a combination of research and experimentation that involves the following five steps:

1. We make an intensive study of the problem situation.
2. On the basis of that study, we map out a course of action for management, which, we think, will improve that situation.
3. We communicate these recommendations to management in a form
such that they can be understood and acted upon. This must be done primarily through informal conversations with executives. Written memoranda
may be submitted also, but they are distinctly supplemental to the direct
person-to-person relationship.*
4. Management takes action along the lines agreed upon.
5. We follow closely every step of management action and make an intensive study of the resulting developments. If events follow the course we
have anticipated, we are in a position to observe just how and why these results were obtained. If the results are substantially different, then we are
in a position to study the factors that accounted for the discrepancies and
gain knowledge out of our own failures.

We have recently established such experimental relationships with
four companies. While it is still too early to report upon our results, we
feel that for the purposes of scientific development, it is exceedingly important to put our conclusions to the test of experience.

For purposes of experimentation, we feel that industry has considerable advantages over the community. Being much more loosely knit in its
structure, the community presents much greater difficulties in the exact
determination of a sequence of human interactions. We are therefore much

_____

*See Alexander Leighton, The Governing of Men (Princeton, N. J.:
Princeton University Press, 1945), appendix, for an excellent discussion
of the limitations of memoranda in influencing executive action.

more likely to find that the experiment succeeds because of actions of people beyond the scope of our observation or that it fails because of factors
whose impact we cannot take account of. In industry, the boundaries of the
social system are clearly defined, and skillful interviewing and observation
can give us a relatively complete record of the sequence of interaction
from the boss down, from the worker up, and through the various staff organizations.

Perhaps the first major social science experiment was carried on in
industry—the test room experiment report in Management and the Worker
—and we feel that continued efforts in this direction will yield rich returns
in the development of the social sciences.

In the second article,[7] Robert K. Bain gives us a most valuable statement concerning social processes and personal experiences in field work
as encountered by a white student in a situation of observation that included both white and Negro employees in a small enterprise in a southern
town. Mr. Bain describes the development of his particular observer-as-
participant role through time, and includes recognition of the impact of the
evaluations made by the people about the field worker himself, his activities, and the various kinds of information he was either viewed as seeking
or was actually seeking.

During the Fall and Winter of 1948-49, the writer made a study of a
laundry plant located in a Southern town. The purpose of the research was
to test and further develop the use of a method invented by Delbert C. Miller for analyzing and rating the social skills required by jobs.[*]

The study or research designed to accomplish this purpose consisted
of several distinct phases, which were as follows: (1) a general descriptive
study of the social organization of the plant; (2) a rating of the social skills
required by the jobs in the plant, following Miller's method; (3) a sociometric study of the interpersonal choices among the workers; and (4) an observational recording of certain time aspects of the interactions between employees, using a simplified adaptation of the Interaction Chronograph method of Eliot D. Chapple.

This article will not be concerned with the results obtained relative to
the main purpose of the research. Rather, it will attempt to gather together certain aspects of the interpersonal relations between the researcher
and those whom he studied to form a case study of the role of the researcher. The value of this case study to the reader will probably be increased in
direct relation to the reader's own field research experience. Undoubtedly
many of the situations reported here are unique, but by comparing them
with those in his own experience, perhaps the reader may gain a fuller understanding of effective roles for the field researcher.

This case study will be presented as an informal chronological account
of the writer's research experiences in the laundry plant. Because it thus
deals with personal experiences, it is hoped that the indulgence will be
granted of using the first person throughout instead of the customary third
person. This should be less awkward and cumbersome.

First, however, I must give a very brief description of the organiza-

7. Robert K. Bain, "The Researcher's Role: A Case Study," Human
Organization, IX (Spring, 1950), 23-26.

*See Delbert C. Miller, "The Social Factors of the Work Situation,"
American Sociological Review, II (June, 1946), 300-314.

tion and personnel of the laundry plant in question. The role of a researcher is determined in part by the general age and sex roles of the society of
which he is a part. To understand my role in the plant, we must know something about the people in the plant as well as about myself.

The XYZ Laundry Plant is owned and operated by the state university
of the Southern state in which the study was made. At the time of the study
the personnel in the plant itself totaled 121, of which 68 were Negro. Wom-
en comprised 71 per cent of the white personnel and 83 per cent of the Negro personnel.* The mean age for all personnel was about 39 years. There
was little variation of this mean when computed separately by race or sex.
All plant personnel were native-born Southerners. Most of them were born
and raised in the local community. All were Protestant. Social class membership probably ranged from Warner's "upper-lower" class to some unde-
termined point in the middle-class range. Whites and Negroes had worked
at the same time in the plant for many years, and the racial situation was
stable. The plant was non-union.

The operations took place in a large well-lighted and ventilated building on one floor. In the front part of the building were located the private
and semi-private offices of the officials and the clerical workers.

Formally, the positions of authority were as follows: superintendent,
plant manager, foreman, supervisors, and workers. Informally, the superintendent and plant manager were nearly equal in authority; in some respects, the plant manager surpassed the superintendent.

Personal data on myself are as follows: I am white, Protestant, and
native born of English-Scotch descent. At the time of the study, I was 26
years of age.

In order to gain admittance to the plant for the study I obtained an interview with the superintendent, explaining to him that I was a graduate student in the Sociology Department of the University and that I wished to make
a study of the social organization of the plant for my Master's thesis. Without questioning me at all, the superintendent replied, "Sure, come right in.
Glad to have you. We don't mind people studying us."

That statement, I found, well represented the attitude toward me which
was shared by the other plant officials. It tended along with my own background and personality and actions, to define in part my role and relations
with the employees. It was, first of all, an attitude of friendliness and trust.
For example, during the first month of the research the plant manager in
particular volunteered much valuable information of a nature which indicated that my discretion was trusted. Nevertheless, at the same time there
was never any particular interest on the part of the plant officials in the
study as such. I might walk into the plant in the morning (I spent a little
over half of each weekday, except Saturday when the plant was closed, in
the plant) and the superintendent would call out, "Well, Bob, how's the study
coming?" (or, in other words, "Good morning,") but there was never much
interest concerning what I was finding out, except for a few tidbits of specific information they might wish to know, or anything to suggest that my study
was considered to be important or valuable. On the part of the employees,
none of them seemed to feel that he had been chosen for anything particularly important as was the case in certain phases of the Western Electric
research, for example. But I am getting too far ahead; let us return to the
research itself.

Having been admitted to the plant, I asked the superintendent to explain
to everyone else who I was and what I was doing. He did this, but in a random, casual manner, although I feel that he acted in good faith. At that time,
I did not see the need for, nor did I request that the superintendent call a

---

*Throughout this article, personnel will refer to all persons working
in the plant; officials to the superintendent, plant manager, and foreman;
workers to those below the rank of supervisor, and employees to both
workers and supervisors.

special meeting of the entire personnel to introduce me and explain my purpose. Even had I realized the need, I doubt if I would have requested such
action, as I would have hesitated to ask for so much on the short acquaintance. As it was, I felt that I could personally fill in whatever information
gaps the superintendent may have left. Later events proved that this decision was wrong.

I was permitted to do my paper work at a spare desk in the semi-private office of the receptionist, who was in daily contact with most of the
plant personnel. This was fortunate. The receptionist (whose job, in addition
to receptionist, was that of payroll clerk, personnel clerk, general information center and other functions) was willing and able to give me valuable information and advice. Although I was careful with her as with everyone else
not to repeat tales or gossip, if by inadvertence or necessity I did repeat to
her any matters of even the slightest confidential nature, her discretion
was to be trusted. Because of the high esteem and trust with which she was
held by other plant personnel, any identification I may have received with
her was to my benefit. Her role in the organization was in many ways similar to the role I tried to play as a researcher; she was friendly with everyone, but close with no group; she associated with high and low alike, but
curried favor with neither.

My first step was to become acquainted with all of the officials and supervisors, to explain my purpose and request permission to study the workers under their respective jurisdictions. The rest of the first week was
spent in drawing a floor plan of the plant, locating on the map machinery,
working space, and personnel. This was done for several purposes. First,
it helped to familiarize myself with the technical operations. Second, it provided an excellent means for meeting the workers and establishing with
them a beginning for a satisfactory definition of my role. As I moved about
and sketched on the map the location of machines, tables, etc., I tried to
meet and talk with each worker, white and colored. I introduced myself
something like this: "Hello, I'm Bob Bain; I'm a student in the Sociology
Department of the University here, and I'm making a study of the plant for
my Master's degree." Then, after learning the name of my informant, I
would ask questions concerning the names of whatever kinds of equipment
were in use, what operations were being performed, and so on. I felt that
requesting such innocuous information would be a good start toward rapport
with the workers. Entering on the map the name and customary working location of each worker greatly helped me to remember names later; I was
soon able to call most of them by name.

As I entered the plant each day, I made it a point to get around and
greet everyone possible, addressing them, white and colored, as "Mister,"
"Miss," or "Mrs." In the case of the colored workers, I wondered if the
whites would resent this breach of customary racial etiquette, but there
was never any resentment that I could detect. I can only ascribe this to the
impartial role I sought to establish. The Negroes apparently like this manner of address. In the case of male Negroes of my own age, I addressed
them by first name.

The reactions of the workers to my presence and questioning were interesting. From the first, apparently none of them altered their customary
work behavior when I passed by, observed them, or talked to them. My interpretation of this appearance was largely determined by my reading of
the research literature of industrial studies. From these sources, I had
gained the impression that usually workers will cease talking among themselves, and will speed up or slow down in such a situation, depending upon
whom they think is observing them. Accordingly, my interpretation was
that the laundry workers were emotionally stable on their jobs and were
neither hostile to nor apprehensive of the plant management. I now feel that
this explanation over-simplifies a complex and varying situation.

From the beginning, I was pleased with the ease with which the workers permitted me to talk with them or observe them. Perhaps this would be
true in most plants of similar size; I do not know. At any rate, I tried to es-

tablish and maintain the role of an impartial, friendly, trustworthy researcher; the following points summarize the conduct designed to assure
this end.

1. As just mentioned, I made it a point to introduce myself to <u>every-</u>
   <u>one</u>, explaining my presence and purpose.
2. I tried to greet everyone upon entering the plant each day.
3. I tried never to become engaged or engage myself in discussions
   of a controversial topic, such as religion, politics, etc.*
4. As soon as I had established contact with anyone having formal or
   informal authority, I solicited their cooperation and requested that
   they aid in spreading the word of what I was doing. I merely asked
   that they "spread the word," but of course what I implied was "favorable word."
5. I promised each person in the plant that I would carry no tales, gossip, or confidential information of any kind from one to another,
   and that in the written thesis their anonymity would be protected in
   the case of confidential information. Both of these promises were
   scrupulously kept.
6. I tried to maintain daily interaction with both officials and employees.
7. Before beginning each phase of the total research, I first discussed
   the phase with the officials and the supervisors, requesting permission to study the workers under their respective jurisdictions
   and soliciting advice concerning the best way to go about securing
   the information needed.

Although most of the plant personnel seemed cooperative and friendly,
there were a few persons who initially viewed my presence with hostility
and suspicion. It was difficult not to simply avoid much further contact with
such persons, but with conscious effort I continued to maintain a friendly
attitude and tried to interact with them as frequently as anyone else. In
most instances, such persons later became most cooperative, and no such
persons continued to be openly hostile.

Conversely, it was equally difficult not to make favorites or to associate too much with those persons or groups who were especially friendly or
cooperative. In times of setbacks or failures, it was especially a temptation
to seek out such people for reassurance. Instead, however, I waited until
nightfall and used my long-suffering roommates for a wailing wall.

Some helpful suggestions concerning practical research techniques
were found in an article by Gardner and Whyte.† Here, the authors tell of
how they learned that the researcher must maintain interaction with both
management and workers. After initially conferring with management con-

---

*In this connection, it may be difficult not to become engaged in such
discussions at certain times. Ordinarily, in entering practically any group
as a participant member, one volunteers more or less subtly certain facts
about himself in order to place himself and to place others. Usually, he
seeks to enter the clique most congenial to his own personality, interests
and ambitions. As a researcher, however, one must (for certain research
situations at least) be as impartial and neutral as possible. Yet, those whom
you are studying will want to place you in an ordinary role. In my own case,
my ethnic and racial background was acceptable. However, my home is in
Washington, D. C., and my predominantly Northern background was obvious.
Upon one occasion the plant foreman quizzed me at some length concerning
my attitudes toward Negroes. Realizing that his purpose was to help define
my role for himself, I permitted a limited discussion and tried to leave
him with the impression that my own position was somewhere between that
of the late Senator Bilbo and of Paul Robeson.

†Burleigh B. Gardner and William F. Whyte, "Methods for the Study
of Human Relations in Industry," <u>American Sociological Review,</u> II (October, 1946), 509.

cerning their research in the plant, they spent most of their time with the workers and neglected to report to management frequently enough, whereupon the officials became noticeably distant and apprehensive that the researchers weren't getting the "true picture." I tried to heed this advice but unwittingly violated it in reverse.

After completing the map of the floor of the plant, I spent a great deal of time in the receptionist's office (which adjoined the office of the superintendent and plant manager) gathering from the files personal data and job history concerning the employees. This was supplemented with information concerning previous work experiences in the plant gathered by informal interviews with the workers themselves. However, I was spending most of my time in the office.

I began to notice a slight "cooling off" on the part of some of the workers. Perhaps I had become a bit too closely identified with the front office and officials, or perhaps it was merely felt that I was too close to their ears. As soon as I fully realized this, I changed my tactics and spent much more time out on the floor, continuing to talk informally with the workers, sometimes asking questions, often just passing the time of day.

A somewhat ticklish situation arose with regard to the superintendent and plant manager. Formally, the superintendent was first in authority. He had risen from the ranks and had been associated with the plant for many years. A few years previous to my study, the plant manager had been hired, creating a new position. The purpose of hiring him was the desire of the university officials to institute more efficient procedures in the plant. Whereas the superintendent was mild and easygoing, the plant manager was businesslike and aggressive. Although the superintendent was nominally the head, actually the plant manager was a greater influence in formulating policy, changing work procedures, and so forth.

From the start, the plant manager was very friendly and helpful to me. As I have mentioned before, he volunteered a great deal of confidential information. Although I was never able to detect any conflict or jealousy between the two officials, I was afraid I might be in the process of being placed in an embarrassing position. Because the plant manager was informally in the position of greater authority, it was easy to fall into the habit of consulting him alone for advice and permission during the various phases of the research. However, I consciously made an effort to consult as frequently with the superintendent, in order not to become a "favorite" of one or the other and thus become embroiled in any jealousy that might possibly exist between them.

When the time came to start the sociometric study (which was about a month after I entered the plant) I felt that I still did not have enough rapport with the workers for such a study. Moreover, there were indications that some of them were getting tired of being questioned. Apparently I had not originally been explicit enough concerning the probable length of the research, and many had thought that it would not take more than a few weeks or a month at the most. They were beginning, I suspect, to wonder just what I was doing that should take so long a time. As I shall mention later, one of my biggest mistakes was assuming that the workers knew what "research for a Master's thesis" meant. The solution (or at least, the partial solution) to this problem was so obvious that I don't know why I didn't think of it before. The solution was to do some work for a change.

I spent the next couple of weeks working on first one job and then another, with both white and colored workers, male and female. While thus working, practically the only questions I would ask were those concerned with skillful performance of the job. I stressed that I was a beginner and that I wanted to learn how to do the job so I could get a better idea of the operations of a laundry plant. The workers were glad to show me how to do the jobs.

It would often happen that we would work for 20 minutes at a time without saying anything. At other times, if there were a general conversation going on, I might enter into it. Working on the jobs proved to be conducive

to more relaxed and informal relations than were possible before. Formerly, I was constantly initiating the contacts, asking the questions. Now, as we
worked side by side, the workers could, in their own sweet time, ask me
whatever questions were on their minds. This often gave me the opportunity to clarify my role.

This participation proved to be of particular value in the case of Negro
workers. I here learned for the first time that most of them had very little
understanding of what I was doing. On several occasions, different colored
women asked me, "Are you studying to be the boss man?" After all, a
"Master's thesis" is outside of the experience of most of the workers,
white and colored. A few of the white workers (but none of the colored) had
friends or relatives attending the university. To most of the Negroes, the
introductory explanation I had given was probably meaningless. None of the
workers had previously experienced any contact, as far as I know, with industrial or sociological researchers. Even my connection with the university probably helped but little to establish my role. Presumably, to most of
the plant workers the mention of scholarly or scientific research called
forth a picture of a musty library complete with bookworms, human and in-
sect, or else a white-coated person bending over a test-tube or an atom-
smasher. The Negro workers particularly were not in a frame of mind during the stiffness and uneasiness of the first introduction to readily understand the limited explanation I did give of my purpose.

Let us recall that I tried to build up the role of a friendly, impartial,
trustworthy researcher. I believe that I succeeded fairly well in establishing the first three aspects, but left much to be desired in establishing the
researcher aspect of the role.

Although I felt that I was liked by most of the Negro workers, at the
same time I never could believe that I was learning directly more than su-
perficialities from them. Even in cases where the information given seemed
to be of an important or confidential nature, I would never be safe in gener-
alizing from it. Any white researcher, I think, must be very careful in interpreting any statements Negro informants make to him. Many Southern
Negroes, and especially working-class Negroes, have very thoroughly
learned their role. Courtesy, even to an "Uncle Tom" extreme, is a large
part of that role. This, together with a carefully non-committal attitude,
may lead the unwary white researcher into a trap. He speaks to the Negro;
the Negro is courteous and friendly. The researcher thinks, "This will be
easy. My informant seems very friendly, and the rapport seems to be good."
He asks questions, but learns very little. He thinks, "This informant can't
be holding back on me, see how friendly he is! Perhaps he just doesn't understand the question." So the researcher proceeds to ask leading questions,
and he gets the corresponding type of answers. And both white and Negro go
away quite satisfied with the interview.

Valuable as this participant observation was in the case of colored
workers, nevertheless I did not learn as much thereby as I did with white
workers. Much of the knowledge gained from participant observation consists not only in hearing statements or observing actions and recording
them, but in imputing to the actors the same sentiments of feelings that the
observer feels or would feel in the same situation. Now, the observer
shares these feelings by what are often very delicate cues or nuances of
expression. Unless one is a Negro or has been raised as a Negro, it is
much more difficult, I think, to learn from participant observation, and the
white researcher should be correspondingly cautious and sophisticated when
he draws conclusions. The same remarks apply, of course, to social class
differentials.

Although the next point should be obvious to any student of society, I
fell into the same error myself. The error is to regard one or a few Negroes as being representative of many or all Negroes. The researcher cannot be too aware of the obvious fact (that he may well know intellectually)
that there are class, status, and role differences among Negroes as well as
whites.

In the plant, a Negro worker made a statement to me that fitted my pre-conceived stereotyped notion of the opinions and attitudes of the working-class Southern Negro. I was all ready to accept and generalize from this statement when, to my dismay, quite by chance another Negro made a state-ment which was the exact opposite. I tried to be rather more thorough from then on.

The sociometric questionnaire was first presented to the white work-ers. It was felt that if they proved willing to cooperate, then the colored workers might be more inclined to participate. As it actually worked out, the sociometric study of the interpersonal choices of the white workers took so much longer than planned that I was unable to include the colored work-ers.

The original plan was to present each worker with a list of all others in the plant of the same race and ask him or her to indicate for each name whether he or she liked, disliked, or felt indifferent toward the person in question, and then to rank the "likes" and "dislikes" in order. This proce-dure was first tried with members of one work group with poor results. Cooperation was difficult to obtain, and many respondents merely said that they liked everyone on the list. I was forced, therefore, to change the meth-od somewhat and ask each worker instead to merely choose from the list the 10 persons he or she liked best. I further thought that if I could inter-view the workers in the privacy of their homes, I could secure better co-operation. Therefore, I went to the members of other work groups, request-ing permission to interview them at home for the purpose of securing infor-mation of a more confidential nature than I had previously gathered. I did not tell them just what this information was, because at the time it seemed that to do so would defeat the very purpose of home interviewing—which was to be able to carefully and fully explain just what information I wanted and why. This was the stupidest mistake I made during the entire research, and it should not require a social scientist to predict what happened.

Here I was, being so mysterious concerning some information I wanted, and here were the workers, wondering what it was all about; on the other hand, there were the people of the work group I had originally talked with, who knew what it was about.

Two days later, I received word that a certain worker was "spreading a rumor." The rumor was to the effect that "Well, I've finally found out what Mr. Bain is here for—he's going to find out who likes and dislikes each other here!" While this was literally true, it was hardly the interpretation I wanted. By sheer luck, the following day I had an opportunity to speak in private with this person. Without mentioning the rumor or the fact that I knew about it, I asked for her advice concerning the best way to go about the sociometric study. I explained what information I wanted and for what purpose, and said that I was afraid I had made a mistake in the manner in which I had introduced the study, and that I felt that perhaps some people were worried about it. She said, "Why, just go ahead and tell them what it's all about yourself, and I think they'll understand." I followed her advice. Furthermore, this person, who had never been very friendly before, was pleasant and cooperative through the rest of the study.

While following her advice, I also realized that home interviewing would be impracticable, so instead I interviewed in the plant, using the mod-ified technique previously mentioned. From then on, cooperation and re-sponse was gratifying, particularly in view of the personal nature of the questions.

In one work group, four of the members of a clique of five persons first declined to participate. Five days later, the four recalcitrant ones came up en masse to participate. I found out that one of the clique leaders had talked the others into cooperating. I thanked this person and asked her why she had done it. She said, "Well, here's how I felt about it, and this is what I told them: if I had a son in the University who was trying to finish his degree, I'd want to see people help him if they could."

I think that this statement contains a clue to part of the role I played in the laundry and a clue to the generally successful research relations I was able to maintain. Apparently, I was never able to completely establish the role of researcher, but instead with the women workers I placed myself, or was placed in, what sometimes approached a mother-son type of relationship. Perhaps many of them identified me with a son they might have had going through college—with either the son or the college or both being, in many cases, imaginary.

At lunchtime, all association with the women workers ceased. Most of them brought their lunch to work, and they would eat in groups, here and there. I had the strong impression that male company was distinctly not wanted at that time. I usually ate lunch with a group of fellow outcaste male supervisors and workers in one corner of the plant. The plant manager occasionally invited me to eat lunch in a restaurant downtown with him. By keeping my ears open, I learned as much from these lunchtime "bull sessions" with the fellow male minority as I did from any interviewing I ever did.

Following the Christmas holidays, the research was continued with the final phase consisting of the timing of the interactions of a sample of workers. At first, this interaction study encountered no difficulties, no one seemed to have the slightest objection. Using a stop-watch and a battery of hand counters, I would observe one person at work for two hours at a time, recording the duration, number, and direction of interactions.

About halfway through this study, the officials of the plant began to lay off a few workers here and there, because the volume of business had slacked off from the wartime peak. Now, here I was, watching certain workers and timing their interactions. Was I a spy from the university? Was I trying to find out who talked too much, or to determine who were the least efficient employees? Logical analysis would seem to render such conclusions unlikely. I had been there months before the layoffs started, and certainly much of the information I had been gathering was already known to the plant officials and would have been useless had it been designed to determine who was inefficient. But these were some of the suspicions which various persons began to entertain. Hostility and suspicion on the part of certain workers became open and obvious.

In an effort to counteract this, I talked with some of the workers so concerned and tried to reassure them. Some of them, still trusting me to a certain extent, admitted that they were afraid that I might be a spy. They seemed ambivalent and perplexed, for one of them told me that if, when I had first entered the laundry, one of the officials could have introduced me to everyone and told my purpose, the situation now would have been much better. I further learned that there had always been a slight, latent suspicion that perhaps I wasn't quite what I claimed to be. Presumably, as long as the workers were emotionally secure these latent suspicions were of little consequence, but once the workers became worried and upset the suspicions came to the fore in an intensified and overt manner. And it had taken me three months to learn this!

I soon found that there was little I could do to reassure the workers so affected. Talking with them did not help. It was emotionally upsetting to me to have persons who had apparently formerly liked and trusted me exhibit rather suddenly suspicious and hostile behavior. In the process of "reassuring" them, my own emotional state subtly appeared. Realizing this, I withdrew. In such a situation, my own problem was of little importance to them. My task was not to cry on their shoulders, but to maintain my balance and let them, if possible, cry on mine. In any event, I could not afford to become emotionally involved with them.

Accordingly, I concluded that the only thing to do was to carry on as usual and act as if I were not guilty and let it go at that. Surprisingly soon thereafter, in about five days' time, the suspicion lessened. I suspect it was through no virtue of mine. I did refrain from making matters worse, such as by acting hurt, complaining to still friendly workers about it, or accusing the hostile ones of treating me unfairly. After all, this problem was as much a part of my data as anything else, and I still had to play the role of an impartial observer. What actually improved the situation was simply the fact, no doubt, that after the initial layoffs, the workers regained their equilibrium sooner than I would have predicted. There remained on the part of a few a slight residue of suspicion, but it did not seriously hamper the completion of the research.

The Medical Profession

The paragraphs quoted here, from Oswald Hall's dissertation, "The Informal Organization of Medical Practice in an American City," illustrate chiefly the subtle effects, as well as the forthright impacts, upon the field worker's role when the information in society he seeks runs the gamut from public to private and when the potential informants are not only of high social status (usually higher than most researchers), but are also quite resistant to being interviewed by any one, let alone a non-member of their profession. The consequences for scientific research on the sociology of medical work, and for reporting results, are also touched upon.

While the "delicate materials" and other specific problems mentioned may be peculiar to the study of the medical profession, every field worker will recognize analogies in field situations more familiar to him, even though he may never have encountered one that would make it so impossible to take the role of participant as observer—let alone that of complete participant.

In his Introduction Dr. Hall writes:[8]

Several peculiar difficulties are encountered in trying to study the medical profession. The status of its members is generally higher than that of the persons making the studies. Since it is usually considered inappropriate to discuss one's important affairs with those of a lower status this limits the kinds of facts revealed. Another limit arises because of the nature of the doctor's work. His usual role is to listen to patients and tell them what to do. This handicaps discussion and hampers interviewing. More important is the fact that the profession has developed a public apologia—a set of fictions which justify the conduct of its members. The individual member uses this as a "line," a device for limiting the discussion. In part those having the relevant knowledge refuse to reveal it to the outsider. Since doctors as a group are highly sophisticated this is usually done gracefully. But more important is the tendency for such groups to suppress or even repress data on the inner working of the group until such facts are completely out of sight.
The following frank revelation by a doctor in a genial mood illustrates the kind of data rarely revealed.

You want to know how I can tell if a patient is good for a thousand, or five hundred or a mere two hundred? Well, I'll let you in on a little secret. When I discuss hospitalization with a surgical case, I ask him what sort of room he wants and about

---

8. "The Informal Organization of Medical Practice in an American City" (Ph.D. diss., Department of Sociology, University of Chicago, June, 1944), pp. 3-6.

what he wants to pay for a room. If the price seems unimportant
to him I then ask whether or not he wants special nurses. If
these are wanted I then ask whether he wants them for the post-
operative period or from the time he goes into the hospital. If he
wants them for both periods, "so as to have company" then my
guess is he's worth a thousand dollar fee. Sometimes I guess
wrong and the patient thinks the fee is out of line. In that case I
ask what he considers fair. Usually they won't try to shave more
than a hundred off. But if I get nine hundred, I should worry.

This doctor would not relish having the authorship of the statement revealed to patients or colleagues. Professional solidarity calls for maintaining silence about the use of, or need for, such devices. Although congenial-
ity in this case broke down the barrier and allowed the doctor to talk un-
guardedly, it still is not possible to identify the source. The reason is two-
fold. The doctor spoke under an implicit guarantee of anonymity. But over
and above that it must be remembered that the ranking members of the
teaching and medical professions (in the community studied) carry on a
common social life, belonging to the same clubs, etc. Any subordinate member of either of these professions who attempted an exposé of professional
conduct would be penalized. At the very least he would be cut off from the
sources of any further information.

It is abundantly clear that not only the gathering of relevant data, but
also their analysis and presentation, pose difficulties. Although the function of sociology is not to expose, yet it proposes a kind of analysis which
requires the use of facts often hidden from the public and sometimes even
from the conscious thinking of the individual actor. Exposé must be used
insofar as it is necessary to analysis, but for the reasons mentioned above
the sources cannot be identified. This draws attention to some of the peculiar problems of verification. In this kind of study it is impossible to go back
to the same person and verify his statements. Actually he would not be the
same person because one re-questioning constitutes a new situation. A subject questioned twice is not the same thing as a subject questioned once.
Verification finds the sociologist caught between the position of the historian and that of the natural scientist. The historian indicates his sources
so that others can verify them. The natural scientist indicates the essential
features of a situation so that others can repeat them. Science repeats the
type and not the unique event. It does not require that penicillin kill the
same germs twice. Verification for the sociologist involves indicating the
typical situation but not repeating identical situations. But there is a unique
problem of protecting the subjects studied. Most of the historian's subjects
are long dead and no longer interested in entering law suits for damage to
reputations. The biologist is free to carry out studies on the gonorrhea spi-
rochete, because the latter does not resent study in the way its host does.
Exposé is an attack on both ego and social position. Hence there are practical limits imposed on the documentation of statements. This is peculiarly
the case in the study of the medical profession in a small community where
many of the niches and positions are unique and discussion of them would
involve identifying specific functionaries.

In Providence, Rhode Island, the setting of the study, there is one main
medical system. Two-thirds of the doctors of the city are integrated into
this system which revolves around one large dominating hospital. For these
doctors almost every position in the system is unique in the sense that discussion of the position would identify its incumbent. The statements of doctors who spoke candidly concerning themselves, or colleagues, cannot be
made public without jeopardizing their reputations or rupturing their relations with colleagues. In many cases it has been necessary, therefore, to
present a specific instance as a generalization, or to change the nonessen-
tial features to preclude identification. This study is based on delicate materials and the treatment of such must likewise be delicate.

The following attempt at verification has been used at many points in
the study. Although no person was found in the community who was interest-

ed in studying professions, there were persons who had had a good deal of acquaintance with the careers of doctors. They had watched certain careers with much sympathetic insight. They had a lot of vicarious "acquaintance with" even though it could not be transformed into "knowledge about." This acquaintance extended to the social world of the doctors concerned; these observers were sophisticated enough to understand that doctors use their medical status to enhance their status in the larger society, and that in a multi-ethnic community they often struggle to rise above ethnic limitations and sometimes to preserve preferred status positions. By discussion it was possible to discover whether the data collected in the course of this study were out of line with the notions held by these observers. The congruence of the two constitutes a kind of verification which is valid for exploratory studies.

Dr. Hall later explains:

Approximately fifty interviews were arranged with representative doctors in the city. Some were formal but the majority were occasions when a doctor generously expanded a luncheon hour or donated an evening. . . . Other interviews were arranged with medical students. Interviews were attempted with persons willing to confide their experience as patients. . . .[9]

On the comparative accessibility of different kinds of information about the medical career, and the consequences of these evaluations for observing and reporting, Dr. Hall writes:[10]

The main elements in a medical career are as follows: (a) the engendering of an ambition, (b) the development of appropriate roles, attitudes, and conceptions of status, (c) formal incorporation into the profession, (d) the accumulation and retention of a clientele, (e) the establishment of a reputation, and (f) acceptance into the "fraternity" of the profession.

All of the above are interwoven in the fabric of a career, but for purposes of analysis they can be considered separately. All of them are social in the sense that their achievement requires the active participation of other persons. Ambitions are not self-generating, establishing a reputation is a reciprocal affair, and acceptance into the fraternity involves positive intervention by other persons on behalf of the candidate.

Three levels of difficulty are encountered in studying the six facets of a career indicated above. In (b), (c), (d), and (e) one can gather objective data and document the steps by indicating things visible to an observer. In the case of (f) one is dealing with a social system known only to its participants and in which the outsider is excluded from the current avenues of communication. Those within interpret gestures in a manner recognized by the members, but to the outsider both the gesture and its meaning are largely unavailable. In the case of (a), the genesis of an ambition, the whole matter is private to the individual concerned and one must depend on his report of what transpires. This chapter deals chiefly with (b), (c), (d), and (e) because they concern a simpler order of facts than do (a) and (f). . . .

From the data of Chapter V three distinctive types of careers emerge. One of these is characterized by its dependence on the institutional structure of medicine. This type of doctor links himself with medical institutions, gives his loyalty to them, and draws a clientele unto him, and a circle of colleagues about him, because of his relations to those institutions. His ambitions are oriented toward the institutional positions; his position in such structures deflects patients toward him; his practice persists because such positions are sheltered from competition. The practice is readily transferred to a new incumbent.

---

9. Ibid., pp. 11-12.

10. Ibid., chapter v, "The Medical Career," pp. 101, 151-52.

A second type practices medicine as a free lance enterprise . . . few or no institutional facilities yielding patients. . . . The practice shrivels as the competitive strength of the doctor declines.

A third type is oriented primarily toward personal relationships. . . . Favors are granted to, and sought from, colleagues on a friendship basis; relationships with patients are kept on a personal level. Such a practice can be transferred only by incorporating a second doctor into the web of friendly relations involving colleagues and patients.

Dr. Hall also describes the larger context of individual careers, distinguishing three types or levels of organization in an American city: (1) ecological, (2) formal structure of hospitals and doctor's offices, and (3) the informal organization, or inner fraternity.[11] Regarding the latter, he explains that the researcher is forced to adopt "an oblique approach" in order to fill out the picture obtained by his interviews in the role of observer as participant:[12]

In the course of time such a system becomes firmly established. It tends to embrace and direct both the symbiotic order and the formal organization. It becomes the legitimate "recognizing" mechanism in the medical community. Both its controls and its decisions are matters of extreme informality. It is so pervasive that when its members are acting most spontaneously they are acting according to its norms. A list of the medical activities over which it exercises substantial control would include: (a) sponsorship to medical school; (b) internships, externships, and staff positions in the dominant hospital system; (c) offices in, and policies of, the local medical association; (d) incorporation into the dominant specialities in the community; (e) access to the multiple offices of the East Side and the referral system employed there; (f) acquisition of consultant status; (g) formulation of the official apologia of the profession. To this system of informal organization the term "inner fraternity" is applied.

Obviously it is not possible to indicate precisely the membership, relationships, or activities of such a group. The group is not an historic group. It does not celebrate its past nor try to glorify its present. Actually its policies and activities are in opposition to the official apologia of the profession. Officially its members act in guild fashion; actually there are unpleasant occasions when decisions must be made and statuses ascribed and preserved. It follows that such a group can be observed only when functioning; at other times there is no organization or machinery visible. Hence the opportunities to observe it are very limited. Moreover it is conventional for its members to deny its existence. Officially the medical profession is a democracy and an area of free enterprise. Membership in the fraternity is an implicit denial of the tenets of faith of the profession.

Consequently it is not possible to analyze the fraternity in direct fashion. The conventional approaches, such as the participant-observer, historical, or analysis of formal structures, are effectively blocked. This necessitated an oblique approach using the following types of data: (a) data on location of offices, (b) data on the status of doctors as gathered from press clippings, reports of meetings, appointments, etc., (c) data on the institutional positions of doctors, and (d) interview material as indicated above.

In the preceding chapter the concentrated group of Yankee specialists was denoted as part of the fraternity. The firmly established members of that category form the core of the fraternity. These men are associated

---

11. Ibid., p. 174.

12. Ibid., pp. 175-77.

with young colleagues, newly recruited, destined in time to inherit the positions of power. Other men stand midway between these two age groups.
This age composition renders the fraternity self-perpetuating and stable.

The fraternity is not limited to the Yankee group. However, none of
the non-Yankee multiple offices discussed in Chapter VI is included. Some
members of such houses are, but only as individual doctors, and not as
members of a recognized group of doctors. . . .

. . . Jewish doctors as a group are excluded. . . .

The Italian doctors . . . have no representation in the fraternity. . . .

None of the Irish multiple offices is incorporated into the fraternity;
however individual members are accepted.

The Public School

For the social sciences, small rural schools, and even fairly large
consolidated schools in some areas, present situations of observation that
are relatively easy of access and may permit the field worker to act in the
role of participant as observer. In large cities, however, for many reasons
the public schools limit and control the entrance of outsiders and require
adaptive approaches in field work much like those found necessary in the
study of factories or other social organizations "with walls around them."

In the following, a young researcher tells in his own words something
of his rationale for field work on a problem which required, in one aspect,
a program of testing and interviewing students in a large city high school.
While his discussion goes beyond strict field work considerations, it helps
to explain the definition of his role in relationships with students, fellow
researchers, administrators, men and women teachers, and clerical employees in the institution. The information he wanted, and eventually gathered, clearly ranged from public to private, and to obtain it he took the role
we call observer as participant and apparently succeeded in maintaining it
with a high degree of consistency, perhaps because this was so clearly desirable in his view of the situation. He points out that adopting this role
does not mean putting on an inflexible pose or the same rigid manner of
acting toward every person in the situation. Rather, he tried to discover
what his role, observer as participant, meant to each new person he encountered and to help that person find a workable definition for their relationship. Failing the latter, he tried to correct a faulty one, if possible, or
tried to get along without having much to do with any person who could not
or would not accept him in some version of that role.

In a study such as this one, and in an institution with an elaborate time
schedule, the field worker finds it advisable to move fast and according to
a plan: he tries to get in, get along, and get out in rather short and well-
defined periods of time. One effect of this is to limit his opportunities to
build relationships more in the direction of complete participant, such as
the ethnographer tries to do. It also requires him to intensify his efforts to

win acceptance in the observer-as-participant position, with emphasis on
observation, to make every move explicit to himself, to keep others reassured of where he is and what he is doing, to make every moment count,
but at the same time, to become and remain in the eyes of the people in the
situation what is sometimes called "a real person." (The latter may be a
role demand peculiar to organizations "producing" people rather than man-
ufactured articles, but something very much like it would be expected of a
researcher in a factory. Perhaps only the words would be different, as in
"a right guy.")

Our field worker-turned-informant begins with his attempt to differen-
tiate himself from the several researchers in his group who administered
tests and questionnaires to groups of students in classrooms:[13]

I have tried to keep away from testing in order to avoid being taken by
the students as a teacher surrogate. I thought that if they didn't have any
identity it would be all to the good.
I felt that since I was going to interview certain members of the senior
class on some problems, some intellectual problems, and I was also going
to have a kind of free interview about their life problems, I wanted to get
as good a rapport as possible with these students. I felt that if they identified me as a teacher or a teacher surrogate that they would not be as free
with me as they might. I wanted them to see me pretty much as a fairly
close contemporary of theirs, someone who has been out of high school for
just a few years and is now in college and is doing some research on which
they could help me. I wanted them to be able to freely discuss their personal lives and their problems with me. If they thought that I was in any way
connected with the school or if they emotionally identified me as a teacher
or a kind of a teacher, they would be less apt to be free. As a matter of fact,
however, this hope of mine has been dispelled by some unfortunate occurrences. Due to some difficulties in the testing schedule it has been necessary for me to talk to—and—while they were administering tests. No
doubt these students who saw me will recognize me again when I interview
them and will therefore connect me with this testing project. To school students, high school or otherwise, a teacher and a tester, I think, are pretty
much the same thing emotionally. I am going to have to depend upon my
own individual efforts now in the interview to break down this picture of
me which they now have.
[He explains the sponsorship of his study; how permission to work in
the school was obtained from the heads of the city public school system;
and how he obtained the co-operation of the high school principal. There
were reasons of convenience for preferring this school as the site for field
work, including the co-operativeness of the principal, but there were also
reasons for preferring it as most representative for the scientific purposes
of the larger study. Access to the most desirable site was therefore an important matter—something precious to be protected with care.]
As an aid to anyone who intends to do research in the city high schools,
I would make the following suggestions:
1. Once you have become established in the school—that is, once the
principal has accepted your research project and has given you permission

---

13. The following passages are from a tape-recorded interview with
an informant who wished to remain anonymous. As the excerpts show, the
field worker's statements were as informal as they were earnest. One part
of his account is summarized in brackets, since he wished also to conceal
the site of his field work.

to work in the school—if at all possible try to get acquainted very closely with some secondary administrative official. He may be the assistant principal, a counselor, or an adjustment teacher or something of the sort. If you can find out who is the principal's "right-hand-man," this should be the person to try to get next to. Usually the principal sees himself as being too busy to spend too much time with you as a researcher. I found it not a good idea to burden them with your little problems if you can at all help it. On the other hand, once having established yourself with one of these more secondary administrative officials you can impress upon him the importance of the study and utilize, insofar as possible, the status of the institution from which you come and you can very often get very close, intensive cooperation.

2. As soon as you can, familiarize yourself with the administrative set-up of the school. Find out where the records are kept, what the records mean, who handles the records, find out which file drawers and which offices contain the kind of information you are interested in, try to look at some of the cards and folders and files that they have on the students so that you are fairly familiar with them. Learn the terms for these different things. Every card, every file, every piece of information in the school has a name for the administrator. It may be a name which you aren't familiar with, but learn these names so that you can communicate with the administrators about these different kinds of information. As an example, out at ——there is a card called a "program card." This is a card which shows in which class each student is at each period of the day. These are called program cards at this school; other schools have different names for them. When you are communicating with these people, it is always a good idea to use their symbol for these cards. Another example is the "cumulative folder." This school calls the folder in the adjustment office in which the student's tests, grammar school record, and so forth are kept the cumulative folder. Other places call it the "file folder," some schools call it the "record folder," some schools call it just "the record." If you don't use the specific term you find very often that you are confusing the people when you are trying to communicate with them, and you create some little tension that is not necessary.

3. Insofar as possible try to get what information you need from the school records about the students yourself. Deal as little as possible with the clerks or the lesser administrative figures. Here are a couple of examples. One, I became known to the clerks in the office, they knew who I was, my status was established, and they did not question my right to be in the office. I then found out where the students' files were and went to these files myself, with their permission, of course, and with their understanding, to get what information I needed from them. Another point is that each semester each student fills out a program card. It would be very easy for the administration to request that a second program card be filled out for you. Then when and if it is necessary for you to get a specific student out of a specific class, you can go to this file which you have, find out what class he is in when, and it will be much easier for you to get this student. As an example, if you want to get a student out of second period algebra in Room 333 all you have to do is to go to whichever administrative official you are dealing with and say you want to take this student out of second period algebra in Room 333. Then it is very simple for him to make out a simple slip of paper which you or he can take to the teacher of the room to get the pupil excused. However, if you do not know what room this pupil is in at the time you want him, it will be necessary to go to the main office and to deal with high school students, usually girls, who help out in the main office and in my experience, they will not understand your request three-fourths of the time. When they do understand your request, they then go to the clerk and the clerk may finally consult someone else and in the meantime, your communications become somewhat garbled, you have four or five people operating on this, and it creates an undue amount of tension. Having your own program cards can be a very good thing.

4. If you are a man working in the school, and of course the obverse would hold for a woman worker, you must recognize that in most school systems, the sex lines are fairly strictly drawn in the faculty. The men teachers and the women teachers do not as a rule mix socially. It is a good idea in my own experience for you to be identified with the social group of your own sex, that is, find out where the men teachers go for a smoke and if you smoke, go there to have one. Chat with them. Become, in a sense, one of the boys. I think a woman researcher would do much the same thing with the women teachers. It is kind of hard to describe, but it seems to me that the proper condition for you to attain socially in the school is that you are at one level accepted as "one of the boys" and not in any sense a threatening figure or a strange figure to these people, so that you can deal with them at a very personal level. However, you must never carry this so far that they fail to have the respect for you that your status as a University researcher demands. Somehow you must keep it before their eyes that you are a status figure without being a threatening one. I can't give any particular clues as to how one attains this, but perhaps if one has this social structure in mind it is easier to work within it. I might give an example of what I mean by this kind of relationship. The men teacher's lounge [has] pin-up pictures. The atmosphere is one of freedom, of masculine conversation about sexuality and about women. Before I was received into this room, I had already created a relationship with a few of the administrators and faculty members such that I was evidently acceptable. However, a number of times in conversations with the gentlemen in this room my opinion as a "psychologist" was asked on some questions. The point that I am trying to get across is that I was accepted as a man and as a social equal, but was [also] seen as an intellectual or as a status superior of some kind. This I think is very desirable, and almost the most desirable way to be seen by the people in the school with whom you have to work. . . . Yes, I think this is very ego-supporting [for the researcher] and a very satisfactory experience to have—this business of being seen as someone higher in a sense in the intellectual hierarchy. There are a few aspects of this which it might be worth while to discuss. . . . Yes, a field worker is in a sense playing two kinds of roles. He must up to a point be accepted as one of the people—as I said before, as "one of the boys"—but he also is defined as a somewhat "lonely creature." He is not completely one of the community or one of the crowd. Well, I would say that there are two kinds of ego support that come from establishing this kind of relationship I was speaking of. One, of course, is this business of being looked upon as an authority figure, an intellectual authority of some kind. There is no doubt that this is personally gratifying, but the second kind of ego support comes from the feeling, "I am operating successfully in this situation" that one gets as a researcher. When one establishes the kind of relationship I was speaking of before, you do get this feeling that you are really being successful in doing what you are trying to do. I suppose one could call this a kind of participant observation. I am really not out at this school to observe in the strict sense of the word, but of course, I do observe and the observations I make very often determine what kinds of activities I'm going to indulge in out at the school, which kind of tests I'm going to give, when I'm going to give them, how many of them at a time, and how much I can disrupt the school's schedule, etc.

Sometimes as an authority figure—or defined as an authority figure—they will ask some questions which it is presumed you can answer better than the questioners. In my experience these questions almost invariably have been the questions to which there is no answer, or at least no answer which is readily available. Such questions as which college should I send my boy to. My boy does such and such in school, what should I do about it, or—I have this kind of a behavior problem with this kid, how do I handle it. I do not in any reality sense ever feel qualified to answer these kinds of questions, but in a sense my job out there is not to answer questions like this but is to attain a certain degree of rapport, and a certain understanding, and a certain social definition in the eyes of these people. So depending upon the situation I will sometimes answer these questions and sometimes not. I'll leave the morals of the situation for you to decide. I don't have any organizing principles by which I can decide whether or not I shall answer a question, or whether or not I shall at a specific time play the role of the authority figure. Sometimes I have used the device of saying, "Well, this thing is so complicated that I don't know the answer yet (or no one knows the answer yet)." Sometimes I have given offhand advice as an expert, but only when I'm relatively sure that the advice cannot be checked up on or cannot be followed. The only illustration I can think of offhand is that once when we got into a discussion of what produces delinquent kids, what can parents do to prevent delinquency, and so forth. I replied with the psychological or social science cliché that if the parents loved the children enough, these things wouldn't happen. This of course is the kind of thing that in a sense is hard to deny, and no one can check up on it and no one can follow up on this and try loving someone enough tomorrow to keep them from being delinquent.

I wish to emphasize that my purpose in answering the questions or in talking to them in this way is not to give them information, or try to in any sense be a teacher or a guide, but is simply to play the social role which is defined and not entirely by me. It is defined in a large sense by what they think a University person is, by what they think a researcher is, and by what they think a scientist is. Incidentally, I have learned never to play the role of a scientist, never to even use the word scientist, never to even use the word scientist with teachers of physics, chemistry, general science, and so forth, because these people very often, I find, have traditions that people from social science are not scientists and I have found it best not to get into debates or arguments about this point.

The Urban Parish

In contemporary American society it is perhaps a bit more common to question the fundamental ways of operating of our important institutions than it has been elsewhere or at other times, although Margaret Mead's report on her revisit to the Manus[14] might give us pause. Each such inquiry, where it touches upon delicate information, faces resistances in its field work, and in publishing what has been learned in the form of data-about-society, ethical problems of reporting arise.

The following is intended to call attention to Father Fichter's interesting studies, without of course attempting to represent the full story of his field work experiences. Instead, we include this excerpt to illustrate at least one kind of resistance (that of the informant who questions the questioner's methods) and also to illustrate how the researcher maintained the anonymity of those who furnished information for an unusual study of a Roman Catholic parish:[15]

Father Schmidt, who was born and reared in the parish and is now a

---

14. Margaret Mead, New Lives for Old: Cultural Transformation—Manus, 1928-1953 (New York: William Morrow & Co., 1956).

15. Joseph H. Fichter, Southern Parish: The Dynamics of a City Church (Chicago: University of Chicago Press, 1951), "Foreword," pp. vii-ix. See also other references in Selected Bibliography under Fichter (1954) and Fichter and Kolb (1953).

high-placed cleric in the diocese, warned me at the beginning of this study:
"The Pastor is going to dislike you because the facts will show that St.
Mary's Parish is a hollow shell of Catholicism." It was a friendly warning,
and at times during the course of our investigation I felt that it might have
been wise to heed it. Social research of an empirical nature makes certain
demands on the virtues of patience and forbearance which are outside the
ambit of technical competence and analytical insight.

As far as I can judge, Father Urban did not come to dislike me, but he
frequently exhibited an extreme distaste for the evidence we uncovered. He
questioned our techniques, our methods, even our arithmetic; but in the end
—like the truth-loving person he is—he accepted the facts. He still disagrees
with some of our interpretations and conclusions. Neither he nor we have
come to the conclusion that his parish is a "hollow shell of Catholicism."
We still think that St. Mary's should be ranked high among the successfully
operating parishes of the diocese.

Every attempt has been made to conceal the location of St. Mary's Parish and the identity of its priests and people. Minor descriptive changes
have been introduced everywhere toward this end, but none of them has been
sufficient to distort in any way the total picture of the parish.

This anonymity, however, has its drawback. It makes it impossible for
us to give due credit to the even-tempered cooperation of the Pastor, Father
Urban, and his two assistants, Father Dominic and Father Paul. We cannot
appreciate sufficiently the forbearance of the Sisters in the school, the offi-
cers and members of parochial organizations, the individuals and families
of the parish. They were aware of our presence from the beginning but not
at all certain of the purpose of our ubiquitous observation and our innumer-
able interviews.

The same need for anonymity does not apply in regard to my competent
and faithful assistants during the twelve months' research. Under assignment, the "raw data" of research were gathered during the week and presented for a thorough group discussion of several hours duration every Saturday morning. . . .

We turn now, in chapter v, to the experiences of some students learning the rudiments of field work at first hand, and for most of them, for the
first time.

V

LEARNING TO DO FIELD WORK

Generally speaking, students are not often introduced to the learning tasks that would fit them for the field work part of the vocation (or avocation) called social science in any manner that systematically sensitizes them to the range of field worker roles as they are distinguished in this book. Instead, they are usually given, or acquire, some models of social science, as presented by their teachers or found in the more widely read monographs and textbooks, and each approaches his own first attempts at field observation with, apparently, some kind of generalized field worker role in mind. At least, this was true of the beginners and even the more experienced graduate students whose adventures help us, in this chapter,[1] to illuminate some of the basic problems encountered by all social scientists in their efforts to build our knowledge of society from "the raw facts of life."

But the generalized field worker role is not the same for all students, of course. Each has his own apperceptions—perhaps that of the role of the detective, or of the journalist, the missionary, the future novelist, the philanthropist, the scholar, or whatever. I even encountered one student who "found himself" after his first few efforts to secure interviews door-to-door in a strange neighborhood and who promptly transferred to another science curriculum that promised a lifetime in the laboratory, safely insulated from most of the personal problems and social processes in the gen-

---

1. As Project Director of the Social Sciences Field Training Project at the University of Chicago in 1951-52, I was aided in the collection of these materials by my co-authors of the privately circulated document, "Cases on Field Work," by Everett C. Hughes et al. (1952), and by the anonymous participants in a special seminar on Methods and Training in Field Observation conducted in the spring of 1952 by Professor Everett C. Hughes and me at the University of Chicago. These materials consisted of personal interviews and field diaries as well as formal course reports by beginning and advanced students in 1951-52 and from earlier years at the University when I was instructor in the Department of Sociology. The analyses, short interpretations, and other comments are drawn from "Cases on Field Work" and from my reception of echoes from the teaching of George Herbert Mead (1934) over more than two decades of association with a few of his direct students and many more of his readers, especially students at the University of Chicago in sociology from 1946 to about 1955. Among the latter one of the best, and certainly one of the most sensitive interpreters of Mead's thinking as it can and does illuminate field worker role problems is Raymond L. Gold (1954; 1958).

eral flux of human affairs.

With a minimum of editorial comment or interpretation, except for
setting the stage and disguising without distorting social identities of people and places, let us permit these "beginners" to speak for themselves,
so that the reader may share their sometimes vague apprehensions of what
was going on in their field work learning experiences, as well as share
some of their self-dramatizations, their problems in sizing up human situations, and their flashes of insight into themselves and others.

The most common learning experiences, mistakes, and dilemmas of
field workers (not to ignore those of their informants) can be classified in
these groups: the rebuff; using cues, insights, and social perceptiveness;
blocking (on the part of the informant); status problems; problems of role
choice; handling emotional involvement; and ethical problems of reporting.
Accordingly, I present the candid revelations of our learners under these
headings, giving the student an opportunity to "speak for himself" in an un-
interrupted passage wherever possible.

The Rebuff

Few people find it easy to accept refusals dispassionately. Quite a
number of people, however, have a nasty habit of saying nay to any stranger
who knocks on the door, caring little if the person is a young, nervous, over-
anxious, beginning field worker. It is bad enough when things don't go well
for the experienced field observer, but it is almost fatal (or seems so) to
the beginner. Here, therefore, are some excerpts from materials in which
students disclose personal reactions to refusals and hard-to-get interviews.

From the field report of beginning student Sonya Heifitz, is an example
of an attempted interview that is rebuffed:

> The big "let-down" I mentioned before occurred this way: I had stopped
> on the northeast corner of _____ Street and _____ Place to take my bear-
> ings and scribble some notes. The apartment building there has a few shops
> several steps into the basement. I found myself directly in front of the win-
> dow of a China Mending Shop, on the corner, where I could clearly see and
> be seen by the people inside. The proprietress, wearing a large apron, was
> talking to another old woman, thin and wearing a coat. They had noticed me
> and were glancing at me curiously every once in a while. I debated going in.
> Part of me was opposed to it, irrationally, because (a) the women looked
> D.A.R.-ish, (b) I don't care for the itsy-bitsy expensive and ornate china
> shown in the window, (c) the owner's name was Josephine T. Snodgrass,
> and (d) I was hungry. The rest of me figured it would be easy to talk to
> them because they were already chatting and curious about me. So I went in.
> So there was a lovely silence, broken by a long "Ye-e-e-es?" from Miss
> Snodgrass, accompanied by the big smile and a slow observant look all over
> me. (I was wearing slacks, like a fool, instead of proper ladylike clothing.)
> Her smile seen close-up didn't look so good—she has yellow teeth. (I can
> picture her chewing very carefully and taking small bites.) I explained, as
> smoothly as I could, what I was doing, and apologized for disturbing her
> with what was not business. The other woman followed her in reactions,

looked at her before adjusting her facial expression. Rapport, however, was impossible to establish. She considered questions about the neighborhood (such as about the general sort of people living there, general occupational type, average size of apartments, average rent) "Terribly personal—disgustingly personal!" I could see the janitor about such things, she said. She expressed indignation with that smile, which by then I called a leer. She kept asking "Why in the world would the University want such information? And who wants it? I simply can't imagine of what possible use or interest that could be to anyone!" I tried to explain about the course and experience in field study, and almost the whole of the social sciences, but it didn't click, and she remained suspicious. She apparently didn't think much of University projects. At the end, she strongly repeated "This is just an average neighborhood—go study some other neighborhood and you'll know all you want about this one. Take one and you have them all." I thanked her with a smile as brilliant, I hope, as her own, and left.

Another beginning student, Arthur Harris, philosophizes about the many refusals he received before finding "two co-operative women":

Not being new at the interviewing game, I wasn't too discouraged with the many rebuffs I met with in trying to fill out my schedules. Besides the many people who are just never home in the afternoon, the refusals the interviewer gets are both monotonously, and amusingly, typical. Most aggravating is that type of female respondent who upon hearing a male's voice outside bars her door shut and will under no circumstances dare open it as long as you remain. This cruel act fosters the necessity of speaking to a slab of wood—something I detest. Then there's the type who opens the door a fraction of two inches and remarks coyly—and at times teasingly, I suspect—that she's undressed and couldn't possibly allow herself to be interviewed. For the sake of harassed interviewers, a comprehensive study should be made of the mid-afternoon incidence of female nudity in urban areas. Likewise, the astonishing number of women who are just about to step into or have just stepped out of a bath cannot be overlooked. Other types range from the "predatory-hostile" who seem to get a perverse gratification from slamming a door in a stranger's face, through the "suspiciously-careful"—getting them to give an adequate response is worse than pulling teeth, and the interview rapidly degenerates into a battle of wits,—to the "over indulgent informer."
On this Tuesday I was fortunate when toward the late afternoon I managed to find two cooperative women who graciously postponed preparing their husband's dinners to answer a few questions.

These student reactions to the rebuff illustrate resentment (Sonya Heifitz) and humorous sarcasm (Arthur Harris), while another, George Dabney, criticizes his own approach as failing to enable potential informants to understand his work:

November 2. Rang seven bells on east side of _____ Street. Score: one interview, four refusals, two not home. Rang another bell on this street. Old woman, evidently prepared to go shopping answered door. I said, "How do you do," and continued to tell her that I was making a survey of families in the area, and asked if the lady of the house had a few minutes to spare me.
This woman called another woman, and asked me in, telling me to sit down and wait arrival of the person called. The woman who came downstairs was also elderly; her manner was very incisive. She wanted to know what I wanted, so I repeated my spiel; she asked impatiently if I was collecting subscriptions, and didn't seem to believe or understand that such was not the case. She wanted to know who this information was for; I an-

swered that it was for myself, that I was trying to learn about the community. I was rather summarily ushered out with the assertion from her that "you don't want any information from us," and the statement that there was "too much of this kind of thing." . . .

I recognize quite clearly that all of my openings have been poor. I am quite nervous and am probably·on the defensive. I have in every instance, by asking for a few minutes of time, given those who are unsure of me the opportunity to dismiss me. I must find some way to clearly state a purpose that is reasonable and without threat to the neighborhood people.

Fear that he is somehow intruding into the personal life of the informant is perhaps the greatest handicap to the field worker. Every occupation presents some problem of mandate and in this instance, it is the question of the field worker's right to inquire. An advanced student, Arnold Gwaltey, tells us in a personal interview how difficult it was for him to approach the man who had recently suffered the loss of his wife and two daughters when a stunting airplane crashed into a crowd of onlookers. In this instance, the fear of intrusion is clearly more a part of the student's definition of the situation before his approach than after his reception by the informant, for the latter defines him differently than he had anticipated:

For instance, you walk up to the house and you know already that this person's wife and two daughters were killed in this airplane crash. And you had heard that he had talked very freely for the first day or so, but you arrive at the fifth day after the crash. The funeral has just been that day. Knowing all this, you've built up quite an emotional tension which doesn't show on the surface, and you've fatigued yourself a certain amount even before you walk in the place. You remind yourself that in previous experiences with persons like this the person has been very willing to talk—in fact, it's done him some good. Then, on the other hand, you think—well, this is the fifth day—no, it was later than that; it was the sixth day or the seventh day after the accident. You've found out from previous experience that people will talk about this for a certain number of days after which it was psychologically possible for them to forget it, see. So then, at that point, they would clam up, where they'd been talking about it like mad previously. Well, you begin thinking about that. Here it is about seven days afterwards and maybe the guy is going to clam up. Then you walk in and the guy makes an excuse—he can't do it at the time. You don't know whether the excuse is real, or cooked up for the occasion. Then you have another period of four or five hours before you have a reappointment with him. In this particular case he still refused, because he says that meantime he's talked to his doctor and his doctor told him not to talk. Well, you still don't know about that. Then later, after it was too late, after you've left the town, we found out that if we had done what we had tried to do, if we had been successful in contacting this priest beforehand, that we could have cleared the road. The guy was a very uneducated person; he couldn't understand what we wanted to do at all. In fact, it was quite difficult to convince him that it wasn't going to cost him money, that he wasn't going to have to pay us for doing this, so that it wasn't going to be put on the radio. All these things, you see, go through your mind. And you know he's a very crucial person, too, a guy that you really want to get, because he's testing out a certain hypothesis that you've had. Then, as you're trying to convince him of all this, you see at the dinner table that he's got three remaining daughters who are looking daggers at you, wondering why in the heck you want to bother the poor, old man who feels so bad about the empty places at the table. That's the sort of emotional strain you are under. That's the sort of thing that's worse than if the person breaks down and cries in front of you. Anyhow, after you think about it, maybe this guy's doctor is right in this particular case; but maybe his doctor didn't say a thing. . . .

It is often a challenge for the field worker to convince the informant that he is not only occupationally, but personally and socially qualified to conduct the interview. Part of an interview with an advanced student, Henry Bachman, shows how he matched wits successfully with a most incredulous person, the wife of the chosen respondent:

The first interview I want to tell you about was where this guy's wife had turned down about five people before me and the research group had decided that it was hopeless. The husband was to be interviewed, but nobody could get beyond the wife. So I made the contacts with the local minister in this southern, rural town where they lived, and I managed to talk with the wife then and she granted me an interview for that evening. And I thought everything was all set. I was kind of ribbing them back there that they didn't know how to get interviews, and that was probably the only reason I went through what they put me through. I hated to come back without it. I went out there and she became hostile again. I had to battle my way past her before I could see her husband. And to both of them I had to start explaining again why I wanted it—all my reasons—and she asked me what my religion was. I am a Baptist, so I thought I'll get around this one without stretching the truth—I'm a Baptist and she is, too. As soon as I said I'm a Baptist she said, "Kneel down and pray, Brother, I'll soon see what you are." I didn't know what to do, whether to call her bluff and go ahead and give her a prayer, or what. Then I got to thinking that no matter what I would do it wouldn't be right—she'd find fault in it. So I just told her that, according to the Bible, it said that don't pray to show that you are a Christian like the hypocrites do; go into the closet where nobody can see or hear you pray. I said that I didn't think I should pray just to show that I was a Christian; it wouldn't be right; it's against my belief. Well, she accepted that, but from then on it was always that the husband would shut up and I'd have to argue with the wife, and just about the time I'd get her around to it, then he'd start in again. And things started going fairly well, so I decided that I'd try to interview the guy alone. And his wife said that this girl, when she came out here, she said that she'd like to talk to her husband alone and I said that I would like to, too. I explained that sometimes the husband sometimes sees something in the storm that he doesn't want his wife or children to hear about—it's not very nice. Or maybe he doesn't want them to keep thinking about the storm because he'd just as soon they didn't hear what was going on. And he pipes up, "I didn't see anything that would hurt them." So I gave up interviewing him alone. In the meantime, I was trying to get this argument on the tape. I had everything all set up and the thing plugged in. She kept pulling out the plug. Every time I'd just walk over as casually as possible and plug it in and she'd just walk over and plug it out. And she had everything situated so that I had to walk clear across the room every time I plugged it in, and she was in a rocking chair over there by the plug. She said, "Who's going to pay for this electricity?" I said, "We will be glad to pay for the electricity." And she said, "It's going to raise my bill by about two dollars and a half." I told her that I was positive that it wouldn't raise it more than fifteen cents, but just to make sure I gave her a dollar. Of course, the more I think about that, the more I think it was a mistake, that I should have given her about twenty or twenty-five cents. But she wouldn't accept the money herself. I had to give the money to her kids. At the same time she wouldn't let me start the interview until I did give the money to the kids. Another thing she argued about is: Why should the Government pay us money to go around and bother people like that, pay us a good salary for it, when they didn't have enough

to live on? That was a kind of rough one to explain. . . . It was just a constant battle to explain why I should be there. And even after the interview,
about five minutes later, he perks up and says, "I don't see why I should
do this." But finally I got it out of him. It was a short interview. But it
turned out that the antagonism was mostly that they had felt they deserved
some help and they didn't get any. And they thought that we were aligned
with the Red Cross, which they despised, or that we might be communists,
and I don't know where they got that idea. . . .

It is a truism, brought home to every field worker who encounters
either rebuff or acceptance from informants, that at a given instant, a person is what he is because of his past experiences and present situation. In
one situation the same people who are eager to talk to the field worker
may be reluctant to do so in other circumstances. An advanced student,
Charles James, points out how the definition of his approach as "intrusion"
depends upon the informants' personal and social organization when they
have experienced a disaster:

When people have had experience at disaster interviewing, they realize
that when the community has been hit hard the whole community structure
is so disrupted, that any routine in the person's life has been so knocked
off kilter, that he has no routine which you're disrupting. If you interview
someone who had a fire in Chicago, he's in an apartment across the street,
he's going back to work tomorrow. Everything is right back on schedule
and he simply doesn't want to be bothered. He has some things he wants to
make up and he can definitely structure things to see which areas in his
life he is so far behind. These people, who have experienced a community-
wide disaster, have been so obliterated they can't see how far they are in
any area. They don't even know what's important to do. They are very
amenable to suggestion, and we could still find this attitude through the
second and into the third week after the disaster in the communities where,
for example, ninety per cent of the houses were flattened. In other communities, which weren't hit so hard, even though an individual might be involved, the community structure was intact and he was back in the swing
of things and had all these things he had to do. But there's a case where
the problem for the interviewer is not as great as you might anticipate.
It's one of those things about disaster interviewing which makes it easier.
[Interviewer: This anomie business—] Well, that's it on a strictly psychological level, but on a sociological level it's, well, sort of the same thing—
the lack of any structure there which they feel bound by, which they feel
obligated to, and which you're interfering with. It's sort of an amorphous
state. But when, a little later, people begin to refuse in the latter stages,
they refuse on the basis: What good is this study going to do me? How is
granting an interview going to help me get back on my feet? I've got this
and that to do, and they stuck by it see, after the third week. [Interviewer:
They were already beginning to get reorganized.] Yes. And when people
refused on that basis after the third week, we never got them, even if we
sent back two or three other people to see them. While if people in the
early stages even thought of this, and they seldom did, you could break it
down with ease, since they couldn't defend excuses well yet. After a period
of time they are right and they know that they can convince you that they
are right. Why are you bothering them? Well, because you want to get
something below a ten per cent refusal rate. . .

Using Cues, Insights, and Social Perceptiveness

Even novice field workers find ways of sizing up people and situations, and these consist mainly of observing "little things" and applying a comparative attitude. Dale Addison tells how he and his student partner worked together on a small survey, and how he himself used his observations to gain insights:

We wanted to map the district at this time and did not want to spend time in interviewing. We did ask passersby occasionally about the buildings and streets in the area. In so doing we always got more information than we asked for, from the sociological standpoint. The voice, manner, and attitude of the person questioned always revealed a great deal on the basis of social definitions of situations. My companion considered most of the people, especially the children, rude, and aggressive. He is from a small town in Texas, and from an American middle class family. I am from a lower class family in a city of about 15,000 in Michigan. It immediately occurred to me that our reactions to the people here were different because of our different backgrounds. I therefore consider it quite valuable to get a number of viewpoints in such a sociological study as this, to help achieve some kind of objectivity about the unconscious bias of observers.

Again, Dale Addison tells of an insight from observations he makes, although he did not go on to test this "provisional hypothesis":

Zounds! A couple of boys about ten and eleven years of age were fighting in the middle of the road as we were questioning some school girls. "Oh, they're a couple of brothers always fighting," said one of the girls with bored disdain. Fighting among the children, and especially the boys, was quite commonly observed but between brothers might seem unusual. This gave me a lead for a number of questions to determine something about the cultural traits of the people in the area. I made a provisional hypothesis that these brothers were from a family of foreign born parents, and their egoistic aggression was a part of their general rebellion to authority in their marginal position.

Clark Brewster provides an example of social perceptiveness, in which he compares and generalizes:

In the lower-middle class area of Tract __ wives seemed to have a great deal of respect for their husbands. This relationship was brought out in their often quoting their husbands on particular issues and referring to him as the head of the family. The relationship was not necessarily reversed from the husband's point of view. Indeed, the men rarely mentioned their wives, usually referring to the rest of the family, the sons and daughters only, when talking about their home life. The men were more prone to use as authorities their male acquaintances, the ministers of the area, their bosses at work, and the principals of the neighborhood schools.
    The latter statement in the preceding paragraph points up another outstanding characteristic of the people interviewed; they all had a healthy respect for any form of authority more powerful than themselves and those forms directly affecting them or potentially affecting them. But they treated any distant, weak, or not directly affecting authority with great disdain. For example, the local Community Council seemed to be held in more reverence than the national government. The local grade school principal was held in more respect than was the faculty at the University _____. But, I am happy to add, the University itself was recognized to be above any but "those Eastern colleges."
    And yet, the subservience to authority evident in the area did not hold with equal pusillanimity for all authority. Respect depended on quality rather than quantity or nearness of authority. The Metropolitan Police, for instance, were held in scoffing ridicule while the United States Marines and

the FBI received the greatest respect and esteem.

Everett Churchill gives us a mixture of cues and insights, and shows some emotional involvement:

As I entered the dark store, a little bell tinkled and in one corner, near a very old table covered with sheets of yellow paper and entry books, a Negress with grey-white hair turned and looked up. There was absolutely no sign of emotion in that wrinkled face, not even an expression of interest. I walked toward the old lady, avoiding a little grey kitten, tapering tail held rigidly in excitement, and a cardboard box of, what appeared to be kitchen utensils in various stages of disrepair.

"Good afternoon. Are you Mrs. Jones?" I hoped she was not, for she was entirely too old to have taken any effective part in PTA work within the last twenty years at least. Her only answer was a swift shake of the head and a rather haughty grunt. "Did Mrs. Jones live here once? I'm looking for her to talk with her about the Schuster school. Could you tell me where she lives now?" The old lady did not appear to be in the least afraid of her visitor, but she certainly wasn't the most friendly person either. Expecting a kindly, weak response to my questions, it was a surprise when the old Negro shakily rose from her chair and walked unsteadily toward the front door.

She almost tripped over the box of pots and pans on her way to the front of the store. She looked around and gave me a scowl as though to take out her bitterness at being old and her embarrassment at being clumsy on me.

I had no idea what she was up to. I had a very disagreeable feeling that perhaps she was going to show me out, though for the life of me, I could not figure out what I had done to upset her.

The kitten at any rate seemed happy and contented. She was over her curiosity in the strange visitor and was now curled up in one of the window display cases licking her front paws. As I looked at the cat, lying in the sun which forced itself through the dusty windows and cleaning herself in the window stage where everything around her was dirty, and disheveled, I felt very morose. Black hats of odd shapes lay around her as they had been thrown, perhaps years earlier, to gather the souvenirs of time. And a pair of brown and white (they had been white) women's pumps stood forlornly in the center of the window "display," reminders of a bygone day of happiness for someone. As I became more conscious of the decadent atmosphere of the old lady's shop, a few lines of a poem I once heard flashed across my mind. It was an ode to "dust":

> You encamp under the earth as a master
> With the pale legions of your scattered empire.
> O rodent, your infinite teeth devour
> The color, the presence of things!

And the old lady was part of it all. I felt sorry for her. But she probably wouldn't exchange her little run-down, dusty store now even if she could. She was part of the dust and the old hats and the kitten washing itself in the window. She couldn't leave now, or change things; it was too late.

She opened the door and the sounds of the street came in upon us. She blinked in the unaccustomed light, then took my hand and pointed that I was to go that way, turn the corner, and there I would find the stairway to the second floor where Mrs. Jones lived. Actually the old lady did not say a word, but somehow she made everything quite plain. Wondering if she could speak at all I thanked her, smiled and turned away. As I did so, she touched my hand again and I turned back to face her. She had a smile on her face that was yet not a smile, for her mouth was still tightly shut. But her eyes darted furtively about my face and were not afraid to ask boldly for what the old lady wanted—and needed. I felt ashamed and mad at myself for not having thought about giving her something. In a show of anger, more at my-

self than at her, I shoved the money at her more rudely than I wanted to
(and felt sorry afterwards).

She took the money but her face was not pleased, and inwardly, I could
not blame her. But it somehow made me mad for the old lady not to be
more grateful. With very confused emotions I turned abruptly and went
around the corner of the house. As I began to walk upstairs to Mrs. Jones'
flat my anger started to subside, and a feeling of pity and sympathy for the
old woman came over me. I could have been more polite. After all, the
only thing that could have been beautiful to her in life, the only thing left
her, was the kindness of those around her.

> Even the light clothes itself in silence
> with your grey covers, my dust.
> Final inheritor of things defunct,
> you go hoarding everything in your
> travelling tomb.

Beulah Sinclair and Horace Carson wrote the following, which provides
several instances of using cues and gaining insights. The two episodes involving two homes, were reported in the same joint report:

Looking at the built-in bookcases, which contained a number of rather
well-thumbed books, I had a better chance to "size her up." In the book
case were volumes on the topics of philosophy, world problems, art, and
several recent novels. On the coffee table were books more appropriate
for younger children, such as Winnie the Pooh. From these books a thought
immediately came to me. It may be far off the track were I to investigate
the family more intensely. The family seemed to be well informed about
and quite aware of what is going on around them. Unlike the books of many
of their contemporaries, who use the bookshelf to impress the guests with
the "first editions" or the "100 great books," these books indicated fairly
clearly that the family did not buy them to impress others, but rather to
really read them and obtain some useful information from them. . . . The
books indicated that the family takes an interest in their children's school
work.

The furnishings of the room, and of the other rooms which could be
seen, showed good taste. Although it is not ultra-conservative, it indicated
that Mrs. Lemontree might be a rather reserved person. The atmosphere
of the whole house seemed to supply the necessary words to a missing
sign—if such a one were to be hung—"Quiet."

One can spot this over-protective attitude which she has over her children. She rationalizes into saying that "they need me." I would assume that
from her rather tenderly and over-exaggerated description of the good
points of her children, she spoils them quite a bit. Needless to say, the big
disappointment of not having her children accepted into the ___ School made
her turn against all private schools. But how did she justify sending her
son to ___ (another private school)? "He's too brilliant for the ___ (local
public) School" was the answer—as if, "in desperation," she had to turn to
a private school to bring out all of the boy's above-average intelligence.
Mrs. Arnold's constant watching-out of her children's work has made her
well-informed about the teachers of the schools, and she seemed to take
great pride in telling me that she was not the usual kind of parent who did
not know much about the schools to which their children go. Knowing her
teachers "well," Mrs. Arnold's [justification for denouncing the teachers
is strong indeed]. If we took her statement as is, we would feel that her
children are above approach in character—"perfect saints and halos." However, Mrs. Arnold's over eagerness in telling the interviewer all about the
"goodness" of her children betrayed her genuineness. . . .

Blocking

"Blocking" occurs when the field observer forces a topic on an informant, or otherwise defines the situation in some way undesirable to him. A
beginner's field report gives his experience in forcing a topic on an unwilling respondent:

> The actual filling out of the interview (questionnaire) took place in the
> hallway and though she was willing to cooperate a number of questions im-
> pressed her as being a little vague or silly. At the end of the questionnaire
> she commented that she wished she had not started it because she did not
> see what significance there was to it. She also thought it was rather per-
> sonal in several instances and she declined to state what her average
> monthly income and expenses were. On the whole, Mrs. _____ was not
> highly opinionated. She could give no reasons for saying that a female law-
> yer would be any different than a male lawyer, or that a Negro lawyer
> would be inferior to a white lawyer.
> Upon completion of the questionnaire, we talked about the neighborhood
> for a few minutes. She showed a strong concern for the fact that many of
> the homes around her were being broken up into multiple family dwellings.
> After this short conversation, I started to leave and she remarked that
> if she had known the real nature of the questionnaire she would not have
> been willing to fill it out. But, as she had been a student of the University,
> at one time, she consented to come down and talk to me. Otherwise she
> said she would not have been interested.

In an opinion survey the field worker may be required to ask questions
which seem to him most inappropriate for a particular respondent. An advanced student, Yvette Monet, looks back on such an experience as good
self-discipline:

> . . . But it happened that, in my mind, the questionnaire was much
> more for upper-middle class and upper class people than for any sort of
> lower class people. When you are facing a colored woman who has seven
> or eight children and just doesn't know how to feed them, philanthropy be-
> comes a little touchy to ask about. So, this was one of my problems. But
> still, the fact that I had to ask these questions as they were written, even
> though I was feeling a little uncomfortable at times, was very good training
> experience, because I knew I could ask almost any kind of question looking
> the people in the eyes. It's amazing. . . .

Richard Rogers, an advanced student, makes the interesting point that
some informants want to be defined as a respondent-statistic while others
want to be treated as an informant-person. If the field worker and the person interviewed do not concur in this definition of the situation, a free exchange of social gestures becomes impossible:

> . . . But these two attitudes—the idea of liking to be or wanting to be a
> statistic, which I think is quite common among people who have a college
> education, and you find a certain number of people in the field who would
> like to say, "Well, I was one of the people in the Kinsey Report." And then
> you find other people who will talk and give you the most intimate details,
> but if they think you are going to make a statistic out of them they don't
> like it. And here's a thing I ran up against in my experience with disaster
> interviewing—I use this experience because it seems to highlight this kind
> of thing—where people in a disaster situation are feeling quite guilty about

their own behavior; what they did do or what they didn't do, or how they did what they did, and really the things they are beating themselves over the head for not doing are the things you couldn't expect any ordinary human being to do. In fact, it's the things which no one ever does, but they have a sort of hero conception in their minds of how people are supposed to act in this situation and, not having lived up to that, they are very guilt-ridden. So, in some cases, after the interview is over, we sort of try to alleviate this sort of doubt. I sometimes say to them, "We find that over ninety per cent of the time people have a such-and-such reaction," but do you think that has any effect on them? Huh-uh. In two cases, specifically, the only two cases where we tried it, the reaction was so bad that we never tried it again. Immediately when the curtain goes down and rapport is gone, they became self-conscious, and they become hostile towards you. And in one case I just happened to run into the respondent the next day and he was still hostile. Maybe it was the fact that he immediately began to feel that, by gosh, he told you an awful lot and maybe you would go further some time and cite a certain case. So we would never cite a case from a previous disaster, or even any statistics. What I think this does is break down this person-to-person relationship. It's no longer a personal interest in him as a person. You are categorizing him; you are putting him in a class. He doesn't want to become a statistic. He really is an individual and wants to remain one. This is the same reaction that people get to a highly structured questionnaire. Here it hasn't been highly structured at all and you haven't gotten this reaction, but just quoting a statistic puts him in a category. Maybe he doesn't want to be like the majority; maybe he'd rather be guilt-ridden for not having been a saint, than to be like everybody else. So, in trying to educate the public on this professional role, should you picture this interviewer as sort of an impersonal institution that never talks back and who will never divulge this information? What kind of picture are you going to paint of this guy? It looks to me like you are going to have to paint the sort of picture which works on the emotional level, which allows them to project any pictures into it that they want, that is favorable to their own particular bent. It's a big order. I don't know how it would be done. But I know that in certain cases, just to know that this is going to be a statistical study is fine, it opens the door. But in other cases it closes the door with a bang. And in rural areas, they are likely to accept it on a personal basis, while in this fancy suburb, where everybody has a pretty high income, two or three big cars in their garage, well, there it was somewhat of an assurance to tell them that they were going to end up as a statistic.

A joint report written by two beginning field workers provides an example of asking about a topic that is meaningless to the informant and of then, incidentally, making a hasty generalization on the basis of the information obtained:

> We telephoned for an appointment with Mr. Edmund Edge, a Block Captain whose name was given to us by Mrs. Jones. But since Mr. Edge was away we asked if we could see Mrs. Edge.
> We went over and Mrs. Edge let us in. There were a number of small children running around. The house looked as if it had recently been extensively renovated and attractively and expensively furnished. The house itself was large and well kept.
> We told Mrs. Edge that we were interested in community life in this area and asked if she could tell us something about it. This got only a slightly confused look from her. So we said we understood that her husband was a Block Captain and perhaps she could tell us how successful he had been. She said that she knew her husband was doing "something like that" but really knew nothing about it. She was plainly eager to help us but she really did not know what we were looking for. We asked her if most of her

friends came from around there and she replied that some do but they know
people from all over the city. We asked a few other inconsequential questions and got no interesting answers, and failed to get her talking.

Mrs. Edge impressed us as being a timid woman. She was the only person we interviewed that actually was ill at ease with us. The other clearly
relegated us in their minds as "young students." However she bore out our
hypothesis that a real integrated community did not exist in our area; rather that these people exhibited the isolationism typical of urban dwellers.

Status Problems

Some of the status problems met by field workers arise in connection
with the ambiguity of their "mandate" to ply their trade. The dream of having a public right to contact and ask anybody about anything is countered by
the reality on many occasions of a field worker's finding himself obliged
to ask questions which are inappropriate to the informant and the situation.
When this occurs, he becomes acutely aware of the status relationship between him and the informant, often feeling that he has "no right" to be there
in the field and wishing that he were both free and able to ask less obnox-
ious questions. The informant, too, may experience much the same problem in such circumstances.

Other status problems arise when the field worker has to interact with
informants whose social characteristics are not congruent with his. In such
instances, he may find himself too self-conscious to play his field worker
role convincingly. Coincidently the informant is likely to define the field
worker as one object in one kind of situation, but as another object in another kind of situation, simply because of the possible audience he represents in each. Needless to say, the mode and tone of the informant's remarks will make the field worker sensitive to these different definitions.
Thus, the social characteristics which the informant ascribes to him,
whether the ascription is correct or not, may lead to the same kind of status problem which occurs when their respective social characteristics are
manifestly different and clearly inhibit their interactions.

When faced with the task of asking "unsuitable" questions, a student
field worker, Frieda Blumner, saw herself confronted with a status problem deriving from a doubtful mandate:

On this study of mental health, I was supposed to find pre-college people to interview, but the questionnaire was long and the language too high-
brow for them. I was infuriated at having to administer it. Imagine using a
questionnaire that takes four hours! Who's going to give so much time to a
stranger? Can you afford to visit with anyone under such conditions?

In the same interview, Miss Blumner gives two experiences which suggest
that people frequently ascribe a status as a confidence man to the field
worker when they do not recognize his claim to have a field work mandate:

Out in [an industrial suburb], we got admitted by a housewife and we asked her a lot of questions about money, income, bonds, etc. This woman gave us the information all right, but as we were leaving her house, up drives a police car, which the woman living with her must have called. Charley, my partner, was horrified, because he feared an arrest might blemish his character. I was scared; yet a little mad. We had Bureau of Census cards and I.D. cards from the University, but the police were doubtful of their authenticity because a number of people had been bothered—questioned—recently. Finally, one of the police said, "You look like you have character," and he let us go. Apparently the woman we interviewed had been bothered before by a couple who might have been con agents and she decided to call the police this time. Another time we went to an apartment in the Gold Coast. The woman seemed to wonder why the Government was paying two interviewers to see her, wasting taxpayers' money. She called the F.B.I. when we left. Fortunately, the F.B.I. knew about us.

In her field diary a beginning field worker, Fay Lipschultz, presents an anecdotal account of a status disparity problem:

The thing that struck me about this whole interchange of phone calls with Mrs. R. was her belief that only she and the former president of the P.T.A. (who must be a friend of hers, judging from the way Mrs. R. rattled off Mrs. G.'s phone number) were the only ones qualified to discuss the organization. Though I suggested a vice-president, secretary, or treasurer as other people I could speak to, Mrs. R. rejected the idea emphatically. She seems to think that only presidents can know what's going on in the organization. . . . I must admit that I felt antagonistic to her from the moment she flashed her automatic smile at me; she is just the smart, clever, clubwoman type who irritates the Hell out of me. However, I thought of my aunt, president of the ___ Club, who under similar circumstances would probably look and act the same and decided the best way I could conduct the interview would be to be as businesslike and objective as possible.

From a point of view opposite to that of Miss Lipschultz, Robert L. Buchman points to a status disparity difficulty he encountered as a novice field worker. In this instance, the field worker looks down on the informant, rather than resenting her:

She is the character of the institution. She is definitely in line with the caricatures one hears about "little theatre" people (à la Helen Hokinson, but somewhat vicious) (pardon my value judgments). From conversation she has an excellent grasp of what she believes constitutes good singing (at least it agrees with what I think); e.g., Caruso could only sing loud; Lanza is not ready; Bjoerling is great, etc. One odd feature was that she didn't know how to pronounce names like Lanza and Bjoerling which leads me to believe she doesn't get much chance to talk to people with a very "high" taste in music, as one could find anywhere on the Campus here.

Mildred Gatewood's field report contains another example of status disparity which shows how ethnic identification enabled the student to listen to views repugnant to her:

From attending the suppers and talking to different members and leaders, the unconscious or unstated aim of the church seems to be providing entertainment for the Germans and the Swedes of the area—so they won't have to mingle with the Poles and Jews there. They really resent the fact that these two nationalities are moving into the area. I don't think I ever heard prejudices expressed so often and by so many people—I even wondered if there was a secret fascist organization within the church that kept these prejudices stirred up. It just so happens that my parents were born in Germany, so when they asked me my nationality I told them I was German; because of this fact they probably did feel much freer to make their remarks.

Another beginner, Clark Brewster, reveals a problem of status disparity, writing in a style that gives a hint of his own apperception of the field worker role (that of a future modern novelist?):

The wind is blowing softly, just enough to jostle the paper in the gutters but not enough to make your pants tighten back against your legs. And up in the next block you can see the kids already lining up in front of the "Atom" for Hoot Gibson in "Renegade Cayuse," although it is only eleven-thirty, an hour before opening time. There along Schiel [Avenue], with the warm sun beating against your neck and making the blood feel good and tingly, everything is quiet and deserted, except for an occasional noisy green and yellow street car and a couple of black youngsters across the street talking loudly and tossing a dirty softball back and forth between them. Maybe it's too early to start, you ask yourself; it was sort of silly to come out during the lunch hour anyway. For some reason you had never thought about these people having any regular lunch hour, in the conventional way. Then you get a little mad at yourself for jumping to such conclusions. You remember you are to be objective in your investigations. Anyway, there is no reason to think these people are any different from you and your kind.

On the corner a little drug store looks invitingly your way. You start toward it, a little glad of the excuse not to have to get started on your assignment right away. About twelve-thirty everyone should be through with lunch and in a good humor to see me, you reflect. Lordy knows, they'll have to be in a good humor to put up with the foolish things I've got to ask them, you say to yourself, smirking. What can I possibly learn about the area from asking people if they remember who their grandmother's aunt on their mother's side was, and if they themselves had been conceived out of wedlock—"Oh, but perhaps you had rather not answer that," you hasten to add when they look just a little uncomfortable.

You're really a little scared, and you've always been a little timid with people, but you won't admit it to yourself. Instead, you try to override your real feelings by loudly condemning the methods, the instructors, and everything else connected with the Sociology Department. In your irritation and nervousness, you order a milk shake, which you can ill afford.

You are agreeably surprised when the proprietor, who is also the "soda jerk," thanks you for your purchase. You were beginning to think people observed such niceties only in the more civilized Southern states, and you certainly had no previous inkling that anything of the kind was possible in Chicago. It made you feel a little better to know that even here in your Tract there was at least one person with whom you had something in common.

The student-author of the following, Arnold Knight, indicates that his problem of status disparity relates to his lack of belief that he has any proper mandate to question strangers, and in discussing this, he discloses his rationalizations of failure to secure interviews and of his final success:

Over Schiel Avenue the blue sky looks down majestically and wonders what in the world all of those aunt-like (?) objects are doing running around as if they don't know where they are going. After being turned away from three doors on Schiel, you begin to wonder yourself where you are going, and why. And after being suspiciously received in only one residence out of seven fruitless attempts to interview, and then only for five minutes, you step aside, stop, and consider the situation. Perhaps the people are hostile because today is Saturday, you think, or perhaps it is because the houses along the West Side of Schiel are in the shade at this time of day, and the atmosphere thus sees and seems a little more suspicious than is normally the case when the interviewer, who knocks on your door, can be contemplated in the full glare of the "sterilizing" rays of the sun. But you are inclined to believe the reason for the people's hostility is more basic. They are hostile because they are afraid of you; they are hostile because their privacy is being disturbed. They are hostile because they are afraid you are selling something or checking up on something for the "authorities"; and they are hostile because this same thing has happened so often before there on wide-open Schiel, and never before have they benefited from interviews, polls, solicitations. They have no reason to believe they will benefit in this case with you. And perhaps they are hostile because their mental and moral selves have built up a fine defensive attitude against any kind of intrusion into their homes or lives. For you see, just across the street is the almost 100 per cent Negro district, with its filth, its indecency, its backwardness. Through long years of fighting elements of the Negro group who seek to invade their Tract—fighting in both reality and in theory—the Schiel citizens have built up a wall between themselves and all "foreigners."

After such reflections, in short order, you find yourself around on Ratcliff, on the sunny side of the street, far away from the Negro district of Schiel.

At the first two houses there is no response to your knockings. On the third attempt you are successful. The lady invites you in, and somehow you get her talking about her family. It really isn't very adamant or hard—everyone likes to talk about himself and his family. But soon you find the maze of lines and boxes, circles, and triangles, etc. on your notebook becoming so entwined, confused, and untranslatable that you might as wee bit well leave. After asking about her husband's mother and father, just out of politeness, you hastily make your retreat, professing bounteous gratitude for the kindness and help (?) of your dear hostess.

Use more paper next time, you tell yourself; not that it does any good. For you get in just the same mess next time.

A sophisticated student, Yvette Monet, reflects upon the beginners' problems in developing the field worker's attitude toward strangers:

This feeling that sociologists have, that they own, so to speak, the whole field of observation, was certainly an experience. I think that I would have gained much more if I could have seen by myself what I could get out of the interviews. You see, after I have talked to people in a neighborhood, I feel I need not consider them as strangers. All these strangers are potential respondents, so why not consider them as respondents right now? This attitude is probably process in my own growth as a sociologist. It would be just a trick of the trade just to get rid of some fear. I think I would gladly interview again for precisely the knowledge that it gives me of all sorts of people in the community. But it takes an awful lot of time. . . .

When experienced field workers join in "shop talk," the question of just what does determine the status relationship between field worker and informant comes up quite often. From a tape-recorded sample of such talk, comes one man's comments on the importance of "audience" as relating to the information sought:

This is another problem that came up in the seminar [on Field Observation] the other day. It's the problem of the audience. What audience does this person have in mind when he's talking to you? What audience does he think you have in mind when you're listening to him? The informant always asks himself, in some way, the question, "What audience can my remarks eventually get back to?" For every type of data asked for, the informant raises this question—and reappraises the status relationship between him and the field worker. This is all part of defining who the observer really is in this situation. He is one thing in one situation because the respondent's remarks are apt to get back to one particular audience, and he is another thing in another situation because the remarks are apt to get back to another audience. The field worker is the same guy and he's talking to the same informant, but in different situations, since the situation changes as the topic of discussion changes. So, there is always this problem of the audience that different people have in the back of their mind at any given point in the interview. Like everything else we've been talking about, these things [e.g., audience changes] happen in every-day life. Keeping in mind this problem of audience, we might make remarks right here which are directed towards a specific audience—the guys in this discussion. We may make remarks which we think are directed towards posterity; we may think we are saying something brilliant which the tape recorder must take down for all men in all times to hear. Or we may drop a remark that will surely get back to a certain number of people that the others of us will see pretty soon. This problem of the audience is a helluva thing when you stop to think about it, because the same people are interacting all the time, but as the mood changes and as other things in the situation change, different audiences come to mind.

Finally, Harvey Hill, an advanced student, writes about an acute dilemma of status disparity:

. . . Another problem also arose in this research. That is, when the interviewer is not accepted for what he represents himself to be, then what? The question is most acute when he is taken to be something else—usually a spy or something equally undesirable. I think this is what happened to me with one informant who first informed me (ignoring my proffered handshake) that this was "a lot of bunk." He went on to discuss his prejudices (which were not the subject being investigated) with respect to Negroes, Jews, Democrats, and a variety of other topics including the lower classes. I think much of this was an attempt to establish whether or not I, as a member of the University, disagreed with him. When I responded in my best non-directive fashion he was considerably encouraged to talk—which he did for two hours. But it was a complete waste of time. After he warmed to me he merely expressed his prejudices more freely although toward the end I think he expressed them less violently. I was first intimidated, then amused, then bored, and finally irritated. Since I realized it was a waste of time and considering my own prejudices on the topics covered, I have since wondered if I shouldn't have told him to go to hell after the first thirty minutes and let it go at that. But supposing it had been very important to get information from this man, what could I have done?

Problems of Role Choice

It will be remembered that we began this chapter by pointing out that students usually have in mind some generalized field worker role, often idealized and loaded with idiosyncratic apperceptions. It is clear that the role choices they discuss, especially among themselves, are not explicitly the same as those in the range of theoretical social roles for field work (from "Complete Participant" to "Complete Observer") used in this book. If we call the latter "master roles," what students talk about are the "lesser roles" or specific role relationships with informants.[2]

In such terms, as well as much more generally in social life, it can be said that wherever there is a status problem, there is also a role problem, and wherever there is a role problem, there is also a status problem. This concomitance exists because statuses, as well as everything else of a social nature, are communicated through roles. This close relationship between status and role should be kept in mind in reading the following cases in which the field worker succeeds, or fails, in some interesting way, in handling his role. Some equally interesting role problems created for informants are also pointed out.

An advanced student, Edward Michaels, in part of an interview he granted, illustrates: (1) how the field worker's role changes as the study progresses, (2) how the field worker drops the role and becomes a person, thus enabling the informant to lose his bothersome role-consciousness and find a common ground of "colleagueship" with the field worker; and (3) how the redefined situation affects the success of the interview:

Getting into this business of taking on a role other than the one which you actually were playing, a superimposed one, as we became a little more experienced, and we did approach more and more toward the master observer role, not in the full sense, but in the sense of having gotten confidence in interviewing, in writing during the interview, and in following cues and themes and so on, that we could gradually try to meet the person more on his own level as an experienced or semi-experienced practitioner within his own field. So you began to play the role of the observer of community newspapers, rather than a student practicing observing community newspapers. Still, there were lapses in there where you'd run into a problem where you'd missed a cue, where you were afraid to bring it back up again—an important theme, and you couldn't find a spot to bring it back in. You were stuck; whereas a master observer would have been able to deal with it. Yet, on this master observer thing, it was pretty much of a case where I was playing my natural role. Now the big thing is this: once I had gotten beyond the initial stages of the interview and had been able to respond meaningfully to the respondent in terms of his field, namely, community newspapers, I could put the pencil in my mouth, or just hold it up in the air, just lean back—talk generally, giving the appearance of: we're no longer interviewing here; we're off the record here—man-to-man, and gradually I became accepted. Yet, when you started to write again, there was a slight retrenching on their part. Sometimes you'd get some of your best material after you packed up your tent, so to speak—you'd stick around for half hour between the office and the door and the guy would walk out to the door with you. There is always the problem of: How in the hell am I going to record this and keep the guy talking at the same time? I mean, what the guy is telling you is gold and you can't whip out a pencil and start jotting it down. So, as soon as you get out, you get out a pencil and start jotting it down. There is one of the problems of observing. It ties in with the business of how much confidence you have in your own retentiveness. You want to get all of the wheat and let some of the chaff go. There's a big fear, then, that you might get only half or quarter of the wheat and botch it up so badly that you wouldn't have anything. So, through gradually getting famil-

---

2. See Raymond L. Gold, "Roles in Sociological Field Observations," Social Forces, XXXVI (March, 1958), 217-23, especially p. 219.

iar, even while still being recognized as from the University, I was gradually recognized as a person, not an expert, but as a guy having a fair acquaintance with the field of community newspapers published in the city. I knew other publishers; I knew the problems from previous interviews—by this I mean that I had accumulated a body of experience from other interviews and I was able to develop sound sociological problems and phrase them to the respondents in terms of their own business problems. That's about the way it went. . . . Now, in some cases I've found that the guy is annoyed, and you weren't too sure what the guy was annoyed about. You didn't know whether he had a pressing appointment and that he wanted to get you the hell out of the way, or whether it was just the fact that you were sitting there in his office with a pencil in the objective sense of an interviewer, or what. Occasionally the guy had indicated some amount of irritability, and you'd scratch like hell to get all the data in, because you weren't coming back there and it would be difficult to establish the thing again. You'd go through the stuff and then put the pencil aside, and the goddam guy wouldn't let you go. (Interviewer: "After a while people begin to feel they have a claim on you.") Perhaps this is the answer: that maybe this thing of elevating them to a higher status, or at least certain aspects of their role. That is, they were a newspaper publisher, and by our structuring the thing in advance, by the phone, by our being from the University, by our sort of formalizing it—making important the purpose of the study: this subjected them to aspects of their role which were normal aspects of the role, namely, let us say for the moment, the guy who puts out 10,000 copies a week, I was perhaps elevating him in his conception to the height of 940,000 copies a day à la Colonel McCormick. This was perhaps quite a strain. However, while the formal structure was operative, there might be irritability because of the overtones of this type of thing. When we dropped the structure, namely, when we put the pencil away, or we smoked a cigarette, and sort of intimated one way or another, either verbally saying, "Well, I've got enough," or "Thanks," and you sort of lean back a little bit, and he may offer to let you stay a while. Well, then perhaps the pressure is off. And here comes in a variable. Maybe the guy felt a superficial fear. A number of these publishers were—I wouldn't say compensating for feelings of inferiority—but were in a way which is characteristic of the occupation, constantly trying to legitimate themselves, you see. So where you dropped the structure, with which they were perhaps unable to accord, then perhaps either from their own personality point of view, that is, from their own psychological personality or their occupational personality—then they would have to legitimate themselves, but on their own level, namely, that of convincing you, and gradually it slid over into a more of a rapport situation than had been present under the structured one. . . .

We have referred elsewhere to the difficulties encountered by those who seek to do field observation in the position of complete participant. In the following document an advanced student, William Schuler, describes his role dilemmas as they occurred while getting in, staying in, getting out, and reporting on a religious sect. His lesser role was that of a potential convert:

Roles were one of my greatest problems. Having very little knowledge of the inner workings of the group, it was difficult to decide in advance upon the use of a particular type of role. Furthermore, once having assumed a role, it was practically impossible to foresee all the implications and complications which would arise by virtue of that role. This meant that I was consistently facing little "crisis situations" which had to be met at the moment of their inception and to which I must make some immediate and satisfactory form of adjustment. These were not always problems of scientific inquiry as such, but concerned a great many personal difficulties as well.

First and probably foremost was the problem of deciding upon the degree of involvement with the group which was necessary and/or desirable to get the necessary data. Coupled with this was the necessity of viewing this role in terms of the repercussions or outcome which may follow as a result of this participation in the group.

Since my main problem was that of learning how the sect brought in new members, the role which befell me was that of going through this process myself. Partially by necessity, I assumed with this the "dumb role" of not knowing anything about the group. Along with this, and here again partially for my own protection and partially due to planned procedure, I decided upon a neutral position between being interested and favorable to the sect and its beliefs, and critical, hostile, and unwilling to become an active participant in the group. On the one hand this gave me entrance into the primary group, and on the other, it allowed me the privilege of withdrawing from participation in certain forms of activity if I so chose.

Aside from the fact that each of these roles would allow for the gathering of a particular type of information, it became increasingly difficult for me to maintain an equal balance between the two different positions. Either I had to become more hostile with a possible outcome of leaving the group too early, or else I had to become more closely integrated into the group with the consequences of becoming more involved.

This problem of involvement was particularly bothersome to me. It was not necessarily the fact of how much I considered it necessary to become involved to get the data I wanted, nor how far the sect would let me go; but most of all it was a personal problem of how far I would allow myself to go. There was, of course, my own conscience and my own moral evaluations. As to the former I was, after all, a spy, and it was difficult to decide just how much of a traitor I would allow myself to be. Then too, as was pointed out in one of the seminar discussions, there was the question of just how much I would humiliate myself or go against my own personal evaluations just for the sake of scientific inquiry. Finally, there was the problem of others. To what extent would I drag my family and friends into this involvement and also what could be the outcome of all this. The group while being legally cleared of subversive charges was still so looked upon by much of the rest of society. In any event they were not considered as a proper association for members of the larger society.

By way of illustration, it was necessary for me to attend rallies where I had to assume the role of the sect member in public places, some of them dangerously close to the University. What if others had seen me and upset the study? Even worse, what if they would misinterpret the fact of my association with the sect? By and large, one's own actions are interpreted in the light of his associations. This was no exception. It was upon more than one occasion that persons close to me advised that "enough was enough." It became increasingly difficult for my family to justify my association with the group and to convince others that I was not neglecting my own family, a criticism often directed against this particular sect. This was especially so when it finally became necessary for me to attend as many as six meetings a week and on some occasions to be with the group two and three full days in succession.

Along with this there is also the problem of the effect a particular role will have upon other persons. Role-taking does not proceed in a vacuum but extends to other areas of life as well, even when it is not so desired. By ways of illustration, my own role in the sect made it necessary that my wife also take some sort of role in relation to this group. In order to spare her of any participation in the group, it was decided that she was to assume a position of hostility to the group, and to my own participation in the group. The outcome of this role was to the effect that, to save my own position in the group, Mrs. S. had to be portrayed in certain uncomplimentary tones. Accepting this definition, the sect offered their understanding, advice, and

sympathy, with a view in mind of either alienating me from her or of winning her over as well. One without any stretch of the imagination can readily see the possible effects of dwelling, month after month, upon any real
or imagined basis for such thoughts. It can without too much difficulty
come to lose its scientific understanding.

Finally there came the problem of breaking off with the group. How
could this be done gracefully and without ill-will? After all, I was not operating on a personal relationship basis. I had received their confidences,
their friendships, and even gifts. Or for that matter, should one even attempt to take these factors into consideration but merely terminate the
study and let "the chips fall as they may?" It is sometimes difficult to separate the two roles of scientist and individual. The line of demarcation is
not always clear.

Reporting involves not only a decision as to what, "of this private information," should be made public but also what could be the outcome of
the reporting. The reporter must take steps to assure against any "com-
pensatory measures" which might be taken by the group under observation.
To a certain extent this can be done through anonymity, although it does
not always work out this way. It is difficult to disguise without also taking
away some of the value. The problem of deciding what should be left out
and in what way the reported material should be handled is especially bothersome to me.

Additional insights into the problems of the complete participant are
provided by Yvette Monet, in a long interview from which passages are reproduced to illustrate: (1) dropping the role to establish colleagueship on
the "level of human beings"; (2) playing an assumed role; and (3) dealing
with one's problems as a potential convert. Unlike some students, Miss
Monet was able to find a role which protected her from conversation. She
also points out her desire, after completing a period of participant observation, to reveal to a fellow employee just who she really is. The reader
may draw his own conclusions about the implications of this hazard:

You can go through a long participant-observation where you see the
person day by day and notice only a particular aspect. If you had thought
more in terms of the proper interview and questionnaire, you would have
covered different fields. And that's why I tried to point out earlier that my
tendency is to restrict myself to participant-observation. I know that's a
perpetual temptation for many starters—laziness. I don't want to take the
trouble of building a questionnaire. And I think that it is also my choice by
nature. I prefer a natural relationship to these improvised ones. . . . Usually, I think that [my success in interviewing] might be quite well a question of having this [French] accent and everything [that is, petite appear-
ance]. I think that people tend to be protective with regard to me and to
treat me rather kindly and gently. (Interviewer: "Which gives them a feeling of superiority.") That's right. I was thinking of that when a professor
asked me what was my experience about studying a foreign country—doing
research in a foreign country. The more I think about it, the more I think
it is a big advantage. But, from the point of view of my role, it's really
easy. Even this problem that we raised the other day about our contacts
with the workers in the factory—I think that I don't have that, because I
know that I don't speak at all the same English as they do. But I explained
to them that I am now doing housekeeping for a schoolteacher and that it is
the teacher who taught me English, and she taught me her English. And it
is true I could ask all these questions in quite a natural way. I can be naïve
in quite a natural fashion. I think it would be extremely tiring to play the
role of the naïve person, because we are rather used to playing the sophis-

ticated than the naïve person, but even when it is natural for me to be naïve, I am still not as naïve as I could and probably should be, even in the
factory situation. . . . I was in a storehouse for a month before working as
a welder, and when I went back to pick up my final check I told the girls
that I was a student. But I promised myself that I would never do that
again. See, I thought I would do that out of loyalty and out of friendship,
too, so not to have concealed anything important from them. But I discovered it was extremely difficult to explain to them what social sciences
meant and what is meant for me to go and live with them in order to understand them really. This understanding of research as a really humane thing
is something which is particular to us, I think, and I don't think it is wise
to explain your interests along those lines to your fellow-workers—so I
won't do it again. I think that it is better to let them take you as just any
human being. I had to go through this experience of knowing that this research is meaningless to them in order to get rid of that idea of being an
intellectual sharing the life of these people. Once only was I tempted to explain myself to someone at the factory where I worked as a welder. There
was there a little girl who was working in order to work her way through
college. And one day she told me that she was majoring in sociology. And
another thing she told me, "But you live on campus of the University of
Chicago." I said, "Yes, it's because my schoolteacher is still taking
courses there during the summer." And she thought that as soon as I make
some money, I should take some courses there and I said, "What good
would it do me, really?" And she was so scandalized that this was my approach to the University of Chicago. So I thought, but really, that's too bad
to betray this young member of the brotherhood of sociologists. . . . [After
explaining how she accounted for her religious past to the members of a
Negro bible ecstatic church she was studying, she went on to remark] That
explains my religious past, but not my religious present, and why don't I
get converted to their religion while I feel so sympathetic to them and en-
joy their sermons and everything so much? I have never been faced with
the direct question, but I know that it's in most of my friends' minds. It's
a real problem, but I think that I am not in the same situation that an American Catholic would be in, since they are not too sensitive to the singing
and things that take place at the church. I am a Mediterranean Catholic,
and for me all these questions of enthusiasm and feeling expressed in
shouting and singing speaks to me, certainly, so I have not this sort of de-
fense of just showing that I am different, because it is not true—I am not
different. Also, the fact that I am a white woman sort of transforms me
into a sort of taboo being, so I think that I am left much more freedom to
join or not to join than I would be in a white church. One of the best ways
to get the kind of rapport with them that I want is just to play my role as a
woman. When I am invited to a family, I just help with the cooking and the
dishes as I would in any other family situation. That is very good, because
it cuts to a great extent the strangeness of my situation.

The problem of choice of role so vividly presented by Miss Monet is
also frankly discussed in the field diary of Sonya Heifitz, who illustrates
how the student discovered that, instead of concealing her ethnic identity,
she could reveal it to her advantage. Thus, her "real" identity is allowed
to become part of her role in the field:

I thought there would be quite a wide variety of statuses represented
here, from the veddy elite near the Lake, to the plain middle class along
the east-west street car line. I thought, too, that there would be some
strong infiltration of Jews, coming eastward, perhaps. I had noticed Jews
along the Boulevard; these looked well-to-do. Anyway, I expected not much
homogeneity throughout the whole area, and this I liked. (More of a challenge, again.)

Maybe I'd better set down something about myself, too—take stock of personal views in order to minimize the degree to which they might color my observations. I'm 21; I'm Jewish. I guess I'm a liberal politically—shan't go into that now. I'm not repulsive-looking; but I seem to get recognized as Jewish most of the time I'm looking for a job. That was one of the reasons I didn't choose a race problem area—I'd identify myself with it too much. I've had too much Jewish background, too, to be sufficiently "detached" in a very Jewish neighborhood. I have too many opinions on those problems. And, for the sake of my soul, I'd better confess that I do not expect to admit that I am Jewish—since I can "pass"—if the question comes up during this study—that is, if the particular situation can be better handled by my not admitting it. I am not ashamed, or a masquerader by convictions. That pretense would be for scientific purposes only. Might even have occasion to do it. . . . Do I sound defensive?

[Later on in the diary, a revelation in choice of role occurs.]

There wasn't much time for interviewing or establishing "rapport" but she did say a few things that are significant—of what, I'm not sure yet. These came up during questions about nationality and religion—of the doctor she goes to and of herself. The doctor is Jewish; she is, too. She is native-born, but her parents are from Germany, her husband's parents from Russia. She said that she had been warned time and again by her husband to let no strangers into the house—and she only opened the door to me because she thought I was her niece at first, and then she let me in because I looked Jewish. She asked me if I were, and I told her and she was relieved. "Everyone to their own kind," she said. I hadn't expected my being Jewish to be an advantage there. . . .

Three other examples of choice of role are taken from student field reports which illustrate: (1) unintentional misrepresentation, not maintained, (2) intentional partial misrepresentation, resulting in failure, and (3) intentional misrepresentation, resulting in the field worker's feeling compelled to pile on even further misrepresentation.

Beginning student Dale Addison shows how he found himself and his companion being taken for persons acting in a role which was known and accepted by the people he was observing:

On Wednesday, bewitching and beautiful, we returned to the tract between five and eight o'clock to notice what we could of community social life after working hours. On all these occasions we asked people we encountered questions about the area, and learned a great deal, though we had no systematic program or selection of problems to work on.

The first one we questioned was a young man on ＿＿ Street. He was distant as most city people usually are when we asked him where ＿＿ Avenue was. When we told him we were trying to "bound the ＿＿ the Census tract" he became quite effusive. He evidently mistook us for Census takers. Here was an observation, a social fact that we immediately discovered. If he represented a typical attitude, most people would be co-operative about the Census. We did not intend, however, to palm ourselves off as Census takers.

George Wood writes in his field diary:

I walked boldly into the office of the principal and was met head-on by a big Irishman who identified himself as Mr. Sullivan, the principal. I produced for his consideration the letter of introduction from Dr. ＿＿ of the University, and he began to give me the sad story about how disrupted his school was at the present time because of the redecorating but was very considerate and listened to me while I told him that I merely wanted to observe a classroom in the most inconspicuous manner possible and would be of no trouble to either the teacher or the pupils. His first, last, and only reaction, however, was one of withdrawal. I had just about convinced him that the painting would make no difference to me and an abnormal situation would be just as valid an observation as a normal one when he suddenly hit upon the solution to all his troubles with me. The letter of introduction was not approved by the assistant superintendent of schools in charge of elementary schools. After that I was a dead duck as far as trying to gain admittance to the classrooms went. He was, as always, courteous, but stiff.

I gave up the idea of trying to persuade him to my point of view and tried to get a little information about the tract from him. The school has a large number of Negro and Mexican pupils, as we already knew. Mr. Sullivan did not have endless sources of information, to say the least, so I did not press him for exact information. I did not admit having more than a passing sociological interest in the area because of his first question of me. When I first introduced myself to him he asked if I had been there once before looking for info. I had not, but my partner had gone to the lunchroom and had got some significant info. from the women there. Evidently the principal had found out about it and was incensed because he had not been consulted. I wonder how much more or less good it would have been for me if I had been more truthful than I was and at least to have admitted being a partner on the team working on the area. I really don't know what his attitude would have been—better or worse.

Student Clark Brewster tells how he created a role problem by misrepresenting himself to a church group and how, feeling that he owed it to them to repay them for their kindness, he was forced to befriend them and offer advice, not as a person in a congenial role, but as one in an assumed role:

The Meeting Place.—The meeting place (of the young people's group of the old Lutheran Church) was immense and very plainly furnished. There were a number of lumpy, seemingly unused cabinets or chests around the walls. Decidedly, at one end of the room were about sixteen chairs arranged in front of a table which had three chairs around it. On the East side of the room one of the windows was open from the top, and the room waxed coolness. I went over and shut the window; the bareness of the place was striking. The plain cream-colored walls, from which was reflected the frosty light from two uncovered bulbs hanging from the ceiling, seemed sterilized in their simplicity, and somehow depressing. The large, high windows, the top halves of which pointed roundly toward heaven in their Gothic ugliness, appeared as huge voids, as openings from this sterilized, repressive plainness to the filth, the licentiousness, and the excitement of the outside, old world.

Under such conditions of environment, it seemed that the meeting could not avoid itself, being plain, drab, uninteresting. It might even be a little "inhuman," I thought to myself, if it were not for the fact that there were a number of very live young girls standing near the door, comparing ideas on who the man in the room was.

I meet the President.—I walked over to where the girls were and asked if the President of the League had shown up yet. It was 7:30 and time for the meeting to get under way. Through the doorway, in the blackness of the hallway outside, came a feminine voice, "Yes, here I am."

She walked out of the shadows and stood in front of me for a second or two before I recovered from the shock of seeing such a lively, pretty young woman in such surroundings. She had a ready smile and an open manner and I soon felt very much at ease standing there talking to her. Or maybe I wasn't exactly at ease, for instead of telling her I was working on a Sociology research problem, I made up a story about being sent out by the Political Science Department to observe group meetings from the standpoint of the political experience they gave their members. Getting in deeper and deeper, I told her the Department had a pet theory that the American youth is not as politically conscious and thus as politically astute as is the youth of such European countries as Germany, Britain, or the Netherlands, but that their counterparts among us are notably the offspring of patriotic souls, I being one of the latter. We were sure that through our observations they in the Department would be proved wrong, and I assured her that if I had a chance to sit through her meeting it would be a valuable aid to me. I don't know why I lied about my identity and my mission except that she was the kind of a girl one doesn't like to hurt, and I had noticed in talking with other people in the area that they instinctively retreated a few steps when one mentioned he was on a survey project of a sociological nature. People seemed to react almost violently whenever the word "social" or "sociology" was mentioned with emotional tendencies varying from one of hurt to one of anger.

In closing.—Before adjourning there was some discussion as to where the next social activity of the club was to be held and what was going to be done. A number of suggestions were made, among them a dance in the Church basement, a wiener roast, a hike, an outing to a Sox baseball game, and an excursion to a museum or bird sanctuary or zoo. The latter was immediately voted down because most of the members had visited all of these institutions in the city. The dance was outvoted by the younger element. Only the boys were in favor of the ball game. So everyone compromised on the hike and wiener roast, to be held the following Sunday near the Lake. Although the older girls did not seem too enthusiastic about the project, they acquiesced. A number of people were assigned different items of food to bring. This is how the observer got saddled with an invitation which couldn't be dodged because it included an order to bring a jar of mustard along.

Before the final prayer and closing, John asked me if I wanted to say a few words, and I said I did. I thanked them for putting up with me and told them what I had come out for and what I had found from sitting in on their meeting. I assured them that American youngsters were just as politically conscious and perhaps more so than the Europeans. I could see they hardly knew what I was talking about and this reminded me of my earlier resolution to tell them a story that they could see and feel and smell, a story that they could climb into themselves and experience, so that they would know where the money they were donating to foreign missionaries went and what it was used for. I told them about a story of Amazon missionaries and evidently they were able to see and to smell and to feel it, a little anyway, for their faces made me feel that I had given them something in return for the experience in living they had given me.

When the field worker himself is inflexible and fails to use the role called for by the situation, he has a problem of role choice which is somewhat different from those previously discussed. In some "shop talk" among four experienced field workers, two of them, John Cook and Richard Herrmann, discussed this problem:

John: I think that most of our speculation in looking at the interviews has been in the way of: What does the formal training do to an interviewer, and what happens with that formal training when he's actually conducting an interview?
Richard: What do you include in "formal training"?
John: Well, I don't know whether we should include only course work, or the literature that he has read—theory, etc.,—and has been influenced

by, but it's safe to say that there's a great and not so good influence vis-à-vis the effectiveness of the interviewer. I mean, he burdens himself by assuming a role from a theory that does not take into account this interplay between people, and he tends to assume the role whereby he responds to every situation in the same way according to a prior concept.

Richard: Would this kind of fellow you're talking about be the person who really conceives of himself as a psychiatrist and he'd be much happier if he were in a clinic, wearing a white coat, with a lot of pens across his chest, and some prescription blanks sticking out of his pocket? And had that kind of relationship with his informants?

John: Yes, that's right. This is where the respondent says, "I shot my mother," and he says, "Oh, you shot your mother?" Or, the respondent says, "I went to get a Coca Cola," and he says, "Oh, so you went to get a Coca Cola?" This reliance on this role that the situation does not call for —it seems to impede the free flow of evidence or information.

The problem of learning to play the field worker role to suit the situation is discussed by student Edward Michaels and an interviewer whose longer experience led him to give some advice:

Michaels: Let me get at something else that was stressed in this course. The instructor made the remark that anthropologists are individuals who have forsaken one allegiance for another one. If you can view it from a very objective standpoint, this seems to imply a certain degree of failing in sociologists. I mean, namely, that we are in this thing for personal satisfactions in terms of, say, a body of doctrine that we can adhere to because it gives us a security as a type of sanity in the midst of a troubled world, and so on, which can operate to the detriment of forming fairly good interpersonal relationships with others. And that has implications for interviewing and observing. To what extent in a course on field work training can you create outgoing, friendly, sociable people able to form quick social relationships? To what extent can people in such a course learn to be introspective and conscious of self in the social situation of the field? Now let's look at it this way: The more experience we have in taking the role, the more we are able to play the role in actuality. This might imply that whatever field of research you are going to do, you've got to know something about it—you can't break into it cold. For someone like you, you've got to be a painter to study painters. That is, you begin to serve somewhat of an apprenticeship in the area before you start doing your interviewing and observing in the scientific sense: that you are going to record and analyze what you put down. But you live within the area for a little while, even if only on a part-time basis, to familiarize yourself with the motions of the role, some of the nuances of the role. You can still be an apprentice when you are doing your observing, as far as the people's responses to you are concerned, but at least you begin to get into the camaraderie like I said before: If the guy begins to swear, you go along with him. But I must have some prior experience in determining how I would play this role of swearing.

Interviewer (in the role of interviewer-colleague): Of course, if you joined in the swearing, and it wasn't congenial to you as a person, the guy might think you are talking down to him. . . . The only solution, as I see it, is to really be a good social scientist. Then you might make a study of some group, and, even though you have never had any experience with that group, you can nevertheless determine how to go about picking up the requisite experience. The next best thing you can do is immediately size up the people and think on your feet, because then you really have to bring all your social science talents to bear, since then you have to compare them with all kinds of possible people you have read about or personally experienced, and do the right thing as a social scientist. You always come into situations which are problematical, and which you have to solve on the spot. I agree, that, ideally, you should have all these preparations—you know, plan out every bombardment before you attack. But failing that, the only thing is to be a good social scientist. And, of course, I here reveal a personal bias, since I think of a good social scientist as a good field worker.

Every observer whose presence and identity are known to those he observes, is to some degree a participant, since there is always some kind of interaction between him and the others. To what extent can the field worker interact with the observed in his occupational role (as field worker), and to what extent can he interact with them in a more informal, personalized way? And how does each kind of interaction affect the kind of information the field worker gets? These questions are explored by Edward Michaels and the same interviewer:

Michaels: Now, on the problem of identifying with the people you study —I'm not talking about identifying in the sense of divided loyalty, loyalty to colleagues and to informants. What I mean is partially identifying to be able to go into the group. That's the thing. If you're somewhat conscious of yourself as a sociologist, as distinct from the demands of your relationships with the group you are studying, where you have a reaction against some form of rejection or another—if this is true, or if this then has a fair amount of validity with reference to other sociologists, as I can see the thing for myself, then you do have difficulties. These are basic psychological difficulties. Here, again, we get to this business of: Can you establish interpersonal relationships which are congenial, that is, where part of you can act as an observer and part of you can sit down and shoot the bull about women, or about sports, or about what-have-you as a person.

Interviewer: Well, I don't know why you can't do that. Thinking about myself, I can usually do it without any trouble. And then when it's over and done with and I go home and hit the sack, I start to count the cracks in the ceiling and think the stuff over in the manner of the social scientist. I then look at myself differently than I did in the course of this prior interaction, you see.

Michaels: Well, what I had in mind is doing your sociological work while you're in the group, or with the persons while you're there.

Interviewer: I don't think you ever really do this even as a participant-observer. I don't think you ever really do this while you are there. I don't think you can function both as a sociologist and as someone completely apart from a sociologist. I think the people you observe will begin to think you are strange after a while. They will begin to wonder about you.

Ordinarily, the field worker interviews one person at a time and learns to play his role accordingly, and he acquires considerable skill in helping the informant play his role in such situations. There are occasions, however, when the field worker is faced with more than one informant, in which case his role and the roles of his informants are somewhat different than in the one-to-one situation. An experienced field observer, Robert Joyce, recalls an incident in which the intrusion of a second informant caused confusion, as neither he nor they recognized the answer to the role problem. Later he realized that, had he defined the situation as one of a group interview, instead of an individual interview, he would have been able to redefine his role and the role of the informants in a mutually satisfactory manner:

Joyce: We were instructed never to interview when there was more than one person in the room, and we tried to follow those instructions. Now once in a while it would happen that the husband or the wife or the grandfather just wouldn't leave the room, so he had to sit there. Well, under this mental set of having just one person in the room, you tended to regard this person as an outsider, and when he did cut in from time to time, it was kind of embarrassing—you didn't know how to handle it. Very often the outsider really would hurt the interview by disputing something the informant had said, and you would still direct your questions at one person and very unrealistically not face the fact that you had a group here. Since then, I've thought it would be a darn good idea if you could direct your questions to both of them as you see fit. By getting them to relate to one another, you might get some consensus out of it, rather than having one person drying the other one up and you not knowing what to do about it.

Interviewer: . . . It would be very valuable to know the relationship between the first and second person. If you are interviewing a guy and a second person walks in the room, if you understood their relationship pretty well, that is, if you knew something about the people in this kind of town, in this kind of family, and so on, you might be able quickly to decide whether it would be helpful or harmful to have this second person here. Take the case of the man and wife, and the second person walks in the room, where there is a relationship between them such that the initial informant can't afford to allow himself to appear inadequate with respect to the situation about which he is being questioned—he has got to be in complete control of things at all times. Well, here might be a case where, if he had previously talked rather freely, but clammed up right away when the second person walked in the room, or he started to give you different kinds of answers—well, here would be a case of the guy using role to protect self. Or, it might be just the opposite thing of where before he was using role to protect self, you could really get him going when the other person entered the room.

Some interesting class, sex, and age problems are disclosed in an interview with Betty Bauer, an advanced student, and the excerpt also serves to introduce some role problems confronting informants:

It is easier to gain entrance into a lower-class home than a middle-class one, but it is more difficult to communicate with the lower-class guys, since they have more difficulty verbalizing their emotions. I guess that they don't have the language to express their deep feelings. They are often embarrassed because they aren't able to communicate their profound feelings. On the other hand, even though it is harder to get in to see middle-class people, those seen are better able to verbalize their emotions, to communicate their feelings to me. Usually, I find it easier to interview women, perhaps because they find it easier to express their feelings, fears, and so on to a woman. Women may find it not so hard to talk to either sex, since doctors and ministers and others who are traditionally receivers of confidences are male. I have tried to interview children as young as age seven, and, by making mistakes, I feel it quite possible to get them to reveal their feelings about disasters. One mistake I made was to get out my pencil and pad after getting a kid in the right stage of rapport by playing with her. She immediately clammed up, because I suddenly took a teacher role when I produced the pencil and pad. I think it is impossible for a girl to interview an adolescent boy, especially if he has done something rather heroic in a disaster. When I tried to interview one, he became so flustered and embarrassed that it was useless for me to go on. To him I was one of the girls at school, and he blushed for all he was worth.

Thomas Newman, an advanced student, records some role problems which both he and his informants have experienced. Noteworthy in these problems is the theme of initial sparring between field worker and inform- ant to define mutually agreeable roles:

In my present research, I'm interviewing businessmen about their at- titudes toward and participation in a gray market.
In order to get the information, I am often faced with mutually contra- dictory roles. For example, sometimes, to make an interview appointment I must assure the businessmen of the importance of my study and there- fore of their co-operation; yet I must also assure them of the harmless- ness of their co-operation and of my innocuousness. This problem is rela- tively easily met; one role or the other may be emphasized as soon as the direction of the respondents' need for reassurance is decided. The prom- ise of anonymity is a way of resolving this conflict.
Other problems of mutually conflicting roles are less easily resolved. The subject matter of my study includes strongly held value positions. I want to indicate to the businessmen that I am sympathetic with them. But if too much sympathy is shown, questions may be answered flippantly. Much of their conversation consists of slogans; therefore, I must raise dif- ficulties to learn to what extent the implications of the slogans are ac- cepted. Sometimes this raises a barrier as soon as they feel I don't "under- stand" them.
Usually they recognize that I'm merely trying to learn how they feel about various issues. This is partly done by raising objections from one, and then another, value position so that it is clear that I'm playing a dev- il's advocate role when I raise objections.
The success of playing a given role is to some extent dependent on whether it is within the repertoire of the respondent as well as within the interviewer's repertoire. That is, the respondent must be able to recog- nize the role which you may think is the right one for the situation.

Some insight into the role problems of informants who have consider- able self-involvement in the role behavior about which they are questioned is given by Charles James in a discussion of "disaster interviewing":

Interviewer: While talking about institutional roles, I think of the case where, after a couple of weeks, the people aren't too receptive toward you field workers. How about the case of guys who had good, institutional roles? I mean like a priest or a physician. How is it to interview these guys within the first two-week period after the disaster? Are they any bet- ter organized personally than others who don't have such a good role?
James: I would say yes—in a number of ways. In the first place, even though in the crisis period they may have completely lost their self-con- cept and also had a terrific conflict as to which role they should act in— whether they were going to act as a doctor or a husband. But after the ini- tial shock is over, as soon as this realization begins to come back to them, they begin structuring the situation very rapidly in terms of this role and thinking up rationalizations for why they behaved the way they did, and painting a nice picture of how they actually acted in the proper role in the right way. As a result, we noticed very definitely that this kind of person is very difficult to interview to find out what they actually did in the situa- tion—very difficult. In fact, we have practically given up interviewing these people if they know you come to them knowing that they are the chief of po- lice, or they are the Episcopal minister, or they are this or that. If they know that you know that, you might as well forget trying to get the kind of

data from them that you've gotten from everybody else, and use them for another type of data. . . .

From an interview with Betty Bauer comes an example of consciously playing a role to create and sustain a mood of recollection in the informant. This role-playing is an attempt by the field worker to divorce sentiment from intellect in herself, while helping the informant to play the desired role:

> . . . Also, in the field, you run into all kinds of emotional interview situations which make interviewing a difficult job. Most difficult to handle, from the standpoint of getting a good interview, is the emotional atmosphere which accompanies the emotional demands made by the respondent. Under these conditions, it is hard to probe, because you become emotional too, and you lose your sharpness—you lose control of the interview situation. It took me quite some time before I learned to remain aloof, while overtly appearing to be sympathetically as emotional as the respondent. By this I mean that I consciously play the role of someone taking the respondent's role for all she's worth, but I am actually playing this role, not taking it. You get people who are in emotional trauma, who are all keyed up and anxious to pour out to you their deep feelings, if only you are a sympathetic and understanding listener. The toughest interview I had was with a woman who talked for four hours and frequently said, "You can't possibly understand," yet demanding that I do understand in spite of its being impossible to do so. There is considerable non-symbolic interaction in the course of these interviews, and it is important to recognize and control it. There was one woman who, when describing humans in a burning plane, many of whom she knew, began to contort her face, and her facial muscles started to twitch. Whether I wanted to or not, I started to go along with her, so strenuously was I taking her role. What happened? Well, I shook my head and then she did too, and we snapped out of it enough to go on with the interview. In non-symbolic interaction, I try to look as emotional as the respondent. Needless to say, such acting is tiring, even though it is consciously done, and I keep it up until I'm exhausted. If the respondent is reluctant to talk, you can sometimes create the proper mood for verbalization of feelings by acting emotional—by taking the role you want the respondent to take—taking it on the non-symbolic level.

Handling Emotional Involvement

Although problems of emotional involvement have appeared in earlier illustrations such as the foregoing, we turn now to a few illustrations to dramatize the need to recognize explicitly that the field worker, in the performance of his role, is always required to be in some degree a sensitive, perceptive person. As such, he is always aware of his self-feelings and of his beliefs, but he has learned either to subordinate them to the demands of his role or to get out of situations where he doubts that his personal make-up is suitable.

A field report by beginning students George Wood and Warren Howard indicates that one of them became so emotionally involved that he failed to obtain further information from the informant. This he blames, however, on his consideration for the interviewee:

A large Negro woman answered my knock and invited me inside rather quickly. (It was cold outside and she didn't want to stand in the doorway.) I explained my connection with the University and my interest in any kind of troubles she might have with discrimination or related topics. The woman was less talkative than any of the other colored people I had spoken with. I do not know the reason for this. Her house was in rather poor condition but no worse than the other houses I have visited. I used the same general technique. Because frequent "proddings" were necessary to keep her talking, I believe the most satisfactory method of recording the interview is to summarize the conversation.

I learned that there were two children both of whom attended ___ Elementary School and stayed for lunch. She thought they could get better lunch there and for less money than she could fix for them at home. They like the school and she knows of no discrimination against them at the school. The children usually play out in the street and in the alley but sometimes during the summer have gone over to ___ Park. They never go in swimming. When asked why she replied, "Oh, they don't like that little pool. When they want to swim they go over to the lake where there is lots of room." I refrained from asking about specific discrimination at the pool because she seemed to be becoming disconcerted possibly over the topic of conversation.

The problem of the field worker whose feeling for the informant overrides his role considerations is presented by Charles James, who discusses his fellow field workers in a disaster study (referring to them as "they"):

Mainly, the problem which they brought to you was not their main one. They did not come to you with a statement that their morale was getting low, or they were getting tired, or getting uneasy, or restless and worried about this and that; or that they had listened to so many sad stories it was getting them down—never did they say that. They would come back with very specific technical problems. But none of these technical problems, I know, is their real problem. Their real problem is that they are afraid to go back and talk to this guy again. They don't want to talk to him again. "We've interfered with his life enough already," they feel. Then from there you get into other things, like why this woman didn't want to pretest, or why you don't want to go back to get the interview in this particular case, where you begin to identify with the respondent, who is exceedingly busy getting in his crop—about all he has left after the disaster. . . .

Edward Michaels summarizes the role and self problem in situations of emotional involvement as follows:

When the informant said something which was personally repugnant to me, it tended to minimize the personal element. You'd go along with it and report it objectively. Sometimes, after the conversation, if the guy happened to be, say, a fairly rabid Negro-hater, I might or might not, as I felt the situation indicated, get a few licks in, but I would still report exactly what the informant said. And there the more personal feelings would come out, but by that time the interview was done with and I didn't particularly care whether the guy was sore at me or not, and maybe I'd be successful in "educating" the guy. But as long as it wasn't a personal insult, the guy could tell me practically anything. I'd be willing to accept it, because this became an objective datum. Sometimes I felt like slapping the guy in the mouth when he said something crude, but there really weren't any personal insults. The only offense I might have taken was the case where the guy was so bigoted and egotistical in his position that you began to get sore about it. That, in a sense, was the point where you became conscious, not of self, but more conscious of role. (Interviewer: "Using role to protect self.") Yah, and you'd have to. Otherwise, you'd just blow up the interview. ... In terms of self, as I saw it, you'd go in there and you'd be conscious of yourself as looking for certain data, that is, a recognition that you are approaching a certain individual in a certain structured social situation. You weren't approaching him in a buddy-buddy way, but in a rather structured way, not overly structured, but formal in the sense that some of the business relations are formal, whether it's contractual or otherwise. Recognizing the importance of inhibiting certain spontaneous reactions of self, because of the necessity of having success in the interview, there was a lot of introspection—introspection in the sense of: Watch it now; don't respond because this will foul up something else. In a sense, you are using role to protect self, that is, you are able to minimize the injury or insult, as the case may be. But, at the same time, you are using the role as a device, that is, assigning to the role a greater importance than the expression of self-feeling. In that sense, you protect the role by using the role to inhibit self. I can't see too much of the mechanism, but introspection is very definitely involved. There is a definite consciousness of one's self in that role. . . .

Ethical Problems of Reporting

Many of the field worker's ethical problems, such as those relating to his "right to inquire" or even his "right to be there," have been illustrated in other contexts in this chapter. An important group of ethical problems as yet not considered from the student point of view has to do with the field worker's task of turning information in society into data about society. This problem area exists because of the claim on one another felt by the field worker and the informant as a result of having entered into a relationship in which confidences are shared. Moreover, the field worker has an obligation to his colleagues, who may wish to investigate the same or similar group or situation at some later time, to leave his informants with an attitude that is favorable to subsequent social science field work. Thus, this centers around the ethics of reporting.

A beginning field worker, Joan Smythe, reports how she handled a problem of an ethical nature. The interview was mainly centered on the informant's views concerning the local school, and about her plans for her children's future education. The informant had talked quite freely, when suddenly her small son entered the conversation. Then the field worker was faced with the problem:

. . . At this point Tommy thrust his face up into mine and said abruptly, "Who are you?" I told him my name, and he said, "What're you writing there?" (indicating my notebook in which I was jotting down his mother's remarks). I explained that I was writing down what his mother said. His mother looked a little alarmed and wanted to know what I was going to do with the information. I explained that it would be handled confidentially for class purposes and she said, "My name isn't going to be on it, is it? Some of the things I've said. . . . I wouldn't want the colored to. . . ." I reassured her that it was relatively confidential and wouldn't trickle back to anyone in the neighborhood.

I thanked her for her helpfulness and took my departure.

How can certain data be reported without revealing the identity of the informants? In a seminar report, Yvette Monet raises the question of concealing the identity of an informant which, if revealed, might cause him to suffer grievous injury to his career:

> The second (course on professions) was at the ___ Clinic of ___ University. I was a client there for several months and decided that the only way to bear it all was to study what was going on. This time I didn't even leave my chair to do my research. I just listened to my student, observed him and his colleagues, asked questions just enough to encourage explanations and confidences. I compared the student's view about the school to the Official Announcements. I analyzed the crisis situation in terms of self-conceptions and roles; my only tool was sympathetic introspection. Only when my paper was written did I see any use for any questionnaire at all: it would have been only to verify some of my hunches and interpretations. In other terms, I accentuated my orientation towards strict participant observation, and "social psychological" analysis.
>
> By the way, this paper revealed to me one of the big problems of the sociologist: I wrote there everything I had seen, heard, understood. I hardly disguised any personality. I suddenly realized that if the school would put its hands on the paper, the student who had given me all my insight would have a very bad time. This problem of what is to be said, and how it is to be said, still puzzles me a great deal.

In another seminar report, Edith Abrams addresses herself to the problem of "putting the finger on" certain informants should certain data be reported:

> The hospitals studied have certain identifying features which were relevant to my selection of them and therefore must be mentioned in some way in the analysis. Those who know where the study was done might well be able to identify the hospitals. There is only one Director of Nursing Service, e.g., in each hospital. How will I be able to tell what the staff nurses think of their Director if individuals can be so easily identified? I imagine persons doing community studies have much the same problem where there are "one-of-a-kind" institutions and individuals.

From his research experiences in industry, another advanced field worker, Harvey Hill, discusses the problem of how much he can tell management to help them with their problems without damaging the informants' (workers') relationship with management. Should the field worker disguise, stretch the truth, lie, or what, when reporting to an "informed-about" group such as management, or even when reporting to a less involved audience such as his colleagues?

> One [problem] was how to keep from putting the finger on any particular informant. Some of the management members who worked with us on the scheduling of the interviewing frequently asked what this person or that person had to say to us. Needless to say, the predictions made by management people as to what was said in the interviews were usually wrong. The people they called "gripers" were usually not so critical as management people expected. Others were more critical. In any case, several times we were pressed to talk about what had been said in the interviews. This we were pledged not to do— and management knew that this was a condition under which the interviewing was done. I resolved the problem by evading

it really, since my solution was to reply to such queries without revealing anything. Nobody was fooled. The point is that in a less favorable situation meeting such management pressures would have to be done in a more constructive manner. I say constructive because management people do not realize that confidence is confidence in an interview and not confidence from everyone except management people known to the interviewer. An interviewer well acquainted with some management persons in a factory where research is being done is very susceptible to being approached for information about this or that situation or individual's feelings. I think a great deal of damage can be done by the interviewer who succumbs uncritically to such pressure, understandable though it may be. On the other hand, complete resistance on the part of the interviewer to such pressure is liable to result in lack of co-operation from management or in terminating the research. The problem is how much can be safely generalized and then transmitted to management—rather than how much of what one informant says can be repeated to management. Pressure for information should be responded to in this fashion. The interviewer never knows what interpretation management will put on anything he quotes from an informant who has been interviewed. The problem becomes one of social skills, one of dealing with people who are trying to get something you don't want to give them. The researcher must convince management that management is being given a complete account of important information although in a generalized way. Information which makes a marked man of someone in a factory should not be reported on—at least by researchers from a university. Yet, this is withholding information from management which is probably of value to them—and if a condition of research is the supplying of valuable information this becomes an ethical problem also. I think that if, in a situation where the researcher cannot trust management to act upon information in what he considers the best way, it should be withheld. It is a decision which is sometimes difficult to make.

I attempt no synthesis of these wide-ranging experiences reported by students except to call attention, in chapter vi, to the training possibilities offered by recognition of the interconnectedness of the "every day" self and role problems that enter into the life careers of all students before (and after) they become social scientists or anything else, and the analogous self and role problems brought to heightened awareness by making them explicit when it is a question of acting responsibly in any of the field work positions outlined in this book.

VI

SOCIAL SCIENCE, TRAINING FOR FIELD WORK,
AND LIVING IN SOCIETY

In many fields of human endeavor it is commonplace for techniques to become crutches for carrying on routine procedures, yet it is equally apparent that the creative worker, especially in the arts, commands mastery of a technical repertoire. Moreover, his creative results are recognized and admired far more widely than are the means employed, although detailed examination of the latter may give employment to some critics and historians. In the sciences, also, techniques can become masters or be retained as comparatively unobtrusive servants. In the social sciences dependent upon field work, however, either extreme seems undesirable, for we need more complete and precise specification of each situation of observation and of the detailed course of inquiry within it, both for building knowledge from exact comparisons and for conducting replications. In such specifications, techniques are important but are by no means the whole story. If they were, training for social science field work might be merely a matter of drill in a few fundamentals. Instead, there can be no simple manual of field work practice.

For one thing, as I have tried to emphasize, field work and learning to do it are at bottom distinctly individual enterprises. This view was not adopted merely for its advantage in simplifying the task of describing and interpreting phenomena of such extraordinary complexity as social processes and personal experiences in field work. This view is also essential in considering pedagogical matters.

It seems doubtful that the selection and development of social science field workers is a task for mass education, although secondary school and college students can doubtless benefit from opportunities to learn skills, sensitivities, and the like that enter into field work but are also more widely useful. In any debate over curriculum offerings to prepare for social science careers, it may be wise to keep in mind that such preparation remains a job of learning done by individuals who are more self-selecting than selected. Moreover, this particular learning task, to be completed with optimum benefits both to society and to the individual in the long run, revolves around the individual's assuming maximum responsibility for his continuous learning of answers to the question, "Who am I?" While seeking these answers seems to be especially important to the social science field worker in his student days, it actually remains equally so throughout his career.

Three aspects of the question, "Who am I, as a social science field worker?" may be briefly put as follows:

1. "What are my social skills, given my intellectual, sensory, and other attributes, and my experience, for gathering information-in-society?"

2. "Who am I (and who might I become) in the eyes of the people in the situation(s) I want to study, and what effect does this have on my acting in roles in relations with them?"

3. "Who am I, again, given the best obtainable estimates of 1 and 2, and in my own judgment and in that of others, (a) What can I do as a field worker to get what information I can out of the situation? (b) Am I as fully willing and ethical as I am able to do this work to get this information for the purposes of a social science?"

That is, what do I bring with me to the situation of learning and doing field work for a social science; how am I evaluated by all others of any consequence to my acting in some field worker role with the aim to contribute to a social science; and, over and beyond my skills, abilities, capacities, or other endowments of good fortune, have I sufficient sensibility to act responsibly to serve both science and society, to meet their real persistent needs, and to help to articulate their emergent aims?

In the first half of this chapter, in our concern with learning and doing social science field work and living in society, major attention will be directed toward the needs of social science. In the second half, concern will be with the same matters, but with emphasis upon the needs of the learner.[1] In this part some hypotheses on the nature of the situation for the design of field work learning experiences are marked out, and in the second part some "ideal types" of students are described with the intention, not of covering the range of students I have encountered, but of providing some useful ways for their teachers and themselves to think about how to design their distinctive individual learning experiences.

Both enterprises, learning and doing, can be called creative. They certainly tend to engage the whole person of the learner or the doer in a series of social situations of varying degrees of complexity and ambiguity. In preceding chapters a few—really a very few—of the kinds of situations, processes, and experiences that occur have been illustrated. Facets, bits and pieces of complex wholes have been touched upon and viewed as well as the perspectives of the social sciences available to us allow, chiefly

---

1. See chapter v, footnote 1.

those of sociology, social anthropology, and social psychology. Other perspectives exist, or will come into being, and all of them are needed to pursue the researches which suggest themselves throughout this book, but which are not herein formally specified.

Being creative, involving whole persons in social processes, the enterprises of doing and learning have all the more need for enlarged and improved communication beyond what they have received to date. And this for two reasons: first, for the sake of building firmer foundations for the social sciences themselves; second, for the sake of future generations of students, whose learning might thus be facilitated. What needs to be communicated is indicated in earlier chapters containing contributions of thoughtful researchers toward a better, tested rationale for field work. Many practical items for the design of learning experiences, as well as for the conduct of field work at a more advanced level, are contained therein, but in the nature of the case, each individual must glean for himself that which is relevant for his needs.

The development of such a tested rationale might well be the task for a community of scholars (to use an old-fashioned phrase suggesting the guild type of organization for work)—not a tightly closed corporation of masters, journeymen, and apprentices but perhaps one of the broadest and most open collaborations offered and required by modern civilization. In short, in this view of social science, the problem is one for all the people to share, each in his chosen measure.

Learning by "apprentices" in this enterprise, even as it is presently constituted, inevitably finds its milieu in groups: it remains a matter of individual effort but actually occurs in much more meaningful relational contexts than the one suggested by the analogy to a limited, scholastic trade union. This is an ever widening context which provides ample room for "amateurs" and even "mavericks": persons who devote themselves to social science as well as persons who offer unconventional but often useful and even wise perspectives. All of these may help to illuminate the odd corners of a complex world.

Such a broad organization could not depend upon rigid regulations and definitive systems. It can operate with a few, loose ground rules and with the participation of all persons willing and able to communicate intelligibly with each other and with ever widening audiences as these assemble. The important ground rules already exist in an unwritten form like that of the British Constitution, in the interactions of men of science and their audiences in free societies. Such rules as these do not require everybody to belong to the same party, for example. They do require a great deal of open-mindedness, however, and much full, fair, and free communication, and their application will profoundly affect the social sciences in the long run, as they already do in the short run affect field work, particularly in role problems and ethics of reporting.

It is justifiable, therefore, to eschew the term "training," and to urge the larger measure of self-discipline suggested in the term "learning." Evidently we are dealing with phenomena of education in society, and specifically with programs for learning how to learn about society.

Today it is difficult to believe that human beings are purely "trained" to be persons—field workers, social scientists, or any other kind. Something much more complex in the way of human development really occurs, and we need to enlarge our comprehension of this thing. In this view, there can be no simple objectives of training for field work in a social science.

It is conventional to discuss training (and even, sad to say, learning) as if specific objectives and training items could be served forth. But full learning in a social science requires individual development of one's own communicable rationale for field work. In a narrow sense, and for purposes which really leave social science and the student out of it, training in techniques can be achieved, without doubt and even with a certain kind of success. In proportion to one's concern over what harm such training may do, both to some students and to the general reputation of social science, the problems indicated deserve attention.

If it is recognized that field work learning is, and must be, only part of the larger learning process of becoming a social scientist, then it is important to consider the fact that there is an active but false dichotomy between theory and empirical research that is recurrent in the social sciences from time to time. It is active in an organizational sense insofar as graduate students reflect it in their reactions to courses; they perceive some instructors as talking about "theory" and others talking about "field work." This dichotomy may even be exaggerated when the two start calling each other names, such as "radical empiricist" and "armchair theorist."

It is false, of course, at a scientific level because it is impossible for valid generalization to exist without some foundation in field observation, just as it is impossible for field observation to proceed without guidance from generalization—at the very least, generalization at the level of classification—useful or not, as it turns out. (An example of the latter is advice to the field worker on what to look for: it may or may not add validity to generalization, but at least it represents the kind of guidance for perception provided by a concept.)

It is doubly false when the working relationships between concepts and acts of perceiving are defined and controlled so rigidly that no new perceptions can be admitted to the company of selected, or even select, data. It can lead to a complete betrayal of the scientific approach.

There is no hope of offering the student an opportunity to become a complete social scientist if he is confronted with making a choice, by a separation of theory and methods courses, between becoming either a theoretician or a technician. The curriculum requires continual reappraisal to make sure that this dichotomy, even if it is denied in the announcements of courses, has not crept back into actual course work.

If we believe that it is "good" for man to understand himself and society, and if we agree that our knowledge of the workings of human society would lead us to predict the failure of efforts to promote the dichotomy between theory and empirical research, then, while we need to combat the waste of resources and harm done to students when such efforts are made, we should do even more to promote the belief that man and society can be best known by close, constant, and comparative observation directed by scientific reasoning and theory which are, in turn, constantly to be re-examined in the light of the observations made. In the nature of the case, because the situation of observation for a social science is particularly complex, we take the view that such a science boils down to knowledge of society, and of self-in-society, resting upon comparable data-about-society which in turn depend upon information-in-society gathered by field work conducted according to a rationale—the more tested and communicable the better—which is appropriate to enlarging and simplifying the knowledge in question.

Such a social science is an activity enlisting the higher mental processes in a very creative enterprise. Scientific advance always presents two sides: a contribution to knowledge that is exchangeable, or communicable, among those who share a body of existing understandings; and a flowering of someone's will to simplify, to render the complex and abstruse more comprehensible, to "make the order of one's thought correspond to the order of things," and, ultimately, to formulate the nature of man and society in terms parsimonious but sufficient to represent their roles in an ordered universe.

Much more than mere specialists, the social sciences need technicians who are also theoreticians and theoreticians who are also technicians, and for this, they also need improved pedagogical arrangements to enable students more rapidly to achieve their own, individual but communicable, syntheses of the interrelated, interdependent phases of any science: concept and percept, generalization and observation, grand theoretical schema and confusing human fact, whatever one chooses to call them.

The working hypotheses for the design of field work learning experiences are interwoven with assumptions in the following statements:

First of all, as I have noted, field workers who remain in the ranks of social scientists are probably more self-selecting than selected (some persevere even when not elected to academic posts), and although very little is known systematically about their professional careers, we are sure that the development of their skills, sensitivities, and the like takes place in describable social matrices—certain relational contexts, in some developmental series for each type, of very great significance to the outcome as measured by their contributions to the social sciences.

Second, it seems clear that the individual can participate actively and intelligently in planning and carrying out a "design for learning," and that the more actively and consciously he makes his choices in such matters, the faster he will progress.

Third, the behavior of field workers could be studied to delineate the "bundles" of skills, sensitivities, sensibilities, and so on, that characterize them, as well as their apparent need and capacity for much sustained social interaction. (There is indicated here a large field for future research which might be marked out as "the psychodynamics of social science field worker roles." The present discussion deals only with outward behavior, describing it in ways which refer questions of inner motivations to future studies.)

What seems to characterize field workers, especially successful ones and fast learners?

Curiosity, particularly what is elsewhere discussed as "process curiosity," appears to be marked among field workers. They are also collectors, especially of fresh records of field observations that convey some breath of life, some flavor of personality or character, some glimpse into the world of the other fellow. They are also puzzle-solvers: they want to know "what makes people (individually or collectively) tick," especially in contemporary situations observable at firsthand. But due to this demand for firsthand observation (or perhaps need for active participation in some role at the scene of interaction), their interest in the historic past, and sometimes even their interest in the contemporary bizarre, tends to be constricted to what they think helps to explain the present and the commonplace.

They seem to be careful reporters rather than brilliantly interesting ones, perhaps because they strive to separate their interpretations from their descriptions. This may make for very dull reading unless one is interested in the particular field situation described, is able to look and listen vicariously along with the field worker and perhaps even to anticipate significances beyond those indicated by the reporter.

They need colleagues. To have done field work one's self enormously increases one's appreciation of another's report, and in private conversa-

tions among themselves field workers can often exchange much of their
learning that could never be fully put into print. (It would, incidentally, be
interesting to see more published efforts to take the reader along with the
field worker, and it may be that an increasingly sophisticated public will
require more of this from social scientists to enable the audiences better
to evaluate the findings. One possible result would be to widen participation in the making of social science.) Thus the field worker needs active
and appropriate colleague relationships, not merely for moral support but
also for furthering his own learning. In fact, the field worker needs and
usually seeks colleagues, at each stage of his development, who are appropriate in the sense that they stimulate him to improve upon his own best
efforts, while he in turn helps them. Finding such learning situations is
one of the lifelong tasks of the social scientist—a kind of field work, in a
sense, to meet the personal needs of the field worker himself.

    More consciously directed attention to the nature of this task might
benefit the learner who wishes to become a social science field worker, for
discovering such colleague relationships will help him to refine his curiosity, perfect his collecting and puzzle-solving abilities, improve his reporting, and strengthen simultaneously both his contributions to, and his own
internalizations of, some better-tested rationale for field observation.
These, in crude form, are some of the dimensions of the career of the social scientist such as might be included in a sociological study of this occupation—another field for future research.

    The learner would do well to examine the models available to him to
mark out what the social science field worker is and to discover what he
may have to go through in order to become one himself. A few guideposts
in the search for useful ways to think about a design for learning what "is"
and "to become" mean and how to achieve such self-educational goals may
be suggested.

    In briefest form, the central question for the design of field work
learning experiences is the ever loaded, "Who am I?" Dealing with this
question requires the active, intelligent participation of the student, with
the student accepting the larger part of responsibility for his own development. The instructor's guidance may consist simply of providing testing
grounds and progressively more complex learning situations (for example,
a variety of experiences ranging from conditions of no sponsorship to conditions of full sponsorship). But what the local learning situation provides
in the way of theoretical nourishment that the student can internalize along
with his own field work learning experiences will guide the choice of such
a series of situations. The latter should fit into some larger design for
learning to become a social scientist. As for the rest, the instructor's task

is one of continuing "field work" on the problems of his learners, and this may well run to counseling as much as to consultation, a fact that the instructor should probably consider before launching such an enterprise if he has had little experience with field work himself.

It is largely up to the student, although the instructor may help, to conduct an assessment, or a series of reappraisals, of the student's answers to the multidimensional question of "Who am I?" along the lines suggested earlier in this chapter.

Individuals who present themselves as students in the social sciences seem to vary enormously in every respect important to this question. Among these are: sex, age, motivation, maturity (in all senses), background and experience, energy level, physical appearance and personal habits, reading and writing abilities, manual dexterity and social gracefulness, sensory equipment and modes of using it, values and expectations, characteristic ways of being aggressive and deferential, and particular suitability on these or any other counts for presently available career opportunities. The reader who needs to can draw up his own list of such items.

The important point is that not only do individual students vary in these respects but so do generations of students in any one university, and so do groups of students in the same year at different institutions of learning. This points to a local and immediate social science research task, one in which students and faculty conceivably might join, to assess their general and individual situations in order to design the learning experiences that seem to be most appropriate, given all or at least the major answers to the questions already suggested under the major one of "Who am I, as a social science field worker?"

Now in order to summarize the developmental paths taken by three "ideal types" of students, Chart 2 (chapter iii) is amplified to represent "Theoretical Roles for Field Work and for Living in Society."

Using the numeration in this chart, we may now recognize three "ideal types" of students distinguished by their approaches to learning (or not learning) how to become field workers for a social science:

Type A.—The person who, like every other student, or person, has been and always will be, something of a Complete Participant (1 [shaded area]) and whose training takes the pattern of moving from (1) to (I) to (II) to (III), and who tends to become a social scientist who emphasizes participation more than observation: a role as social scientist which may be labeled II/III or Participant as Observer over Observer as Participant.

Type B.—The person who, like those of Type A, is a Complete Participant (1 [shaded area]), but who never gets beyond reporting as a person in that role—that is, never moves to Complete Participant (I). He remains

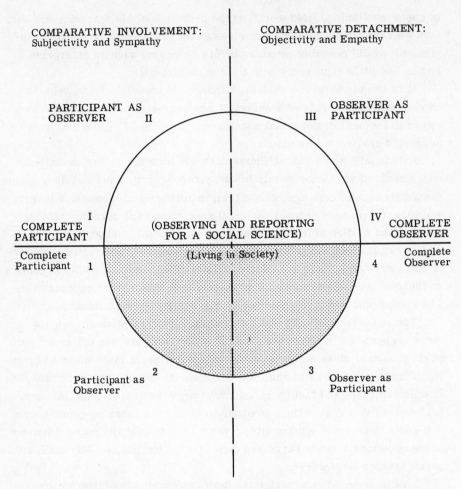

COMPARATIVE INVOLVEMENT: COMPARATIVE DETACHMENT:
Subjectivity and Sympathy   Objectivity and Empathy

PARTICIPANT AS   OBSERVER AS
OBSERVER   II   III   PARTICIPANT

I   IV
COMPLETE   (OBSERVING AND REPORTING   COMPLETE
PARTICIPANT   FOR A SOCIAL SCIENCE)   OBSERVER

Complete   (Living in Society)   Complete
Participant   1   4   Observer

                  2   3
Participant as   Observer as
Observer   Participant

Chart 3. Theoretical Roles for Field Work and for Living in Society

completely ethnocentric, never becomes a social scientist, and even as an
ordinary member of his part of his society, he tends to be a poor natural
observer (hence, a poor informant in the eyes of any field worker who encounters him).

Type C.—The person who, for some reason, starts as a Complete Observer (4 [shaded area])—or at least seems to prefer this role early in life
—and whose training or development is likely to take the pattern of moving
from (4) to (IV) to (III), so that he becomes a social scientist who emphasizes observation more than participation: a role which may be labeled
III/II, or Observer as Participant over Participant as Observer.

In real life, of course, there are many more combinations and permu-
tations of these developmental patterns than these three, but the purpose
of this oversimplification is to stimulate more research as well as more

self-study. For example, it may be true that the most versatile social scientist is one whose repertory of roles for research and for living in society has developed out of much thought and practice along all three lines of development so that in his private life, he used Type B learnings, but as a social scientist finds it easy to oscillate along the entire range, using Type A and Type C lessons.

Chart 3 also points to many other possible correspondences between observing society and living in society. There seems to be a close relationship between learning to be a person and learning to be a social science field worker. If so, that is a fact of deep significance and far-reaching implications for those social sciences whose best and perhaps only "instrument" in the situation of observation is a very human individual—the lone field worker. The very foundations of such a social science must begin here, and no amount of effort to improve our methodology can accomplish its goal if the method-user himself is overlooked or glossed over, along with his role relations in his society and in his scientific work.

In view of this, it is important to examine even more closely the learner himself and some of the processes and experiences through which he develops the attitude, the role, and the self-conception of a social science field worker. Both instructors and students ideally learn from each other in the course of teaching and doing field work, and clearer recognition of role and self problems can help them to arrive at better understandings of themselves and of other field workers at any stage in their careers.

Three important dimensions of the process by which an individual becomes a field worker are: (1) developing the attitude of the social science field worker; (2) developing the role of the social science field worker; and (3) developing the self-conception of the social science field worker. While development along these three dimensions proceeds concurrently, for purposes of this exposition they may be discussed in this order and interrelated logically in the sequel.

How does an individual come to understand the attitude of the social science field worker and incorporate it into his perceptive, emotional, and intellectual apparatus? To begin to answer this question, we would need to know, first of all, what social science is and what social scientists do in and out of the field; second, what kind of attitude the social scientist has toward the social world; and third, we would need to know something about the learner as well as the learning process.

The disciplines of the social sciences are engaged in building a systematic body of knowledge of society which contains data-about-society. Each of these disciplines has its particular range of problems-about-society, which it investigates in the field as problems-in-society. From the

study of the latter, each learns about the points of view, the dilemmas, the
crises, the wants and wishes, and the like of the groups under investigation.
This study yields information-in-society. When this information is subjected to scientific treatment, categorized and analyzed, it is thereby
translated into answers (some of them highly tentative) which, at the level
of data-about-society, amount to attempts to resolve scientific problems-
about-society. The latter include questions of viewpoint, dilemmas, crises,
wants and wishes, and the like in the discipline itself—and, in addition the
consumers of social science.

When the student begins his training for a social science, he finds that
the discipline he has entered has an esoteric language for describing and
conceptualizing large areas of social life which are commonplace to him, or
which he has heard about in commonplace terms. He soon learns that there
is something peculiar about his discipline, for it takes a rather special
view of the world of human social activity, does it in an uncommonly detached way, and then doggedly orders its findings into an abstract system
of concepts in order continually to re-examine the world with its special
view. He may ask himself, "Why take such a narrow-minded view of human
behavior and go through all the bother of collecting a systematic body of
data-about-society?" After all, the student may add, "I should think that
there certainly must be more than enough knowledge of society in the huge
libraries of books at our disposal—why not just distil a few basic formulas
to explain whatever we want to know about society, especially anything we
might want to know about our special view of society?"

And then, when he is required to leave the campus to do field work, he
is prone to become at least a little uneasy about his "science": "They want
me, of all people, to help them construct the discipline. Why, I thought this
stuff came from books!" What I want to point out here is that every student,
no matter how intelligent he is or how much fore-knowledge he has of the
social science he enters for training, experiences a kind of reality shock
when he begins to learn the raw facts of what may become his lifework, as
only the initiated can know them. While the beginning student usually thinks
he knows at least a little bit more than some people about human behavior
(having read some of the classic works in his discipline), he now finds that
social scientists truly have a scientific attitude in their view of society,
and that they do not get their knowledge about society simply from books,
but get it the hard way—by observing human social activity and participating in it! Reality shock occurs in many different ways, a succession of
little ones or a great one that may be overwhelming, but in some degree
and at some stage every professional has encountered it.

Let us continue to view the student at that point in his career when he is beginning to achieve a firmer intellectual grasp of social science as represented in his discipline. Having learned that his fellow-students, however blasé they tried to appear, were just as shocked as he, and having begun to build colleague relationships with them as well as with, perhaps, his instructor, he feels somewhat prepared to tackle the field work assignments which lie immediately ahead of him. Perhaps the instructor, aware of the beginner's problems, since he himself has been through some like them, has advised the student to prepare himself for field work by self-study, as by working through his own social autobiography to increase his understanding of himself as an individual in society.

To his surprise, the student finds that the concepts of his discipline enable him to make some sense out of his past and present everyday experiences, and that, reciprocally, his experiences strengthen his comprehension of the concepts. He continues to interrelate concept and percept in his introspections, discovering more and more about his self: how it became what it is, how he relates his self to others, how he interacts with others and to what effects. This self-knowledge, the instructor has suggested, will help him to understand how others (especially informants) got to be what they are. The student may be a little doubtful about this, especially if he has always thought himself quite a sophisticated observer of human conduct, but let us suppose he decides to humor the instructor by testing this notion.

Although we have not paused to label them as such, the significant segments of attitudinal development have already appeared in the learner's behavior. He is starting to learn that: (1) the concepts of his discipline are rooted in observation at firsthand; (2) the viewpoint of his discipline derives from sets of interests, hence problems for research requiring field work and other research procedures in their investigation; (3) the members of his discipline are amazingly sensitive to people in accordance with their scientific interests in people; (4) the concepts of his discipline, being rooted in reality, help him to gain a better understanding of social interaction, especially that in which he takes part; (5) the relationships he has with colleagues (on all levels of authority or competence) aid him in getting over the rough spots in his training and in reappraising himself as a social scientist-in-the-making; and (6) his curiosity about people undergoes refinement and becomes subject to more control when observing them scientifically.

Shortly after entering the field, the novice field worker may experience reality shock as never before, or again. He makes mistakes, creates dilemmas, and feels acutely ambivalent about the social science attitude. Only a week or so before he was quite confident, but now he is rather bewildered about a number of things. The deficiencies in his attitudinal development are painfully exposed, although he does not always recognize them for what they are. He may find some or all of the following questions personally bothersome at this stage:

1. What is it that we social scientists look for when observing this group of people and sizing up its members?

2. Why haven't the rules of this field work game been made more explicit by the instructor?

3. And even when the rules are clear, why do I find it difficult to accept some of them?

4. What kind of audience should I have in mind when planning and securing interviews or making any other necessary observations?

5. How can I convince myself, on the one hand, and the people I approach for information, on the other hand, that this field work business is worthwhile to science and society?

6. How can I sharpen my knowledge of social science concepts as they are rooted in the behavior of living, acting people in the field?

7. How can I translate our scientific problems-about-society into problems-in-society as I enter the field, and get the two sets of problems to interact after the investigation gets under way?

8. Why can't I always remember that we social scientists look at behavior from the standpoint of the actor?

9. Why do I have trouble interacting with people who have certain social and personal characteristics?

10. To what kinds of people do I look, sound, smell, etc., at least nearly the way I do to myself? Just what kind of individual do different kinds of people think I am, both as a person and as a field worker?

11. Doesn't the instructor like me any more?

12. If my fellow-learners have any of these problems, they certainly conceal them. Why are they so reluctant to sit down with me and talk over our field work problems? Talking frankly about them would surely help us to deal more effectively with them.

13. How can I be sure that I am making progress in developing a professional attitude toward myself and others?

14. I am so confused now that I'm not even sure any more what social science is. In my present state, what kind of information will I get, and how can I report it?

Along with the confusion that attends attitudinal development, the student field worker also encounters role problems. The process by which an individual learns to act as a field worker is revealed in the patterning of these problems, which can be summarized in general form. Developing the attitude of the social science field worker involves primarily learning to <u>take</u> the role of the social science field worker toward self and others. Developing the role of the social science field worker involves primarily learning to play the role in a manner that is congenial and convincing to self and others. Learning to incorporate the attitude of the social science field worker prepares the student for learning to communicate the attitude through the field worker role. The attitude of the field worker is the very stuff out of which the role is constructed—when the role is conceived in its pure form. But because the role is or becomes a part of a person's social identity, it has to be understood in this larger context. We therefore must ask ourselves the following about the role of the student field worker: (1) What is there about a person's social identity that has relevance for his learning to play the role of the field worker? and (2) What personal and situational demands of the field—that is, the situation of observation—present themselves as problems to the person, simply because he expresses his social identity in that situation through the role of the field worker and his social identity now carries the developing attitude of the field worker?

Before entering the field to seek out people for the information they might have on the subject matter of his current assignment, the student field worker was fairly sure that he had an adequate answer to the question, "Who am I?" But now, acting in the role of the field worker, he is no longer sure of the answer. While puzzling over this question, he may ask himself: "How am I supposed to represent myself to these people? Should I tell them that I am merely a student learning to do field work, or should I make up some story about being an old hand at this sort of thing? Can I really get away with misrepresenting myself, or should I play it straight? Can I really act like an experienced field worker? How is one supposed to act? For that matter, how is a beginner supposed to act? The instructor advised us to be ourselves, to treat people like human beings, to act in a warm and sincerely interested way, but isn't all that rather vague? Why isn't there a handbook . . . ?"

It is difficult for the student at this stage to comprehend that playing the role of field worker is not the same as playing a set role in a stage play or a ritualized, or routinized, role in an institution or an office. There is no set plot; there are no lines to memorize; there is only a more or less structured exchange of social gestures which unfolds spontaneously in the course of the interactions between the field worker and the informant. Consequently the student's wish for a handbook can never be fulfilled.

Social gestures are the field worker's stock in trade, and he must play his role by exchanging them with the informant. Some of these may be simple and stereotyped, as in the "phatic communion" found all over the world in one form or another (in our society, "Nice day today, isn't it!" or some such comment on what affects everybody), but social gestures range all the

way to the highly complex and subtle, as in those exchanged in securing
secrets from an in-group member. The exchange always takes place, of
course, in a social setting but one which changes in form and content as
the kind of information sought changes. The exchange also varies according to the social identity (actual or believed) which each participant
ascribes to the other. As in any other area of social interaction which is
not highly institutionalized, communication between the field worker and
the informant in their respective roles is built up as it proceeds, never
before. To attempt to anticipate what a person having the informant's social identity will do and say is very helpful to the student, but such antici-
pating is a matter of learning a great deal more about comparative social
organization and about social psychology, among other things, and as such
it becomes a part of the attitude of the social scientist. As part of the attitude, anticipation may take explicit form in tentative hypotheses which are
tested while "sizing up" or "sounding out" the informant. When the student
recognizes the importance of this anticipation, and begins to deal directly
with these and other requirements of his attitudinal development, he is then
facing the realities of developing his role as social science field worker.

The realities of role development are nowhere made more striking to
the student than in the field. It is there that he faces again and again the
learning tasks discussed and illustrated in chapter v. These problems (the
rebuff, problems of role choice, handling emotional involvement, etc.—all
seven categories) not only occur in the student's development of his role,
but they are also role problems even to the most experienced field worker.
They are never completely "solved" to the satisfaction of all concerned in
every (or perhaps any) field situation. Learning to identify his role to himself and to others is an unending process, because the identification problem changes with the field situation, and no two field situations are ever
precisely the same. Accordingly, learning who he is as a field worker becomes, for the student, a matter of learning what his major occupational
role problems are, determining how his personal role problems intervene
to modify the occupational ones, and then guiding himself toward a resolution of the remaining conflicts by taking the attitude of the social scientist
toward himself and others. In addition, as he gains in experience, his more
effective use of the comparative method begins to be helpful in reducing
the uniqueness of each new encounter.

Let us now consider the occupational and personal learning tasks in
the role development of each of the three "ideal types" of students described earlier in this chapter.

Type A describes the kind of person who, in any role he plays, is always and foremost a human being and who wants both to be known as such

and to know others as such. No role is really congenial to him. At every opportunity, he sets the role aside and attempts to establish with the other a very "earthy" colleague relationship: a relationship of human beings. By continually gravitating toward the level of sentiments (or affect) in interactions with others, he cannot help but lose detachment, at least to some degree. He may achieve a mastery of the attitude of the social science field worker, but he never reaches the point where he can remain aloof long enough to play the role in a personally satisfying way.

In contrast to Type A, Type C describes the individual who finds it both congenial and convenient to play a wide variety of roles. Roles are congenial because they permit him to have interaction without great personal involvement. They are convenient because they enable him to participate in an extensive social world by selecting the roles which accord with the demands of the situation. He sees others in terms of social characteristics, while Type A sees others in terms of the human characteristics of other individuals and social groups. Each type has a self-conception which corresponds to his view of others and his attendant role relationships with others. Each type may also attain an intellectual mastery of the attitude of the social science field worker. But since the attitude receives expression through the person's self, which is the basic idiosyncratic element in role-playing, the role receives from the self a differential emphasis and form both in everyday life and in field work activity. The person who lives more as a participant than as an observer (and vice versa) does so for reasons of self. As a person, the field worker should be aware of these determinants of the role as he plays it, not only to take account of the kinds of relationships which he finds it congenial to enter or create, but also to take account of the kinds of information and hence the kinds of data which these relationships yield.

Type B describes one who has a parochial view of the world and has not learned how to take the role of the out-group other, except in terms of the roles familiar to him because they are played by the in-group others. And since a person must be able to take a role before he can play it, he lacks both the attitudinal and the role development needed to become a social science field worker. Like Type A, he is foremost a person, but he is unable to make any other an ethnic colleague in the way in which Type A makes any other a human colleague. Ethnic sentiments and human sentiments overlap, but do not correspond. What is difficult about Type B, in the view of his instructors, is the task of shifting his attitude in the direction of either Type A or Type C. Indeed, in the case of the ideal type as defined, the attempt by definition fails, but in practice, because some accident of fate or consequence of inner motivation may intervene to affect a

Type B student's life, it may occasionally and surprisingly succeed.

Having examined the development of the attitude and the role of the student field worker, we are now ready to examine the development of his self-conception. The primary consideration in this development is the incorporation of the field worker's role into the self-conceptions of the student. Moreover, it is at this point that we must also consider the development of process curiosity, because it is the most important single component of the field worker's attitude, which in turn comprises the essential stuff, together with the self, out of which the role of the field worker is developed. This may be discussed in terms of the learning of the generalized student, rather than separately for the three "ideal types," because the lessons from his development apply equally well to the developmental tasks of any selected type of student.

No assumption can be made about the development of process curiosity in the attitude of the student field worker, because not every student has this kind of curiosity when he begins field work—at least, not the kind pointing his attention to persons or social groups. (Occasionally a student turns up whose process curiosity, such as it is, would be better served in another curriculum.) If we were to endow the generalized student field worker with process curiosity, it would do more violence to him than our knowledge of student field workers allows. But to go to the opposite extreme and claim that the student who does not have process curiosity when he enters a social science requiring field work training cannot learn it would be to do more violence to this discussion than our present hypotheses allow. For it appears, simply enough, that process curiosity can be learned. The learning task for some students, such as those of Type B, is in many respects one of re-socialization. But that is not to say that the task is impossible or has never been accomplished. In its widest sense, ethnocentrism which includes role consciousness is an attitude which training opportunities, new experiences, and an awakened curiosity can enable some to "learn away." If any student is curious enough about society and about self in society to attempt seriously to work through his social autobiography and to consider questions of the kind raised earlier, then he can learn and utilize process curiosity.

As a way of looking at the world, process curiosity in its fundamental sense is opposite to ethnocentrism. The person who observes human behavior and situations with an earnest intention of discovering and understanding the viewpoints of the actors and the processes by which those viewpoints arise and persist, not only cultivates and uses process curiosity, but has much in common with anyone else who utilizes it. At bottom the employment of process curiosity is the employment of roles. This is true because a person learns to take the role of the other by playing the role of a sincerely and sympathetically interested human and social being. Those who characteristically and naturally employ roles in this way have a self-conception to which their role of natural observer is congenial. (The idea, expressed in the language of Chart 3, is that such persons move skilfully and comfortably along the entire range from complete observer to complete participant when they play field worker roles.)

How does this kind of self-conception develop?

There is ample reason to believe that curiosity, as such, is part of human nature. Indeed, from early infancy through later maturity, it is curiosity (including such forms as anticipation, interest, and expectation) which gives one a zest for living and learning. But for its genesis, process curiosity had to wait until culture contacts became numerous, even commonplace, and until communications among differing societies and cultures enabled people to understand one another's everyday behavior. Process curiosity thus begins as essentially neighborly curiosity, as a kind of folksy interest in the meaning of neighbors' activities. It arises and flourishes in social settings containing and making accessible to view divergent ways of life, where some individuals are likely each to seek continually for clarification of the question, "Who am I?" This clarification comes about through frequent social intercourse with varied others, leading one to examine and re-examine the others in order to understand self, and vice versa. Now, what happens to the self-conceptions of those who attempt to clarify the question, "Who am I?" under these conditions?

It appears that, since such an individual continually seeks from others the answer which would tell him who he is, the self becomes open-ended, that is, ambiguous. Accordingly, ambiguity of self is the common element in the self-conceptions of those who utilize process curiosity, because a sincere interest in the viewpoints of others, especially of very different others, is both the cause and effect of seeking clarification of the "Who am I?" question. Because varieties of experience are endless in a socially heterogeneous community, or in the course of an itinerant existence, the individual's self-conceptions always retain enough ambiguity to keep his curiosity in process.

In view of all this, it is evident that the ethnocentric person never needs to ask himself who he is, because he already knows. For him life is well patterned, and the objects in his little world are clearly defined. He may, as many people more or less happily do, live out his entire life in this manner. But if, and especially if at a relatively early age, he gets into a situation which makes the way of life of culturally different people clear to him from their point of view, he then begins to examine his own style of

life by examining self, and ambiguity of self then has a chance to develop.
The personal confusion and discomfort which accompanies the beginning
of this ambiguity diminishes with each new set of experiences with different others, for then the individual persistently re-examines self and
others, discovering more and more of the answer to the "Who am I?" question. Yet, once the process starts, it never ends. Thus this ambiguity of
self is a socially adaptive, as well as a necessary, characteristic of those
who learn and utilize process curiosity.

Many students, while not completely "ethnocentric" in their outlook,
enter training for field work with a rather narrow range of experiences
and a corresponding curiosity which is in the early stages of becoming
process curiosity. Moreover, they have not yet learned how to cultivate it,
as part of taking responsibility for their own intellectual, social, and professional development. It should now be more clear, in the light of the
foregoing analysis, how experiences in field work can enable such students
to broaden and sophisticate their outlook on human behavior, and how, in
the context of their whole training this enables them to incorporate the attitude of the social science field worker.

As we have suggested, the field worker's role is not always congenial
to the self-conceptions of all those who have incorporated the attitude of
the social science field worker. How, then, can we explain, for our generalized portrait of the student field worker, how the student incorporates
the field work role into his self-conceptions? How, in other words, can we
suggest the manner in which this "student" learns to play the field work
role naturally, convincingly, and effectively?

The answer is really not so difficult when one notes that the role of
the field worker is not always, or equally, congenial to the student, or
even to the "old-timer," in all the field situations in which he participates.
In one field situation, the field worker may have a problem of status disparity, in another a problem of emotional involvement, whereas a colleague, as he discovers, may have different problems, or these in different degrees, in the same situations. Acting in such situations, which are
problematic to the individual, tend to be defined by him as "dirty work,"
since dirty work is the individual's definition of his relationship to the situation. The field worker can, however, learn to appraise his competence
to play his role in any problematic situation, and, if necessary, he can
even ease out and recommend that he be replaced by a colleague whose personal make-up is more suitable to the demands of the situation. When the
student becomes sufficiently aware of his role repertory to make such an
appraisal and recommendation, he has developed not only the attitude of
the field worker, but also the role, and it can then be said that, however

congenial the role as broadly conceived is to his self-conceptions, he has incorporated it therein. The point is that field workers are neither completely born nor completely made; instead, they are always becoming. The becoming process starts when the individual becomes aware that he is personally and socially identified as a field worker. The process is endless, however, because he continually gets into new situations which require clarification of his social identity, and hence of his personal identity or self.

Thus, the challenge of field work to those who engage in it is not only that of developing an appropriate self-conception but also that of maintaining it when pursuing information on "unexplored" social frontiers, that is, areas of society which have not yet been studied by the individual or by his colleagues. For the professional social scientist there is, in addition, the matter of reconstituting his self-conception from time to time through the stages of his career. In proportion to the rate at which such a career is becoming institutionalized in our society, certain kinds of field work will probably come to be regarded as "dirty work" for the advanced professional but appropriate for juniors, as part of their "initiation" into some social science trade. Such tendencies to structure the occupation and the stages of the professional career may be expected to permeate the entire social science enterprise, and the consequences will deserve reappraisal from time to time, especially by creative persons who can discover ways to turn the disadvantages of a current state of affairs into opportunities for scientific advance.

The challenge of field work as a learning process is a challenge for all the social sciences, since the ones we have kept in mind depend upon field workers for the information and ultimately for the data upon which they rest their special knowledge of society. Clearly, the advance of a social science depends on more and better field work, both the conduct and results of which society finds acceptable—not barely sufferable. And so we come full circle—a social science must include not only a science of field work but also the activities of preparing students to carry out its task by learning its fundamentals in appropriate situations of observation.

SELECTED BIBLIOGRAPHY

This bibliography contains two types of material: first, a brief review of the literature on field work and suggestions for further development of a bibliography on this subject; and second, topics and selected references (coded as they are in the author list); with an alphabetized author list of selected references (each coded to indicate its classification in the topic list).

I have sought mainly to include the more accessible published materials in which field workers not only give their findings but also describe their research operations in some detail, especially with attention to social processes and personal experiences. I have also listed a few items in the vast and growing literature of the more technical or prescriptive sort —which might be called "how-to-do-it" items—but I have been primarily interested in the social interaction aspects of field work which, until very recently, have not been so fully and frequently reported as their scientific importance seems to warrant. I do not offer this bibliography as complete or definitive but rather as "a sampler assortment," and I point to the various bibliographic tools the reader may use to build his own library or reference file.

In the eyes of some scientists in other fields, social scientists—and perhaps especially sociologists—are overly concerned with methodology. Perhaps this is because, all too often, a narrow concern with a specialized technique of field observation has been emphasized without sufficient consideration of the social context of its use. For purposes of delineating the broader aspects of methodology in the social sciences employing field work, it is interesting to trace from its thin beginnings to its growing richness the literature which shares this point of view.

The Literature on Field Work

A library classification scheme developed in 1906 by Juul Dieserud[1] of the Library of Congress for the "Science of Anthropology" provided no place for methodology. Dieserud's discussion of the literature of anthropology, ethnology, and social science shows that the writers then were more concerned with questions such as "What is anthropology?" and "How does it differ from ethnology and social science?" than they were with any

---

1. See author list for information on all titles mentioned herein.

questions about how information was to be obtained.

Among the early social surveys, the monumental Life and Labour of the People of London (1902-4) is rich in observations, including many on the difficulties of obtaining the information desired. Charles Booth sought to record observations that could readily be translated into numbers, so that the data could be ordered according to numerical relations, and he gives a further account of his researches in two papers published in the Journal of the Royal Statistical Society (1887, 1888).

However, in the first two decades of the twentieth century, the published reports of social scientists give little on field work problems and experiences. When such matters were dealt with, the information was apparently regarded as incidental and so taken for granted that it was buried in footnotes and asides. An important exception is the long methodological note (pp. 1-86) to be found in Thomas and Znaniecki's The Polish Peasant in Europe and America (1918).

In the 1920's notes on methods began to appear in forewords or prefaces. Since 1929, when the Lynds devoted the first chapter of Middletown to "The Nature of the Investigation," there has been an increasing tendency on the part of field workers to report, or at least to mention, their methods. Descriptions of informants (and even the observers' self-descriptions) began to appear, and means of obtaining information, of achieving rapport, of protecting the anonymity of the people studied, of dealing with bias in field observation and many other problems began to receive fuller treatment in more prominent positions, such as introductory chapters or appendixes. (For a few examples see: Margaret Mead, The Changing Culture of an Indian Tribe [1934]; Bronislaw Malinowski, Coral Gardens and Their Magic [1935]; J. T. Salter, Boss Rule: Portraits in City Politics [1935]; and John Dollard, Caste and Class in a Southern Town [1937; 2d ed., 1949].)

Before 1940 few writers included theoretical discussions of field work problems and experiences. Two notable exceptions are Margaret Mead (1933; 1934; etc.) and Bronislaw Malinowski (Supplement I, in Ogden and Richards, The Meaning of Meaning, 1923). Malinowski's theoretical orientation and reflections upon his own experiences can be found not only in his own works, but also in his introductions to the works of others. (See, for example, his Preface to Facing Mount Kenya by Jomo Kenyatta [1938].)

With the publication (1941) of The Social Life of a Modern Community by Warner and Lunt (Volume I of the "Yankee City Series") more detailed reports on research operations, giving the general theories which guided field operations and some account of the researchers' learning experiences, began to make their appearance.

Full accounts are still rare, considering the large number of field

studies published and still coming off the presses. Whyte's Street Corner
Society (1943; 2d ed., 1955) is one of these rare studies, as are Cora
DuBois' The People of Alor (1944), Myrdal's An American Dilemma (1944),
and Hollingshead's Elmtown's Youth (1949). Perhaps the fullest reports of
this nature will be found in recent and future doctoral dissertations by social science students whose reports are based upon their own field work.

When specialized techniques have been used, especially if they employ
new inventions or revivals of old ones, the published reports usually devote
considerable attention to explaining their designs and applications. Case
studies, questionnaires, schedules, and the like are tools now described
and sometimes critically evaluated in textbooks. Other recent reports describe the use of electronic devices in interviewing, photographic means
of recording observations, and "projective techniques" such as the "TAT,"
for eliciting responses. (An early use of electronic recording is described
by David P. Boder [1949], and by 1951 the use of projective techniques was
incorporated in a doctoral dissertation on movie stars as popular hero
images by Frederick Elkin, to cite just two.)

The literature on such techniques and devices is voluminous and growing. It is accessible through such library tools as Public Affairs Information Service, Psychological Abstracts, Sociological Abstracts, Education
Index, and published subject bibliographies. For this reason, and because
a more comprehensive listing would be out of place in this book, the references for the topics under "Methods and Techniques" are limited to a few
which indicate at least some of the inventions and ideas of social scientists
seeking more effective tools for the study of the individual in society and
of society as a whole.

From 1920 to the present, numerous volumes have appeared which
deal generally with "methods" in making studies employing field observation. To select a few of these, we may begin with F. Stuart Chapin's Field
Work and Social Research (1920), in which he emphasizes historical, statistical, and case study techniques in his outline of field work methods. In
1925 there appeared Florian Znaniecki's The Laws of Social Psychology
and Vivien Palmer's Field Studies in Sociology: A Student's Manual.
Charles H. Cooley's essays, at least those which had appeared in journals
during the 1920's, were collected and published in 1930 in his Sociological
Theory and Social Research. The Webb's Methods of Social Study (1932)—
see excerpts in chapter iii of this book—and Paul Radin's The Method and
Theory of Ethnology (1933) were published early in the 1930's. Among the
most recent general books are the new edition of Scientific Social Surveys
and Research by Pauline Young (1949); Anthropology Today: An Encyclopedic Inventory, prepared under the chairmanship of A. L. Kroeber (1953);

E. E. Evans-Pritchard's discussion of modern field work in his Social Anthropology (1951); Marie Jahoda and others, Research Methods in Social
Relations (1951); Research Methods in the Behavioral Sciences (1953), edited by Leon Festinger and Daniel Katz; and Sociology Today, Problems
and Prospects (1959), edited by Robert Merton, Leonard Broom, and
Leonard S. Cottrell, Jr. There is no single volume presenting a comprehensive historical account of the development of theories and methods of
field work.

As pointed out in the introduction by Professor Hughes, the social survey was an early method of doing field work on a large scale in contemporary situations of considerable complexity, though still in situations involving, as central problems, "conditions of the poor" and the like. By
1912, Paul Kellogg was able to write on "The Spread of the Survey Idea."
As the "survey idea" spread geographically, however, it also widened in
meaning. Contemporary literature and popular thought employ the word
survey in community planning, industrial planning, opinion polls, and so
on. Much of the literature is concerned with specific technical problems
such as "errors in surveys" and "hard-to-reach individuals," and survey
methods are now clearly differentiated from those used in the more intensive and long-continued field study of a social group or community.

The use of the survey approach in planning and polling led to studies
of interviewing techniques. Beginning in the mid-twenties one finds such
articles as: Emory Bogardus, "Methods of Interviewing" (1924-25); R. S.
Woodworth, "Psychological Experience with the Interview" (1925); Mary
Van Kleeck, "The Interview as a Method of Research" (1926); H. L. Myrick, "The Non-Verbal Elements in the Interview" (1928); and B. V. Moore,
"The Interview in Social Industrial Research" (1930).

During the 1930's the literature continued along these lines, but toward the end of this decade the social scientists reported more on such aspects of interviewing as "insight" and "securing rapport," perhaps reflecting developments in psychotherapy. During the next decade, there were
many careful analyses of interview methods, techniques, and results. Problems of bias, of training interviewers for surveys, and matters of sampling
techniques were discussed, as well as "depth interviewing," "non-directive
interviewing," "detailed interviews," "idea-centered question," "focused
interview" and "the psychology of the interview." It seems quite logical
that the next step should have been, as it was, the study of the interviewer
himself and his effect on the interviewing process. (See, for this and studies on many other matters, Interviewing in Social Research [1954], by Herbert Hyman and others.)

The widening uses of the social survey in the 1930's also led to studies of research design, methods of observation, case study, techniques of questionnaire design, and related problems. William Healy's "The Contribution of Case Study to Sociology" had appeared in 1923, the same year in which Edward Lindeman described the method of "participant-observer" in his book, Social Discovery. "Case study" is a common procedure in all scientific fields, of course, and the underlying notion of participant observation must have been present when the first human group met another group (strangers) at some vague and ancient boundary. Indeed, in 1898, Gabriel Tarde proposed a kind of voluntary association of amateur sociologists, in various localities throughout the length and breadth of France, who would report their observations of "little changes" in custom and law (Les Lois sociales, 1898; translated, 1899, as Social Laws: An Outline of Sociology).

What appears to be new is the increase in what amounts to self-criticism: since the 1930's social scientists are more and more tending to raise questions about their own and others' techniques, methods, and even persons and professional ethics. Meanwhile, the use of these techniques and methods is reported in education, human relations, industrial relations, as well as in social surveys, and anthropological inquiries, and in sociological research there is increasing use of new techniques of attitude measurement, content analysis, personality study, and even of methodological approaches derived from mathematics and statistics (for example, the "Q-technique" developed by William Stephenson, 1953).

It is no news that the social scientists continue to be concerned with methodology, but it may be news that so much effort is going into the careful re-examination and refinement of methods and techniques and that there is a growth of interchange between academic and applied fields such as psychiatry, social work, education, and industrial relations. Progress in fields like the latter is important to the academic disciplines and vice versa, but in order for this to mean growth and not mere change, it is to be hoped that the interchanges will involve more than symbol-stealing and slogan-waving.

Social scientists face an enormous widening of their audience, once confined to faculty in-groups, docile students, or sect-like adherents of social movements, but now much enlarged to give many a new twist to the question, "How do you know?" It is no longer sufficient to say, "I was there." Instead, the question from a respected audience now asks for a spelling-out of the reply in terms such as these: "I planned to do this study in these ways; I encountered these obstacles, and found these opportunities; I modified my thinking in this manner with these results; this is what I believe went on; here is what I learned; and finally, this is what I suggest it means."

In other words, to the extent that a research project explores new ground, or old territory with new instruments, just to that degree is it desirable today to give a "natural history" of the research project itself, which necessarily includes some account of who the field worker was before he did his work, what he became during it, and who he is, as a result of this learning, at the end of it. Since this is an open-ended process at least to the limits of mortal life, the "natural history" of any project will never be completely written, even with the best will in the world. Yet, if social scientists learn to approach and solve this problem in some way analogous to that in which they have had to face and solve the problem of recording "everything," namely, by selecting explicit priorities, there will be good reason to hope that the study of society will become the science of society.

Below, I have listed sources which helped bring some titles in the author list to my attention. These sources vary greatly in subject, coverage, kind of information given, and choice of subject entry. Bibliographies and references to other literature in these items were made to yield further sources. Even so, I became aware that the selection was quite random, even when it was not clearly idiosyncratic, and I became convinced that bibliographic organization of social science literature is a large task in itself. Some of the difficulties and some of the suggested solutions are discussed in connection with the references in Part II below.

A special source for materials for future development of this bibliography is the Human Relations Area Files ("HRAF") in the libraries of the co-operating universities associated with that project. (See the Preface to George P. Murdock et al., Outline of Cultural Materials in "Behavior Science Outlines," Vol. I [3rd rev. ed., 1950].) An incomplete set of these files was examined in 1952 at the University of Chicago in order to find statements by field workers on "social interaction" methodology and their personal experiences in field work. At that time I found very few items (actually only 5 items out of all those representing 150 processed sources) with the kind of information I was seeking, but the appropriate categories exist in that filing system so that, in due course, if a social scientist publishes information of this sort and if his book or monograph is processed by HRAF, what he has to say about the social processes and personal experiences of field work will be readily available.

Apart from the HRAF system, access to social science literature is so far a rather hit-or-miss proposition. Librarians and bibliographers regularly deal with problems of recording, organizing, locating, and transmitting the records of scholarship in all areas of knowledge. These problems are especially difficult in the social sciences, partly because of the broad scope of the field covered by these disciplines, partly because of their own overlapping, and because of their several systems of interrelations with quite diversified fields not logically, or even historically, except most recently, connected with them. (An example is that of the interconnections of the physical sciences with biology and anthropology due to the successful radiation-dating of fossils and other remains of early man. Further interconnections between field work and applied sciences that might otherwise seem quite distinct are suggested by Rowe in his article, "Technical Aids in Anthropology: A Historical Survey" in A. L. Kroeber (ed.), Anthropology Today [1953], pp. 895-940.)

Faced with such problems, the graduate schools in librarianship are beginning to use some of the methods of social science, and not simply in self-defense. By the use of participant observation and case studies, they are investigating the types of situations in which bibliographic services are being used. The original project from which this book stems was in fact used as "a case study" in a Master's thesis by Miss Dorothy Kittel, of the Graduate Library School of the University of Chicago, "A Case Study in Bibliographic Method in the Social Sciences" (1954). The staff of that project not only benefited from her able collaboration in helping to compile this bibliography, but were also gratified in being able, for once, to act as "subjects" in someone else's study.

The researchers in librarianship are trying to find out how the communication process works within groups and among groups of different levels and with different interests in our society. By analyzing literature into "information units," they hope to develop well-organized descriptive devices for social science and other literature. Classes of these information units can then be identified briefly, coded, and made more easily accessible.[2]

For today's scholar, the flood of literature precludes the possibility of knowing all, or even most, of what is going on in his field—even if it is only one aspect of one discipline within the social sciences. From the librarian-bibliographer's point of view, this dilemma can be partially taken care of by adequate abstracting services, by good bibliographic organization, and by the development of better methods for disseminating information among scholars. Also, of equal importance in our society is the dissemination of the results of the social scientists' investigations and think-

---

2. For further discussion of this work see Margaret E. Egan and Jesse M. Shera, "Foundations of a Theory of Bibliography," Library Quarterly, XXII (1952), 125-37 and Bibliographic Organization edited by Shera and Egan (Chicago: University of Chicago Press, 1951). Growing uses of computers, electronic "memories," etc., are leading to promising advances in this field.

ing to other groups of scholars, to educators and students, to the technicians who do the planning in our society, and to the lay public. By pursuing
investigations along the lines indicated, access to graphic records through
bibliographies should become more adequate and more effective. The information, derived from field work with living people and conceptualized
by social scientists, will increase the individual's knowledge of himself
and of society. Such knowledge should enable the individual in society, and
society as a system of interacting individuals, to select with greater understanding desired goals and means of achieving them.

From the social scientist's point of view, this version of the librarian-
bibliographer's outlook merges with his own. And there is, and can be more
of, a continuous communication process involving the "knowledge-about"
that is found in books and the "knowledge-of-acquaintance" that is gained
by simply living in society, as well as in doing field work.

Suggestions for Further Development of Bibliography

A bibliography may consist simply of author and title listings, or it
may be annotated, or it may offer abstracts of the literature in a given
field such as appear in the periodicals Psychological Abstracts, Sociological Abstracts, and the short-lived Social Science Abstracts (1928-32). Another form is that of the bibliographical review, such as that of Floyd N.
House's article, "The Logic of Sociology," American Journal of Sociology,
XXXII (1926-27).

If bibliographies already do these things, why are we concerned about
further development? What are some of the problems of searching for literature in the social sciences? First of all, any one bibliography will be
found sadly lacking in comprehensiveness. Since there is no single periodical giving author and title listings of all books, periodicals, and pamphlets,
published in the social sciences, the searcher must examine and compile
his own lists from at least Psychological Abstracts, Public Affairs Information Service Bulletin, Education Index, Sociological Abstracts, International
Index, and perhaps others in order to find most of the current literature.
In each source the classificatory headings differ, as do the kinds and
amount of information supplied. For the older literature the social scientist may or may not have access to a library card catalogue, and to the
printed catalogues of the Library of Congress or the British Museum. But
in any library catalogue, only the major aspects of the subject of the book
can be indicated. This means that the searcher, if he wants information on
a somewhat obscure subject, must spend much time going through literature of little or no interest to him.

For the beginner in a social science, some systematic instruction in how to use a library and how to build a bibliography should be as much a part of his training as his practice in field work. The more advanced student may well benefit from opportunities to collaborate with others in the improvement of bibliographic services—librarians, bibliographers, publishers, and distributors of graphic materials, as well as other scholars in his own and other fields. Below are listed some references which may provide an introduction to the problems and possibilities of such collaboration.

Egan, Margaret B., and Shera, J. H. "Foundations of a Theory of Bibliography," Library Quarterly, XXII (April, 1952), 125-37.

Shera, J. H., and Egan, Margaret (eds.). Bibliographic Organization. Papers presented before the Fifteenth Annual Conference of the Graduate Library School. Chicago: University of Chicago Press, 1951.

United Nations Education, Scientific, and Cultural Organization. Library of Congress. Bibliographic Services: Their Present State and Possibilities of Improvement. Prepared by Verner W. Clapp, Washington, 1950.

_____. "Notes on the Development of the Concept of Current Complete National Bibliography," by Katherine C. Murra, in Bibliographic Services, Washington, 1950.

_____. Bibliographical Survey. National Development and International Planning of Bibliographical Services. Paris, 1950.

_____. Meeting on Improvement of Bibliographical Services, Paris, 1950. Delegation from the U. S. Report, by Jesse H. Shera. Chicago: University of Chicago Press, 1951.

University of Chicago. Graduate Library School and the Division of the Social Sciences. "Bibliographic Services in the Social Sciences," Library Quarterly, XX (April, 1950), 79-100.

Bibliographic sources found helpful in surveying the literature on field work are listed below.

Periodical and Serial Publications

Agricultural Economics Research. U. S. Department of Agriculture, Bureau of Agricultural Economics. Quarterly.

American Anthropologist. American Anthropological Association. Bi-monthly.

American Journal of Orthopsychiatry: A Journal of Human Behavior. American Orthopsychiatric Association. Quarterly.

American Journal of Sociology. University of Chicago Press. Bi-monthly.

American Sociological Review. American Sociological Association. Bi-monthly.

Employment Security Review. U. S. Department of Labor, U. S. Employment Service, Bureau of Employment Security. Monthly.

Harvard Business Review. Harvard University, Graduate School of Business Administration. Six times a year.

Human Factor. See Occupational Psychology.

Human Organization. Membership, Society for Applied Anthropology.
Quarterly.

International Journal of Opinion and Attitude Research. (World Association for Public Opinion Research.) Social Sciences, Publisher. Quarterly.

Journal of Abnormal and Social Psychology. American Psychological Association, Inc. Quarterly.

Journal of Applied Anthropology. Now Human Organization, q.v.

Journal of Applied Psychology. American Psychological Association, Inc.
Bi-monthly.

Journal of Applied Sociology. See Sociology and Social Research.

Journal of Consulting Psychology. American Psychological Association,
Inc. Bi-monthly.

Journal of Educational Psychology; devoted primarily to the scientific
study of problems of learning and teaching. Monthly.

Journal of Higher Education. Bureau of Educational Research, Ohio State
University, Columbus, Ohio. Monthly.

Journal of Personnel Research. Now Personnel, q.v.

Journal of Psychology; the general field of Psychology. Quarterly.

Journal of Social Issues. Society for the Psychological Study of Social Issues, 347 Madison Avenue, New York 17. Quarterly.

Journal of Social Psychology; political, racial, and differential psychology.
Quarterly.

Journal of the Royal Statistical Society. London. Quarterly.

Occupational Psychology. National Institute of Industrial Psychology, London. Quarterly.

Oceania; devoted to the study of the native peoples of Australia, New Guinea and the Islands of the Pacific Ocean. Membership. Quarterly.

Personnel. American Management Association. Bi-monthly.

Proceedings of the Academy of Political Science. Academy of Political
Science, Columbia University. Semi-annually.

Psychiatry; journal for the operational statement of interpersonal relations.
Quarterly.

Psychological Bulletin. American Psychological Association, Inc. Bi-
monthly.

Public Opinion Quarterly. Princeton University, Princeton, N. J. Quarterly.

Public Personnel Review: the quarterly journal of the Civil Service Assembly of the U. S. and Canada. Quarterly.

Review of Education Research. American Educational Research Association. Five times a year.

Social Education. National Council for the Social Studies. Monthly.

Social Forces. The University of North Carolina, Chapel Hill, N. C. Quarterly.

Social Science Review. University of Chicago Press. Quarterly.

Social Work Journal. American Association of Social Workers, 130 E. 22d St., New York 10. Quarterly.

Sociological Review. (Institute of Sociology) frequency not given. Le Play House Press, Ledbury, Herefordshire, England. Irregular.

Sociology and Social Research: an international journal. University of Southern California, Los Angeles 7. Bi-monthly.

Sociometry. American Sociological Association. Quarterly.

Sudan Notes and Records. P. T. 50. Finance Dept., Khartoum, Egypt. Irregular.

Teachers College Record. Teachers College, Columbia University, New York 27. Monthly.

    Indexes, Abstracts, etc.

Bibliographic Index. 1937—.
    A listing of bibliographies found in books and periodicals, arranged by subject, issued quarterly by the H. W. Wilson Co., and cumulated into annual volumes.

Bradshaw, F. F. "The Interview: A Bibliography," Journal of Personnel Research, V (July, 1926), 100-103.

Buros, Oscar K. (ed.). Research and Statistical Methodology; Second Yearbook of Research and Statistical Methodology. The first volume covers books, 1933-38, the second covers 1939-40. The arrangement is by subject and the volumes contain excerpts from reviews of the literature.

Columbia University. Bureau of Applied Research. Bibliography of the Literature Concerning the Use of Interviewing in Selected Fields. Prepared under contract with the Human Resources Institute, Air University, Maxwell Air Force Base, Montgomery, Alabama. No date. Dittoed.
    An annotated list of the literature on interviewing arranged by the following subjects: opinion and attitude research; social science research other than opinion and attitude research; social case work; personnel appraisal and selection; legal investigation. Plans have been made for supplementation and revision.

Culver, Dorothy C. Methodology of Social Science Research: A Bibliography. Berkeley: University of California Press, 1936.
    A bibliography of material published in English from 1928-35. Includes bibliographies on: methodology of special fields, sources of materials, collection and analysis of data, including the survey, questionnaire, interview, case study, etc.

Eaton, Allen. A Bibliography of Social Surveys. New York: Russell Sage Foundation, 1930.

Education Index. H. W. Wilson Co.
A monthly index similar to other Wilson publications. The major area covered by this index to periodical literature is, of course, education, but many allied subjects are included.

House, Floyd N. "The Logic of Sociology," American Journal of Sociology, XXXII (1926-27), 271-87.

International Index to Periodicals.
A quarterly index to American and foreign periodicals published by H. W. Wilson. One of the most comprehensive indexes to foreign literature available in the U. S.

Jones, D. Caradog. Social Surveys. London: Hutchinson's University Library, n.d.

Murdock, George P. et al. "Behavior Science Outlines." See especially Vol. I, Outline of Cultural Materials, 3d rev. ed. New Haven: Human Relations Area Files, Inc., 1950.

Psychological Abstracts.
A monthly publication prepared by the American Psychological Association. Almost every item listed is abstracted. There is an annual name and subject index.

Public Affairs Information Service Bulletin.
An indexing service issued by Public Affairs Information Service, Inc., weekly with an annual cumulation. It indexes current books, documents, pamphlets, periodicals in political science, government legislation, economics, sociology, etc.

Social Science Abstracts.
Established in 1928, issued monthly, and discontinued in 1932 because of lack of funds. It dealt with the whole field of the social sciences and covered the whole of social science literature, including foreign as well as American materials.

Sociological Abstracts. 218 E. 12th St., New York 3, New York. Quarterly.

University of Chicago. Committee on Education, Training, and Research in Race Relations. Inventory of Research in Racial and Cultural Relations. Chicago: The Committee.
A periodical list of research projects, completed and in progress, with abstracts describing the research. Arranged alphabetically by author with a comprehensive subject index.

Wirth, Louis (ed.). Eleven Twenty-six: A Decade of Social Science Research. Chicago: University of Chicago Press, 1940.

Young, Pauline V. Scientific Social Surveys and Research. 2d ed. New York: Prentice-Hall, Inc., 1949.

The scholar interested in the long history of man's efforts to understand his social world will certainly wish to add, to all of these suggestions for development of bibliography, The Encyclopedia of the Social Sciences (New York: Macmillan Co., 1933, 1948).

References According to Topics

Code for Classification of References

Classification of each reference in the alphabetical author list is indicated in the left-hand margin of that list for each item. The code used is as follows:

A. Discussions of Field Work in Reports of Field Studies

B. Reports Based upon Field Work

(A selection of articles, monographs, etc., that do not always elaborate on field work experiences or processes)

C. Stages of Field Work

1. Planning

2. Doing

3. Analyzing Results and Publishing (including ethics of reporting)

4. Interdependence of These Phases of Field Work and the Advance of Knowledge in the Social Sciences

D. Methods and Techniques

1. General discussions and texts

2. The survey

3. The questionnaire

4. The interview and interviewing techniques

a) The interview

b) Interviewing and recording (especially phonographic recording)

c) Analysis and evaluation

5. The case study method

6. Participant observation

7. Tests and schedules

8. Research design

E. Not Classified

A. Discussions of Field Work in Reports of Field Studies

Anderson, E. (1937); Anderson, N. (1923); Bakke (1933, 1940); Banfield (1951); Booth (1902-4); Bowen (1954); Carpenter and Katz (1929); Caudill (1958); Chalmers et al. (1954); Chandler (1948); Cottrell (1940); Davis and Dollard (1940); Davis, Gardner, and Gardner (1941); Dollard (1937, 1949); DuBois (1944); Eggan, D. (1952); Ekvall (1939); Embree (1939); Evans-Pritchard (1931, 1937); Fei (1939); Festinger et al. (1956); Fichter (1951, 1954); Firth (1929, 1936); Ford and Stephenson (1954); Fortes and Evans-Pritchard (1948); Frazer (1950); Gillin (1946); Glick (1951); Hall, O. (1944); Hall, S. W. (1939); Hicks (1946); Hogbin (1934); Hollingshead (1949); Hsu (1943); Hughes (1928, 1931, 1943); Hughes et al. (1958); Hunter (1936); Jones, A. W. (1941); Junker (1939); Kellogg (ed.) (1909-14); Kenyatta (1938); Kimball and Pearsall (1954); Lazarsfeld and Thielens (1958); Leighton

(1945); Lewis (1951); Little (1951); Lynd and Lynd (1929, 1937); Malinowski (1930, 1932, 1935, 1938, 1950); Mead, M. (1932, 1949, 1956, 1959); Miller, P. A. (1953); Myrdal (1944); Powdermaker (1939); Radcliffe-Brown (1948); Redfield (1941); Redfield and Villa (1934); Richards (1932); Roethlisberger and Dickson (1943); Rogler (1940); Rosten (1941); Salter (1935); Sanders (1949); Seeley et al. (1956, 1957); Sherman and Henry (1933); Tax (1932); Thomas, D. S., and Nishimoto (1946); Thomas, W. I., and Znaniecki (1918, 1927); Thrasher (1926, 1936); Wagley and Galvai (1949); Walker and Guest (1952); Ware (1935); Warner (1937, 1958); Warner, Junker, and Adams (1941); Warner, Havighurst, and Loeb (1944); Warner et al. (1941, 1942, 1945, 1947, 1959); Webb, S., and Webb, B. (1898); West (1945); Whitehead, T. N. (1935, 1936, 1938); Whyte (1941, 1955); Wilson, G., and Wilson, M. H. (1945); Wilson, M. H. (1951); Wisdom (1940); Zaleznik, Christensen, and Roethlisberger (1958).

B. Reports Based upon Field Work
(A selection of articles, monographs, etc. that do not always elaborate on field work experiences or processes.)

Arensberg (1942); Arensberg and Kimball (1940); Ashton (1952); Barton (1949); Beaglehole, E., and Beaglehole, P. (1941); Beals (1946); Benedict (1934, 1948); Benney (1946); Blumenthal (1932); Booth (1887, 1888); Bowers, A. W. (1950); Burnett (1951); Childs (1943); Elkin, A. P. (1953); Fortes (1949); Fortune (1932); Gersjuritson (1947); Goffman (1959); Goldschmidt (1947); Hall, O. (1946, 1948, 1950, 1951); Hughes, E. C. (1958); Hughes, E. C., and Hughes, H. M. (1952); Hughes, Hughes, and Deutscher (1958); Junker and Loeb (1942); Kittel (1954); Kulp (1925); Lang (1946); Miner (1939); Osgood (1951); Park (1950, 1952, 1954); Parsons (1936); Pierson (1942); Redfield (1930); Saunders (1954); Tax (1951); Warner and Associates (1947); Weslager (1943).

C. Stages of Field Work

1. Planning
   Bain, R. K. (1950)

2. Doing
   Bain, R. K. (1950); DeGraer (1929); Halbwachs (1925, 1949); Trice (1956).

3. Analyzing Results and Publishing (including ethics of reporting)
   Fichter and Kolb (1953); Little (1951); Ogden and Richards (1930).

4. Interdependence of These Phases of Field Work and the Advance of Knowledge in the Social Sciences (see also D-1)

Barnes (1924); Bernard (1919, 1933); Bierstedt (1949); Gee (ed.) (1929); Gillin (ed.) (1954); Hobhouse et al. (1915); Larrabee (1945); Lasswell (1937, 1939); Lee (1951); McLaughlin (1926); Merton (1945, 1947, 1948, 1949, 1957); Murdock et al. (1950); Park (1926); Rignano (1928, 1929); Shils (1948, 1949); Sibley (1951); Simmel (1950); Small, A. W. (1920, 1922, 1924-25); Smith and White (eds.) (1929); Spicer (1946); Useem (1950); Webb, S., and Webb, B. (1898); Von Wiese (1924); Wirth (ed.) (1940); Znaniecki (1925, 1934, 1948, 1952).

D. Methods and Techniques

1. General discussions and texts

Arensberg (1954); Bartlett et al. (eds.) (1939, 1946); Bennett (1942, 1948); Bernard (1934); Blankenship (1946); Bogardus (1924, 1936); Bossard (1950); Bowers, G. A. (1925); Bowers, R. V. (1954); Brunner (1957); Bureau of Applied Social Research (1957); Burgess (1945); Cantril (1944); Carr (1948); Chapin (1920, 1947, 1948); Chapple (1952); Chapple and Coon (1942); Cobb (1934); Cohen and Nagel (1944); Cooley (1930, 1931, 1956); Dobbs

(1947); DuBois (1937); Durkheim (1947, 1950); Eaton (1951); Eby (1950); Ellwood (1907, 1916, 1933); Elmer (1939); Evans-Pritchard (1951); Festinger and Katz (1953); Fry (1934); Gardner and Whyte (1946); Gee (ed.) (1929); Gee (1950); Gillin (ed.) (1954); Goffman (1959); Gold (1954, 1958); Good et al. (1938); Goode and Hatt (1952); Gottschalk et al. (1945); Greenwood (1945); Guilford (1936); Guttman (1944); Hall, O. (1951); Hamalainen (n.d.); Hart, C. W. (1947); Hart, H. (1921); Hatt (1951); Henderson (1894); Hollingshead (1948); House (1926-27, 1929, 1935, 1936); Hughes (1950, 1958); Hughes, E. C., and Hughes, H. M. (1952); Human Organization, Editors of (1949—); Jahoda, Deutsch, and Cook (1951); Kaufmann (1944); Keith (1942); Komarovsky (ed.) (1957); Krech and Crutchfield (1948); Kroeber (ed.) (1953); Larrabee (1945); Lawrence (1950); Lee (1951); Leighton (1945); Lerner (1958); Lewin (1948); Lewis (1951, 1953); Lindzey (ed.) (1954); Linton (ed.) (1945); Linton (1945); Lundberg (1929, 1942); Luszki (ed.) (1958); Mark (1958); Mayer (1941); Mead, G. H. (1934); Mead, M. (1933, 1949, 1952); Mead, M. and Métraux, R. (1953); Merton (1945, 1947, 1948, 1949, 1957); Merton, Broom, and Cottrell (1959); Murdock (1953); Murdock et al. (1950); Nadel (1951); Odum (1929); Ogden and Richards (1930); Palmer (1926, 1928); Park (1950, 1952, 1954); Park and Burgess (1924); Parten (1950); Piper and Ward (1930); Pollack (1952); Radin (1933); Rice (ed.) (1931); Richardson (1952, 1953); Richmond (1917); Ross (1928); Rowe (1953); Ruesch and Bateson (1951); Searles (1948); Sells and Travers (1945); Sewell (1949); Shils (1948, 1949); Sibley (1951); Simmel (1950); Small (1910, 1920); Smith and White (eds.) (1929); Sorokin (1948); Spahr and Swenson (1930); Spicer (1946); Spencer (ed.) (1954); Tarde (1898); Taylor (1948); Thrasher (1926, 1928, 1936); Trice (1956); Useem (1950); Waller (1934); Warner (1936); Warner et al. (1941); Warren (1955); Webb, S., and Webb, B. (1932); White (ed.) (1956); Whitehead, A. N. (1925 and 1948); Whitney (1942 and 1950); Whyte (1941 and 1955, 1959); Von Wiese (1924); Willems (1951); Wilson, M. H. (1948); Wirth (ed.) (1940); Wissler (1932); Wolff (1944, 1945, 1952); Young, K. (1940); Young, P. V. (1949); Znaniecki (1925, 1934, 1948, 1952).

2. The survey

Blumer (1948); Campbell (1946); Deming (1944); Dobbs (1947); Dodd (1944, 1947); Feldman et al. (1951-52); Gosnell and DeGrazia (1942); Houseman (1949); Jones, D. C. (1941, 1949); Katz (1941, 1946); Kellogg (ed.) (1909-14); Kellogg (1912, 1928); Lundberg and Larsen (1949); Park (1928); Shaw and McKaye (1942); Skott (1943); Stouffer et al. (1949); Streib (1952); Stringfellow (1949).

3. The questionnaire

Bain, Reed (1931); Blankenship (1943); Cantril (1944); Carpenter and Katz (1929); Cavan (1933); Elkin, F. (1951); Ellis (1947, 1948); Jenkins (1941); Lazarsfeld (1935); McNemar (1940 and 1946); Parry and Crossley (1950); Payne (1951); Rugg and Cantril (1942); Sletto (1940); Vernon (1939 and 1946).

4. The interview and interviewing techniques

a) The interview

Ackerman and Jahoda (1950); Allport (1935); Anderson, E. (1937); Becker, H. (1949); Bell (1929); Berdie (1943); Bereman (1943); Bevis (1949-50); Bingham and Moore (1941); Birdwhistell (1952); Blackburn (1941); Boder (1949); Bogardus (1924-25, 1925, 1934); Borg (1948); Bossard (1950); Campbell (1946); Caplow (1956); Carr (1930); Cavan (1929); Chapin (1943); Chapple (1953); Clark (1949); Edmiston (1944); Elkin, F. (1951); Ellis (1947, 1948); Fearing (1942); Fenlason (1950, 1952); Franz (1942); Freeman (1944); Garrett (1942, 1951); Gee (1929); Gill et al. (1954); Gorden (1954); Gross and Mason (1953); Guest (1947); Harriman (1935); Hartman (1933); Heneman and Paterson (1949); Hill and Ackiss (1945); Himler (1946); Hyman (1950, 1951); Hyman et al. (1954); International Journal of Opinion and Attitude Research (Symposium, 1948—); Jones, A. W. (1941);

Kahn and Cannell (1957); Katz (1941); Kay and Schick (1945); King (1944); Kinsey et al. (1948, 1953); Krause (1950); Krugman (1956); Lasswell (1937, 1939); Lazarsfeld (1944); Link (1943); Maccoby, E. E., and Maccoby, N. (1954); Marshall (1944); Mead, M. (1949); Merton and Kendall (1946); Merton et al. (1952); Moore (1929); Myrick (1928); Nadel (1939); National Opinion Research Center (NORC) (1945); Oldfield (1941); Otis (1944); Paul (1953); Queen (1928); Reckless and Spelling (1937); Rice (1929); Richmond (1917); Riecken (1956); Riesman and Benney (1956); Riesman and Benney (eds.) (1956); Roethlisberger and Dickson (1943); Rogers (1942, 1945); Rose (1945); Reusch and Bateson (1951); Skott (1943); Smigel (1958); Steiner (1955); Stringfellow (1949); Symonds (1938, 1939); Thompson and Demerath (1952); Udow (1942); Van Kleeck (1926); Wagley and Galvai (1949); Webb, B. (1926); Wechsler, J. (1940); Whyte (1951, 1953); Williams (1945); Wilson, G., and Wilson, M. H. (1945); Womer and Body (1951); Woodside (1945); Woodworth (1925); Young, P. V. (1935).

    <u>b)</u>   Interviewing and recording (especially phonographic recording)

Bevis (1949-50); Boder (1948); Corner (1944); Fisher (1950); Greene (1948); Heard (1950); Womer and Body (1951).

    <u>c)</u>   Analysis and evaluation

Childs (1943); Feldman et al. (1951-52); Hart, C. W. (1948); Lorie and Roberts (1951); Ludeke and Inglis (1942); Ogden and Richards (1930); Sheatsley (1950, 1951); Womer and Body (1951).

5.   The case study method

Allport (1942); Anderson, N. (1923); Blumer (1939); Cavan (1929); Gaw (1943); Gottschalk et al. (1945); Hamalainen (n.d.); Healy (1924); Hillpern et al. (1949); Krueger (1925); Lazarsfeld and Robinson (1940); Maxcy (1942); Shaw (1927); Shaw and McKay (1942); Stouffer (1941); Symonds (1945); Waller (1934); Young, K. (1940).

6.   Participant observation

Argyris (1952); Arrington (1943); Bader (1948); Becker, H. S. (1958); Benney (1946); Eaton and Weil (1951); Kluckhohn, F. (1940); Lindeman (1923); Lohman (1937); Miller, S. M. (1952); Palmer (1926); Schneider (1950); Tarde (1898); Thomas, D. S., et al. (1933).

7.   Tests and schedules

Elkins, F. (1951); Greene (1941); King (1944); Kluckhohn, C., and Rosenzweig (1949); Krech and Crutchfield (1948); McNemar (1940, 1946); Maller (1944); Sletto (1937); Thurstone and Chave (1929); Vernon (1939 and 1946); Wechsler, I. R., and Bernberg (1950).

8.   Research design

Chapin (1947); Green and Mayo (1953); Hart, C. W. (1947); Hobhouse et al. (1915); Hogbin (1934); McCormick and Francis (1958); Sargent and Smith (eds.) (1949); Stephenson (1953).

E. Not Classified

Bosanquet (1906); Dieserud (1908); Egan and Shera (1952); Kittel (1954); Mead, M. (1959); Park (1904); Shera and Egan (eds.) (1951).

Author List

-A-

D-4   Ackerman, N., and Jahoda, M. Antisemitism and Emotional Disor-
      der. New York: Harper & Bros., 1950.

D-5   Allport, Gordon. The Use of Personal Documents in Psychological
      Science. New York: Social Science Research Council, 1942.

D-4   _____. "Attitudes," in A Handbook of Social Psychology, edited by
      Carl Murchison. Worcester, Mass.: Clark University Press,
      1935.

A   Anderson, Elin L. We Americans: A Study of Cleavage in an Amer-
D-4   ican City. Cambridge, Mass.: Harvard University Press, 1937.
         A study of the way groups with different cultural back-
      grounds adjust to old and new loyalties. Methods are discussed
      in Appendix A.

A   Anderson, Nels. The Hobo: The Sociology of the Homeless Man.
D-5   Chicago: University of Chicago Press, 1923.

B   Arensberg, Conrad M. The Irish Countryman. New York: Macmil-
      lan Co., 1942.

D-1   _____. "The Community-Study Method," American Journal of Soci-
      ology, LX (1954), 109-24.
         A critical review of the use of the method, in a special is-
      sue of this journal devoted to the study of the community.

B   Arensberg, Conrad M., and Kimball, S. T. Family and Community
      in Ireland. Cambridge, Mass.: Harvard University Press, 1940.

D-6   Argyris, Chris. An Introduction to Field Theory and Interaction The-
      ory. New Haven: Yale University, Labor and Management Cen-
      ter, 1952.

D-6   Arrington, R. "Time Sampling in Studies of Social Behavior," Psy-
      chological Bulletin, XL (1943), 81.

B   Ashton, Hugh. The Basuto. London: Oxford University Press, 1952.

-B-

D-6   Bader, Carolyn. "Standardized Field Practice," International Jour-
      nal of Opinion and Attitude Research, II (1948), 243-44.

D-3   Bain, Reed. "Stability in Questionnaire Response," American Jour-
      nal of Sociology, XXXVII (1931), 445-60.

C-1   Bain, Robert K. "The Researcher's Role: A Case Study," Human Or-
C-2   ganization, IX (1950), 23-28.

A   Bakke, E. Wight. The Unemployed Man: A Social Study. London:
      Nisbet, 1933.
         The field work for this study was done while living among
      unemployed working-class people in Greenwich, London.

A   _____. Citizens without Work: A Study of the Effects of Unemploy-
      ment upon the Worker's Social Relations and Practices. New

Haven: Yale University Press, for the Institute of Human Relations, 1940.
    A study of readjustment problems faced by unemployed
American workers and their families and the resources which
they bring with them to this task. In the Preface (p. vii), there
is a statement of how the data were obtained: participation, intensive case studies, and interviews.

A   Banfield, Edward C. Government Project. Glencoe, Ill.: Free Press,
        1951.
            At the outset the author states that the approach used in this
        study is what Charles H. Cooley called "the life study method."
        The files of the Farm Security Administration, interview notes
        of another social scientist, and the author's observations and in-
        terviews were the sources for the data.

C-4   Barnes, Harry E. Sociology and Political Theory. New York: Alfred
        A. Knopf, 1924.

D-1   Bartlett, F. C., et al. The Study of Society: Methods and Problems.
        London: Kegan Paul, Trench, Trubner & Co., 1939; 2d ed., 1946.

B   Barton, R. F. The Kalingas: Their Institutions and Custom Law.
        Chicago: University of Chicago Press, 1949.

B   Beaglehole, Ernest, and Beagelhole, Pearl. "Pangai, Village in Ton-
        ga," Memoirs of the Polynesian Society, XVIII. Wellington, New
        Zealand: The Society, 1941.

B   Beals, Ralph L. Cheran: A Sierra Tarasca Village. Smithsonian In-
        stitution, Institute of Social Anthropology Publication No. 2.
        Washington, D.C.: Government Printing Office, 1946.

D-4   Becker, Howard. "The Regimented Man: Interviews with German Of-
        ficials," Social Forces, XXVIII (1949), 19.

D-6   Becker, Howard S. "Problems of Inference and Proof in Participant
        Observation," American Sociological Review, XXIII (1958), 652-
        60.

D-4   Bell, E. P. "Interviewing, Its Principles and Functions," Proceed-
        ings of the American Society of Newspaper Editors, V (1929),
        169-75.

B   Benedict, Ruth. Patterns of Culture. New York: Houghton Mifflin
        Co., 1934; Mentor Book, 1948.

D-1   Bennett, John W. "The Study of Cultures: A Survey of Technique and
        Methodology in Field Work," American Sociological Review, XIII
        (1948), 672-89.

D-1   Bennett, John W., et al. "Food Culture in Southern Illinois—A Pre-
        liminary Report," American Sociological Review, VII (1942),
        645-60.

B   Benney, Mark. Charity Main. London: Allen & Unwin, 1946.
D-6   A study of industrial relations in a British coal field, based
        on researches undertaken by the author in his capacity of Indus-
        trial Relations Officer in the Ministry of Fuel and Power.

D-4   Berdie, R. "Psychological Processes in Interviewing," Journal of

Social Psychology, XVIII (1943), 3-31.

D-4 Bereman, Joel V. "Intensive Non-Directive Interviewing as a Meth-
     od in Social Research," State College of Washington, Research
     Studies, IX (1943), 37-44.

D-1 Bernard, Luther L. The Fields and Methods of Sociology. New
     York: Farrar & Rinehart, 1934.

C-4 _____. "The Objective Viewpoint in Sociology," American Journal of
     Sociology, XXV (1919), 298-325.

C-4 _____. "Sociological Research and the Exceptional Man," in Socio-
     logical Problems and Methods: Papers Presented at the Twenty-
     Seventh Annual Meeting of the American Sociological Society,
     December 28-31, 1932. Chicago: University of Chicago Press,
     1933.

D-4 Bevis, Joseph C. "Interviewing with Tape Recorders," Public Opin-
     ion Quarterly, XIII (1949-50), 629-34.

C-4 Bierstedt, Robert. "A Critique of Empiricism in Sociology," Amer-
     ican Sociological Review, XIV (1949), 584-92.

D-4 Bingham, Walter V., and Moore, Bruce. How To Interview. 3d ed.
     New York: Harper & Bros., 1941.

D-4 Birdwhistell, Ray L. Introduction to Kinesics (An annotation system
     for analysis of body motion and gesture). Washington, D.C.: De-
     partment of State, Foreign Service Institute, 1952.
          Useful in sensitizing observers and interviewers to body
     movements and gestures that have significance for attitude or
     affect.

D-4 Blackburn, Julian. "The Psychology of the Interview," Sociological
     Review, XXXIII (1941), 154-58.

D-3 Blankenship, Albert B. Consumer Opinion and Research: The Ques-
     tionnaire Technique. New York: Harper & Bros., 1943.

D-1 Blankenship, Albert B. (ed.). How To Conduct Consumer and Opinion
     Research. New York: Harper & Bros., 1946.

B   Blumenthal, Albert. Small-Town Stuff. Chicago: University of Chi-
     cago Press, 1932.
          Early example of field work in a small community.

D-5 Blumer, Herbert. An Appraisal of Thomas and Znaniecki's "The
     Polish Peasant in Europe and America": Critiques of Research
     in the Social Sciences, I. New York: Social Science Research
     Council, 1939.

D-2 _____. "Public Opinion and Public Opinion Polling," American Soci-
     ological Review, XIII (1948), 542-49.

D-4 Boder, David P. I Did Not Interview the Dead. Urbana: University
     of Illinois Press, 1949.
          In studying displaced persons in Europe, the author made
     use of the intensive psychological interview, recording it on a
     wire recorder. In the Introduction he reports his methods of
     getting the interviews and of solving language problems.

D-1   Bogardus, Emory S. Introduction to Social Research. University of
      Southern California, School of Research Series, No. 14, Social
      Science Series, No. 17 (1936).

D-1   _____. "What Is Sociology?" Journal of Applied Sociology, IX (1924),
      57-62.

D-1   _____. "The Social Explorer," Journal of Applied Sociology, IX
      (1924), 143-47.

D-4   _____. "Methods of Interviewing," Journal of Applied Sociology, IX
      (1924), 456-67.

D-4   _____. "The Social Research Interview," Journal of Applied Psychol-
      ogy, X (1925), 69-82.

D-4   _____. "Interviewing as a Social Process," Sociology and Social Re-
      search, XXX (1934), 770.

A   Booth, Charles. Life and Labour of the People of London. 16 vols.
      London: Macmillan & Co., 1902-4.

B   _____. "The Inhabitants of Tower Hamlets (School Board Division),
      Their Condition and Occupations," Journal of the Royal Statis-
      tical Society, L (1887), 326-401.

B   _____. "Condition and Occupations of the People of East London and
      Hackney," Journal of the Royal Statistical Society, LI (1888),
      276-399.
          The two JRSS papers contain the first account of Booth's re-
      searches, an explanation of the background and preliminaries of
      his monumental survey, and also a description of the methods
      used.

D-4   Borg, L. "Interviewing School," International Journal of Opinion and
      Attitude Research, II (1948), 393.

E   Bosanquet, Helen D. The Standard of Life and Other Studies. London:
      Macmillan & Co., 1906.
          See also her Bernard Bosanquet (1924).

D-1   Bossard, James H. S. "The Study of Family Life: A Methodological
D-4   Postscript," chapter x in Ritual in Family Living: A Contempo-
      rary Study by James H. S. Bossard and Eleanor S. Boll. Phila-
      delphia: University of Pennsylvania Press, 1950.

A   Bowen, Elenore Smith. Return to Laughter. New York: Harper &
      Bros.; London: Victor Gollancz, Ltd., 1954.

B   Bowers, Alfred W. Mandan Social and Ceremonial Organization.
      Chicago: University of Chicago Press, 1950.

D-1   Bowers, G. A. "Issues in Research Methods," Journal of Personnel
      Research, IV (1925), 155-61.

D-1   Bowers, R. V. "Research Methodology in Sociology: The First Half-
      Century," in Method and Perspective in Anthropology: Papers in
      Honor of Wilson D. Wallis, edited by R. F. Spender. Minneapo-
      lis: University of Minnesota Press, 1954.

D-1   Brunner, E. The Growth of a Science: A Half-Century of Rural Soci-

ological Research in the United States. New York: Harper &
Bros., 1957.

D-1   Bureau of Applied Social Research. Twentieth Anniversary Report:
       Research and Training Program and a Bibliography of Publica-
       tions and Reports. New York: Columbia University, 1957.

D-1   Burgess, Ernest W. "Sociological Research Methods," American
       Journal of Sociology, L (1945), 474-82.

D-1   _____. "Research Methods in Sociology," in Twentieth Century Soci-
       ology, edited by G. Gurvitch and W. E. Moore. New York: Phil-
       osophical Library, 1945.

B   Burnett, Jean. Next Year Country: A Study of Rural Social Organiza-
       tion in Alberta. Toronto: University of Toronto Press, 1951.

-C-

D-4   Campbell, Angus. "Polling, Open Interviewing, and Interpretation,"
       Journal of Social Issues, II (1946), 67-70.

D-2   Campbell, Angus (Issue Editor). "Measuring Public Attitudes," Jour-
       nal of Social Issues, II (1946).

D-1   Cantril, Hadley. Gauging Public Opinion. Princeton: Princeton Uni-
D-3   versity Press, 1944.
            Deals in part with questionnaire construction for opinion
       surveys.

D-4   Caplow, Theodore. "The Dynamics of Information Interviewing,"
       American Journal of Sociology, LXII (1956), 165-71.
            One of a number of articles of interest in this issue which
       is entirely devoted to "The Interview in Social Research."

A   Carpenter, Niles, and Katz, Daniel. "A Study of Acculturization in
D-3   the Polish Group of Buffalo, 1926-1928," University of Buffalo
       Studies, VII, Monographs in Sociology, No. 3 (1929).
            The use of certain questionnaire schedules and the kinds of
       information they would produce are discussed in the section on
       "Objectives and Methods," pp. 103-6. On p. 133 there is a brief
       discussion of the advantages of using a lengthy questionnaire.

D-1   Carr, Lowell J. Situational Analysis: An Observational Approach to
       Introductory Sociology. New York: Harper & Bros., 1948.
            Note that earlier, shorter text is preferable to the later edi-
       tion.

D-4   _____. "Experimentation in Face to Face Interaction," American So-
       ciological Society Publication, XXIV (1930), 174-76.

A   Caudill, William. The Psychiatric Hospital as a Small Society. Cam-
       bridge: Harvard University Press, for the Commonwealth Fund,
       1958.

D-4   Cavan, Ruth S. "Topical Summaries of Current Literature. Interview-
D-5   ing for Life History Materials," American Journal of Sociology,
       XXXV (1929), 100-115.

D-3   _____. "The Questionnaire in a Sociological Research Project,"
       American Journal of Sociology, XXXVIII (1933), 721-27.

A   Chalmers, W. Ellison, et al. Labor-Management Relations in Illini
         City. 2 vols. Champaign: University of Illinois Press, Institute
         of Labor and Industrial Relations, 1954.
             See especially Vol. II, Appendices (on methodology, etc.).

A   Chandler, Margaret K. "Social Organization of Workers in a Room-
         ing House Area." Ph.D. dissertation, Department of Sociology,
         University of Chicago, 1948.

D-1   Chapin, F. Stuart. Field Work and Social Research. New York: Cen-
         tury Co., 1920.

D-1   _____. Experimental Designs in Sociological Research. New York:
D-8   Harper & Bros., 1947.

D-4   _____. "Some Problems in Field Interviews when Using Control
         Group Technique in Studies in the Community," American Soci-
         ological Review, VIII (1943), 63-68.

D-1   _____. "The Main Methods of Sociological Research," Sociology and
         Social Research, XXXIII (1948), 3-5.

D-1   Chapple, Eliot D. "The Training of the Professional Anthropologist:
         Social Anthropology and Applied Anthropology," American An-
         thropologist, LIV (1952), 340-42.
             See also the companion article by Margaret Mead.

D-4   _____. "The Standard Experimental (Stress) Interview as Used in In-
         teraction Chronograph Investigations," Human Organization, XII
         (1953), 23-32.
             This describes a specially designed form of interviewing in-
         tended to produce materials for an "evaluation of the personality"
         of the interviewee, partly by standardizing the conduct of the in-
         terview itself. See also the author's miscellaneous essays as edi-
         tor of Human Organization (Summer, 1951 through Spring, 1956),
         dealing with various problems of field work.

D-1   Chapple, Eliot D., and Coon, Carleton S. Principles of Anthropology.
         New York: Henry Holt & Co., 1942.
             Includes an explicit, systematic statement of the principles
         of social anthropology, as developed since the work of W. Lloyd
         Warner.

B   Childs, I. L. Italian or American? New Haven: Yale University
         Press, 1943.
             A study of second generation males of Italian origin which
         combines participant observation with systematic interviewing.

D-4   _____. "The Use of Interview Data in Qualifying the Individual's Role
         in the Group," Journal of Abnormal and Social Psychology,
         XXXVIII (1943), 305-18.

D-4   Clark, C. "Unsettled Problems," in The Polls and Public Opinion,
         edited by N. C. Meiers and H. W. Saunders. New York: Henry
         Holt & Co., 1949. Iowa Conference on Attitude and Opinion Re-
         search, University of Iowa, 1949.

D-1   Cobb, John C. The Application of Scientific Methods to Sociology.
         Boston: Chapman & Grimes, 1934.

D-1   Cohen, Morris R., and Nagel, Ernest. An Introduction to Logic and

Scientific Method. New York: Harcourt, Brace & Co., 1944.

D-1   Cooley, Charles H. Sociological Theory and Social Research. New
      York: Henry Holt & Co., 1930.
         See chapter v, "A Study of the Early Use of Self-Words by
      a Child," especially "In What Sense Is 'I' a Social Conception?"

D-1   _____. Life and the Student: Roadside Notes on Human Nature, Soci-
      ety and Letters. New York: Alfred A. Knopf, 1931.

D-1   _____. The Two Major Works of Charles H. Cooley: "Social Organi-
      zation" and "Human Nature and the Social Order." With an Intro-
      duction by Robert Cooley Angell. Glencoe, Ill.: Free Press, 1956.

D-4   Corner, B. J. "Studies in Phonographic Recording of Verbal Materi-
      al," Part IV, Journal of Applied Psychology, XXVIII (1944), 89-98.

A   Cottrell, W. Fred. The Railroader. Stanford, Calif.: Stanford Uni-
      versity Press, 1940.
         A description of methods appears in the Preface.

                              -D-

A   Davis, Allison; Gardner, Burleigh B.; and Gardner, Mary R. Deep
      South: A Social Anthropological Study of Caste and Class. Chi-
      cago: University of Chicago Press, 1941.

A   Davis, Allison, and Dollard, John. Children of Bondage: The Person-
      ality Development of Negro Youth in the Urban South. Washing-
      ton: American Council on Education, 1940.
         See especially the authors' notes and "The Subject and Its
      Setting" (pp. xv-xxviii). Also the sections on interviewing tech-
      niques and establishing rapport, pp. 68-72, 99-100, 179-80.

C-2   De Graer, Albert. "L'Art de guérir chez les Azande," Congo, X
      (1929), Part 1, 220-21. Bruxelles: Goemare, 1929.
         This reference is listed to illustrate what may be found on
      field work in Human Relations Area Files: the item describes
      the field worker's use of a role already made legitimate (his
      role as a physician investigating sleeping sickness) to obtain
      professional secrets ("very powerful remedies") from native
      practitioners.

D-2   Deming, W. Edwards. "On Errors in Surveys," American Sociolog-
      ical Review, IX (1944), 359-69.

E   Dieserud, Juul. The Scope and Content of the Science of Anthropol-
      ogy. Historical Review, Library Classification and Select, An-
      notated Bibliography; with a List of the Chief Publications of
      Leading Anthropological Societies and Museums. Chicago: Open
      Court Publishing Co., 1908.
         The Preface is dated December 1, 1906, Library of Congress,
      Washington, D. C. The author's classification has three parts:

                  1: General
            100-1000: Somatology or Physical Anthropology
           1000-4000: Ethnical Anthropology

      and under "General" appears "Methods"—"50: General; 51:
      Measurement (Anthropometry); 55: Instruments; 61: Illustration
      (Photography, etc.); 65: Statistics." There is no explicit mention
      of field work or field observation as such.

D-1 Dobbs, H. A. C. Operational Research and Action Research. New
D-2   York: Institute of Ethnic Affairs, 1947.

D-2 Dodd, S. C. "On Reliability in Polling," Sociometry, VII (1944), 265-
        82.

D-2 _____. "Standards for Surveying Agencies," Public Opinion Quarter-
        ly, XI (1947), 115-30.

A   Dollard, John. Caste and Class in a Southern Town. New Haven:
        Yale University Press, 1937, 2d ed.; New York: Harper & Bros.,
        1949.
            The first three chapters (pp. 1-41) discuss choice of a site
        for a research project, research methods, and the problems of
        bias. The Preface to the Second Edition (1949) contains a state-
        ment bearing upon the ethical problems of reporting: the author
        refers to losing his friends in "Southerntown" when the book was
        first published, but he concludes that publication "had little ef-
        fect on town or people."

A   DuBois, Cora. The People of Alor: A Social-Psychological Study of
        an East Indian Culture. With analyses by Abram Kardiner and
        Emil Oberholzer. Minneapolis: University of Minnesota Press,
        1944.

D-1 _____. "Some Psychological Objectives and Techniques of Ethnogra-
        phy," Journal of Social Psychology, VIII (1937), 285.

D-1 Durkheim, Emile. The Division of Labor in Society. Translated by
        George Simpson. Glencoe, Ill.: Free Press, 1947.
            In the Preface to the first edition Durkheim discusses what
        kinds of information can be obtained by the use of observation
        (pp. 34-38).

D-1 _____. The Rules of Sociological Method. Glencoe, Ill.: Free Press,
        1950.

-E-

D-6 Eaton, Joseph W., and Weil, R. J. "Psychotherapeutic Principles in
        Social Research," Psychiatry, XIV (1951), 439-54.

D-1 _____. "Social Processes of Professional Teamwork," American So-
        ciological Review, XVI (1951), 707-13.

D-1 Eby, Kermit. "Research in Labor Unions," American Journal of So-
        ciology, LVI (1950), 222-29.

D-4 Edmiston, Vivian. "The Group Interview," Journal of Educational
        Research, XXXVII (1944), 593-601.

E   Egan, Margaret B., and Shera, J. H. "Foundations of a Theory of
        Bibliography," Library Quarterly, XXII (1952), 125-37. See
        also Shera & Egan (1951).

A   Eggan, Dorothy. "The Manifest Content of Dreams: A Challenge to
        Social Science," American Anthropologist, LIV (1952), 469-85.
            Provides an example of field worker's using position of Ob-
        server as Participant to get private information. Also deals with
        ethical problems including those of publishing "such intimate
        data."

A   Ekvall, Robert B. Cultural Relations on the Kansu-Tibetan Border. Chicago: University of Chicago Press, 1939.
This book is a kind of autobiographical field report of one who was born more or less as a complete participant, who later returned as a special kind of complete participant, and who finally, in this book, reports, largely from the viewpoint of participant as observer.

B   Elkin, A. P. Social Anthropology in Melanesia: A Review of Research. New York: Oxford University Press, 1953. (Published under the auspices of the South Pacific Commission.)
An invaluable review of research in the large area of Melanesia, this provides a source for references to monographs of the kind every student field worker will find helpful in learning about how to structure one's field work tasks anywhere in the world.

D-3
D-4   Elkin, Frederick. "A Study of the Relationship between Popular Hero Types and Social Class." Ph.D. dissertation, Department of Sociology, University of Chicago, 1951.
D-7

D-3
D-4   Ellis, Albert. "Questionnaire versus Interview Method in the Study of Human Love Relationships," American Sociological Review, XII (1947), 541-53; and XIII (1948), 64-77.

D-1   Ellwood, Charles A. Methods in Sociology. Durham, N. C.: Duke University Press, 1933.

D-1   _____. "Sociology: Its Problems and Its Relations," American Journal of Sociology, XIII (1907), 300.

D-1   _____. "Objectivism in Sociology," American Journal of Sociology, XXII (1916), 289-305.

D-1   Elmer, Manuel C. Social Research. New York: Prentice-Hall, 1939.

A   Embree, John F. Suye Mura: A Japanese Village. Introduction by A. R. Radcliffe-Brown. Chicago: University of Chicago Press, 1939.

A   Evans-Pritchard, E. E. Witchcraft, Oracles and Magic among the Azande. Oxford: Clarendon Press, 1937.

D-1   _____. Social Anthropology. Glencoe, Ill.: Free Press, 1951.

A   _____. "Mani, A Zande Secret Society," Sudan Notes and Records, XIV (1931), 105-48.

-F-

D-4   Fearing, F. "Factors in the Appraisal Interview Considered with Particular Reference to the Selection of Public Personnel," Journal of Psychology, XIX (1942), 131-53.

A   Fei, Hsaio-Tsung. Peasant Life in China. London: Routledge; New York: E. P. Dutton & Co., 1939.

D-2
D-4   Feldman, J. J., et al. "A Field Study of Interviewer Effect on the Quality of Survey Data," Public Opinion Quarterly, XV (1951-52), 734-61.

D-4   Fenlason, Anne F. Essentials in Interviewing for the Interviewer Offering Professional Services. New York: Harper & Bros., 1952.

D-4   Fenlason, Anne F. "Anthropology and the Concepts of Culture,"
      Social Work Journal, XXXI (1950), 178-82.

D-1   Festinger, Leon, and Katz, Daniel (eds.). Research Methods in the
      Behavioral Sciences. New York: Dryden Press, 1953.

A   Festinger, Leon; Riecken, H. W.; and Schacter, S. When Prophecy
      Fails. Minneapolis: University of Minnesota Press, 1956.
            See also article, "The Unidentified Interviewer," by H. W.
      Riecken (1956).

A   Fichter, Joseph H., S.J. Southern Parish. ("Dynamics of a City
      Church," Vol. I.) Chicago: University of Chicago Press, 1951.

A   ____. Social Relations in the Urban Parish. Chicago: University of
      Chicago Press, 1954.

C-3   Fichter, Joseph H., S.J., and Kolb, William L. "Ethical Limitations
      on Sociological Reporting," American Sociological Review, XVIII
      (1953), 544-50.

A   Firth, Raymond. Primitive Economics of the New Zealand Maori.
      New York: E. P. Dutton & Co., 1929.

A   ____. We, the Tikopia. London: Allen & Unwin, 1936.

D-4   Fisher, H. "Interview Bias in the Recording Operation," International
      Journal of Opinion and Attitude Research, IV (1950), 393.

A   Ford, Thomas R., and Stephenson, Diane D. Institutional Nurses:
      Roles, Relationships and Attitudes in Three Alabama Hospitals.
      University: University of Alabama Press, 1954.
            See especially Section II, "The Field Worker, the Hospitals,
      and the Communities," and pp. 15-20 inclusive.

B   Fortes, Meyer. The Web of Kinship among the Tallensi. London:
      Oxford University Press, 1949.

A   Fortes, Meyer, and Evans-Pritchard, E. E. (eds.). African Political
      Systems. London: Oxford University Press, for the International
      Institute of African Languages and Culture, 1948.

B   Fortune, Reo F. Sorcerers of Dobu: The Social Anthropology of the
      Dobu Islanders of the Western Pacific. London: G. Routledge &
      Sons, 1932.

D-4   Franz, J. G. "The Psychodrama and Interviewing," American Soci-
      ological Review, VII (1942), 27-33.

A   Frazer, Sir James G. "Preface" to Argonauts of the Western Pacific
      by Bronislaw Malinowski. New York: E. P. Dutton & Co., 1950.

D-4   Freeman, Graydon. "Using the Interview to Test Stability and Poise,"
      Public Personnel Review, V (1944), 89-94.

D-1   Fry, Charles L. The Technique of Social Investigation. New York:
      Harper & Bros., 1934.

-G-

D-1   Gardner, Burleigh, and Whyte, William F. "Methods for the Study of
      Human Relations in Industry," American Sociological Review,
      XI (1946), 506-12.

D-4   Garrett, Annette. Interviewing: Its Principles and Methods. New
      York: Family Welfare Association of America, 1942.

D-4   _____. "Interviewing and Social Work" in Communications: The So-
      cial Matrix of Psychiatry by Jurgen Ruesch and Gregory Bate-
      son. New York: Norton, 1951.

D-5   Gaw, Esther A. "Case-Study Techniques," Journal of Higher Educa-
      tion, XIV (1943), 37-40, 58.

D-1   Gee, Wilson. Social Science Research Methods. New York: Apple-
      ton-Century-Crofts, Inc., 1950.

D-4   Gee, Wilson (ed.). Research in the Social Sciences: Its Fundamental
D-1   Methods and Objectives. New York: Macmillan Co., 1929.
              Includes articles by Robert E. Park, Clark Wissler, Roscoe
      Pound, John Dewey, Charles A. Beard, and others.

B   Gersjuritson, M. J. Trinidad Village. New York: Alfred A. Knopf,
      1947.

D-4   Gill, M. W., M.D.; Newman, R., M.D.; and Redlich, F. C., M.D. with
      the collaboration of Margaret Sommers, M.D. The Initial Inter-
      view in Psychiatric Practice (Yale University School of Medicine,
      Dept. of Psychiatry). New York: International Universities Press,
      1954.

A   Gillin, John. Moche, a Peruvian Coastal Community. Washington:
      Smithsonian Institution, Institute of Social Anthropology, Publica-
      tion No. 3, 1946.

C-4   Gillin, John (ed.). For a Science of Social Man. New York: Macmil-
D-1   lan Co., 1954.

A   Glick, Ira. "The Study of a Marginal Religious Group." Master's
      thesis, Department of Sociology, University of Chicago, 1951.

B   Goffman, Erving. The Presentation of Self in Everyday Life. Garden
D-1   City, New York: Doubleday & Co., 1959; a Doubleday Anchor Orig-
      inal, A 174.
              See also "Communication Conduct in an Island Community"
      (Ph.D. dissertation, Department of Sociology, University of Chi-
      cago, 1953).

D-1   Gold, Raymond L. "Toward a Social Interaction Methodology for So-
      ciological Field Observation." Ph.D. dissertation, Department
      of Sociology, University of Chicago, 1954.

D-1   _____. "Roles in Sociological Field Observations," Social Forces,
      XXXVI (1958), 217-23.

B   Goldschmidt, Walter. As You Sow. New York: Harcourt, Brace &
      Co., 1947.

D-1   Good, C. V.; Barr, A. S.; and Scates, D. E. The Methodology of Educational Research. New York: D. Appleton-Century, 1938.

D-1   Goode, William J., and Hatt, Paul K. Methods in Social Research.
       New York: McGraw-Hill Book Co., 1952.

D-4   Gorden, Raymond L. "An Interaction Analysis of the Depth-Inter-
       view." Ph.D. dissertation, Department of Sociology, University
       of Chicago, 1954.

D-2   Gosnell, Harold, and DeGrazia, S. "A Critique of Polling Methods,"
       Public Opinion Quarterly, VI (1942), 378.

D-1   Gottschalk, Louis; Kluckhohn, Clyde; and Angell, Robert C. The Use
D-5   of Personal Documents in History, Anthropology, and Sociology.
       New York: Social Science Research Council, 1945.

D-8   Green, J. W., and Mayo, S. C. "A Framework for Research in the
       Actions of Community Groups," Social Forces, XXXI (1953),
       320-27.

D-7   Greene, E. B. Measurements of Human Behavior. New York: Odys-
       sey Press, 1941.

D-4   _____. "New Training Device-Candid Recordings," Employment Se-
       curity Review, XX (1948), 24.

D-1   Greenwood, Ernest. Experimental Sociology: A Study in Method.
       New York: King's Crown Press, 1945.

D-4   Gross, Neal, and Mason, Ward S. "Some Methodological Problems
       of Eight-Hour Interviews," American Journal of Sociology, LIX
       (1953), 197-204.

D-4   Guest, Lester. "A Study of Interviewer Competence," International
       Journal of Opinion and Attitude Research, I (1947), 17-30.

D-1   Guilford, J. P. Psychometric Methods. New York: McGraw-Hill
       Book Co., 1936.

D-1   Guttman, Louis. "A Basis for Scaling Qualitative Data," American
       Sociological Review, IX (1944), 139-50.

-H-

C-2   Halbwachs, Maurice. Les cadres sociaux de la mémoire. Paris:
       Librairie Félix Alcan, 1925.
              Also see his Mémoire et Sociéte (Paris: Presses Universi-
       taires de France, 1949). Concerning what we have called the
       field diary, Halbwachs suggests that it provides "a later conver-
       sation with oneself."

A   Hall, Oswald. "The Informal Organization of Medical Practice in an
       American City." Ph.D. dissertation, Department of Sociology,
       University of Chicago, 1944.

B   _____. "The Informal Organization of the Medical Profession," Ca-
       nadian Journal of Economics and Political Science, XII (1946),
       30-44.

B   _____. "The Stages in a Medical Career," American Journal of Soci-
       ology, LIII (1948), 327-36.

B   ____. "Types of Medical Careers," American Journal of Sociology, LV (1950), 243-53.

B   ____. "Sociological Research in the Field of Medicine: Progress
D-1   and Prospects," American Sociological Review, XVI (1951), 639-44.

A   Hall, S. Warren. Tangier Island: A Study of an Isolated Group. Philadelphia: University of Pennsylvania Press, 1939.

D-1   Hamalainen, A. E. "An Appraisal of Anecdotal Records," Contribu-
D-5   tions to Education, No. 891, Columbia University Teachers College, n.d.
       This reference is intended to call attention to the considerable literature on the use of anecdotal records in education, which can be found in Education Index (H. W. Wilson Co.) and in specialized bibliographies in that field.

D-4   Harriman, P. L. "An Objective Technique for Beginning the Interview with Certain Types of Adults," Journal of Applied Psychology, XIX (1935), 717-24.

D-1   Hart, Clyde W. "Some Factors Affecting the Organization and Pros-
D-8   ecution of Given Research Projects," American Sociological Review, XII (1947), 514-19

D-4   ____. "Bias in Interviewing," Proceedings of the American Philosophical Society, XCII (1948), 399.

D-1   Hart, Hornell. "Science and Sociology," American Journal of Sociology, XXVII (1921), 364-83.
       Outlines five inductive methods for use in sociological research, but asserts the superiority of the statistical method.

D-4   Hartman, G. W. "The Interview as a Research and Teaching Device," Journal of Applied Psychology, XVII (1933), 205-11.

D-1   Hatt, Paul K. Reader in Urban Sociology. Glencoe, Ill.: Free Press, 1951.

D-5   Healy, William A. "The Contribution of Case Study to Sociology," Publications of the American Sociological Society, XVIII (1924), 147-55.

D-4   Heard, Alexander. "Interviewing Southern Politicians," American Political Science Review, XLIV (1950), 886-96.

D-1   Henderson, Charles R. A Catechism for Social Observation: An Analysis of Social Phenomena. Boston: D. C. Heath & Co., 1894.
       Described by Pauline V. Young (1949), p. 24 as "a small book . . . to give essentials and to provide simple techniques of procedure for hosts of untrained investigators—among them civic clubs, women's clubs, churches, commercial bodies, and others determined to study their own communities at first hand." Henderson was one of the charter members of the Department of Sociology at Chicago and was a student of crime, recreation, and cities.

D-4   Heneman, H. G., and Paterson, D. G. "Refusal Rates and Interviewer Quality," International Journal of Opinion and Attitude Research, III (1949), 392-98.

A　　Hicks, Granville. Small Town. New York: Macmillan Co., 1946.

D-4　Hill, Mozell C., and Ackiss, T. D. "The 'Insight Interview' Approach to Race Relations," Journal of Social Psychology, XXI (1945), 197-208.

D-5　Hillpern, Else P.; Hillpern, Edmund P.; and Spaulding, Irving A. Bristow Rogers: American Negro; A Psychoanalytic Case History. New York: Hermitage House, 1949.

D-4　Himler, L. E. "Psychological Aspects of Interviewing," NOMA Forum, XXI (National Office Management Association), (1946), 15-21.

C-4　Hobhouse, L. T.; Wheeler, C. G.; and Ginsberg, M. The Material
D-8　Culture and Social Institutions of the Simpler Peoples. An Essay in Correlation. (The London School of Economics and Political Science. Series of studies in economics and political science, No. 5 of the "Monographs in Sociology.") London: Chapman & Hall, 1915.
　　　　This classic work tested the hypothesis that a society's technology determines the form of its family and political institutions, as well as certain kinds of values, by the comparison of some 650 primitive societies. They found some correlations, but not such complete ones as some theorists might have expected. Their data, however, came from reports based on field work of less than a satisfactory sort. Their method, that of comparison, employs the variety of human societies or cultures as the social scientist's laboratory; it is important as one approach to, or simulation of, experiment in the social sciences.

A　　Hogbin, H. Ian. Law and Order in Polynesia: A Study of Primitive Le-
D-8　gal Institutions. With an Introduction by Bronislaw Malinowski. New York: Harcourt, Brace & Co., 1934.

A　　Hollingshead, A. B. Elmtown's Youth. New York: John Wiley & Sons, 1949.

D-1　_____. "Community Research Development and Present Conditions," American Sociological Review, XIII (1948), 136.

D-1　House, Floyd N. The Range of Social Theory: A Survey of the Development, Literature, Tendencies and Fundamental Problems of the Social Sciences. New York: Henry Holt & Co., 1929.

D-1　_____. The Development of Sociology. New York: McGraw-Hill Book Co., 1936.
　　　　See especially chapter xxxiii, "Sociological Theory and Social Research."

D-1　_____. "The Logic of Sociology," American Journal of Sociology, XXXII (1926-27), 271-87.

D-1　_____. "Viewpoints and Methods in the Study of Race Relations," American Journal of Sociology, XL (1935), 440-52.

D-2　Houseman, E. E. "Design of Samples for Surveys," Agricultural Economics Research, I (1949), 3-10.

A　　Hsu, Francis L. K. Magic and Science in Western Yunan: The Problem of Introducing Scientific Medicine in a Rustic Community.

New York: Institute of Pacific Relations, 1943.

A   Hughes, Everett C. The Growth of an Institution: The Chicago Real
       Estate Board. Chicago: Society for Social Research, 1931.

A   ____. French Canada in Transition. Chicago: University of Chicago
       Press, 1943.

B   ____. Men and Their Work. Glencoe, Ill.: Free Press, 1958.
D-1

A   ____. "A Study of a Secular Institution: The Chicago Real Estate
       Board," Ph.D. dissertation, Department of Anthropology, Univer-
       sity of Chicago, 1928.

D-1   ____. "Institutions," in New Outline of the Principles of Sociology,
       ed. A. M. Lee. 2d ed. rev. New York: Barnes & Noble, Inc.,
       1950.

B   Hughes, Everett C., and Hughes, Helen MacGill. Where Peoples
D-1   Meet: Racial and Ethnic Frontiers. Glencoe, Ill.: Free Press,
       1952.
            See p. 16 for "the anthropological way of working" (that is,
       field work); pp. 131 ff. on sociological field work; p. 139 on so-
       cial rhetoric.

A   Hughes, Everett C.; Hughes, Helen MacGill; and Deutscher, Irwin.
B   Twenty Thousand Nurses Tell Their Story. Philadelphia and
       Montreal: J. B. Lippincott, 1958.

D-1   Human Organization, Editors of. (Formerly, the Journal of the Soci-
       ety for Applied Anthropology.)
            Beginning with the Winter issue of 1949 (VIII, No. 1), there
       have appeared in this journal a series of articles and notes, all
       of interest to field workers, and some especially presented in
       the series, "Field Methods and Techniques," by various authors.
       The editors (C. M. Arensberg, E. D. Chapple, and since summer,
       1956, William F. Whyte) have maintained this interest in their
       editorial pages and have stimulated many debates or discussions
       about field work, particularly on the matters of ethics in the pro-
       fessions concerned. For example, see the issue for Fall, 1951,
       Vol. X, pp. 3-4, "Editorials: Field Work—Anthropology's Indis-
       pensable Approach" and "Developer of the Personality."
            The first of these editorials expresses concern over a tend-
       ency for young anthropologists not to engage in field work or,
       when they do, to take on a kind of summer-tourist approach to
       the field and to believe, thereby, that they have had adequate
       field experience. "Any tendency of workers in anthropology and
       related fields to regard field work as secondary to library re-
       search creates a very great danger for a discipline whose funda-
       mental strength has been based upon the primacy of the field ap-
       proach."
            The second editorial answers the question of "Why should
       one go into anthropology?" with a development of the idea that
       professional anthropology, through field work, helps to develop
       a mature personality as effectively (perhaps even more effec-
       tively) as the analytic sessions in training therapists.

A   Hunter, Monica. Reaction to Conquest. London: H. Milford, 1936.
       (See also under Wilson, Monica Hunter.)

D-4   Hyman, Herbert. "Problems in the Collection of Opinion Research Data," American Journal of Sociology, LV (1950), 362-70.

D-4   _____. "Interviewing as a Scientific Procedure," in The Policy Sciences: Recent Developments in Scope and Method, ed. Daniel Lerner and Harold D. Lasswell. Stanford, Calif.: Stanford University Press, 1951.

D-4   Hyman, Herbert, et al. Interviewing in Social Research. Chicago: University of Chicago Press, 1954.

-I-

D-4   International Journal of Opinion and Attitude Research. "Symposium on Interviewing Problems," II (1948), 68-94; III (1949), 435-46, 587-90; IV (1950), 80-90.

-J-

D-1   Jahoda, Marie; Deutsch, M.; and Cook, S. W. Research Methods in Social Relations. New York: Dryden Press, 1951.

D-3   Jenkins, J. "Characteristics of the Questionnaire as Determinants of Dependability," Journal of Consulting Psychology, V (1941), 164.

A
D-4   Jones, Alfred W. Life, Liberty, and Property: A Study of Conflict and a Measurement of Conflicting Rights. New York: J. B. Lippincott & Co., 1941.

D-2   Jones, D. Caradog. Social Surveys. London: Hutchinson's University Library, 1949.

D-2   _____. "Evolution of the Social Survey in England since Booth," American Journal of Sociology, XLVI (1941), 818-25.

A   Junker, Buford H. "Methods for the Study of Personality in Negro Society, Part I. Negro Personality in the Social Context." Proceedings, Third Biennial Meeting of the Society for Research in Child Development. Washington, D. C.: National Research Council, 1939.
        A research paper on the study later published in the book, Color and Human Nature (1941), by W. L. Warner, Buford H. Junker, and W. A. Adams.

B   Junker, Buford H., and Loeb, Martin B. "The School and the Social Structure in a Midwestern Community," School Review, L (1942).
        A paper reflecting some of the field work in "Hometown" later incorporated in the book, Who Shall Be Educated? (1944), by W. L. Warner, R. J. Havighurst, and M. B. Loeb, and other publications.

-K-

D-4   Kahn, Robert L., and Cannell, Charles F. The Dynamics of Interviewing: Theory, Technique, and Cases. New York: John Wiley & Sons, Inc., 1957.

D-2
D-4   Katz, Daniel. "The Effect of Social Status or Membership Character of the Interviewer upon His Findings," Psychological Bulletin, XXXVIII (1941), 540.

D-2 _____. "Survey Technique and Polling Procedures as Methods in Social Science," Journal of Social Issues, II (1946), 62-66.

D-1 Kaufmann, Felix. Methodology of the Social Sciences. New York:
Oxford University Press, 1944.

D-4 Kay, L. W., and Schick, J. H. "Role Practice in Training Depth Interviewers," Sociometry, VIII (1945), 82-85.

D-1 Keith, George. "Research—A Tool of the Administrator," Social
Service Review, XVI (1942), 641-49.

D-2 Kellogg, Paul U. "The Spread of the Survey Idea," in Academy of
Political Science, Organization for Social Work. Proceedings,
II (1912), 475-91.

A   Kellogg, Paul U. (ed.). The Pittsburgh Survey. 6 vols. New York:
D-2   Russell Sage Foundation, 1909-14.
        Includes description of the methods of this "first" among
social surveys in the United States. For family life in Homestead, see the volume by Margaret F. Byington, Homestead: The
Households of a Mill Town (1910).

D-2 Kellogg, Paul U., and Deardorff, S. "Social Research as Applied to
Community Progress," First International Conference of Social
Work, Proceedings. Paris, 1928.

A   Kenyatta, Jomo. Facing Mount Kenya: The Tribal Life of the Gikuyu.
With an Introduction by Bronislaw Malinowski. London: Secker
& Warburg, 1938.
        Malinowski's introduction points out that the idea of a "na-
tive anthropologist" was strongly resisted in some scientific
circles.

A   Kimball, S. T., and Pearsall, Marion. The Talledega Story: A Study
in Community Process. University: University of Alabama
Press, 1954.
        Includes, as Appendix A, Kimball's "Some Methodological
Problems of the Community Self-Survey."

D-4 King, Morton, B. "Reliability of the Idea-Centered Question in Inter-
D-7   view Schedules," American Sociological Review, IX (1944), 57-64.

D-4 Kinsey, Alfred C., et al. Sexual Behavior in the Human Male. Philadelphia: W. B. Saunders Co., 1948.

D-4 _____. Sexual Behavior in the Human Female. Philadelphia: W. B.
Saunders Co., 1953.

B   Kittel, Dorothy. "A Case Study in Bibliographic Method in the Social
Sciences." Master's thesis, Graduate Library School, University of Chicago, 1954.

D-7 Kluckhohn, Clyde, and Rosenzweig, J. C. "Two Navajo Children over
a Five-Year Period," American Journal of Orthopsychiatry, XIX
(1949), 266-78.

D-6 Kluckhohn, Florence R. "The Participant-Observer Technique in
Small Communities," American Journal of Sociology, XLVI
(1940), 331-43.

D-1   Komarovsky, Mirra (ed.). Common Frontiers of the Social Sciences.
       Glencoe, Ill.: Free Press, 1957.

D-4   Krause, Luise. "Problems of Interviewing with Older People," in
       "Personal Adjustment in Old Age," by John Hair, et al. Joint
       Master's thesis, Department of Sociology, University of Chicago,
       1950.

D-1   Krech, David, and Crutchfield, R. S. Theory and Problems of Social
D-7   Psychology. New York: McGraw-Hill Book Co., 1948.

D-1   Kroeber, A. L. (ed.). Anthropology Today: An Encyclopedic Inven-
       tory. Chicago: University of Chicago Press, 1953.

D-5   Krueger, B. T. "Technique of Securing Life History Documents,"
       Journal of Applied Sociology, IX (1925), 290-98.

D-4   Krugman, Herbert E. "Interviewing Ex-Communists in the United
       States," Public Opinion Quarterly, XX (1956), 473-77.

B   Kulp, Daniel H., II. Country Life in South China: The Sociology of
       Familism. Vol. I, "Phenix Village, Kwantung, China." New
       York: Teachers College, Columbia University, 1925.

                                 -L-

B   Lang, Olga. Chinese Family and Society. New Haven: Yale Univer-
       sity Press, 1946.

C-4   Larrabee, Harold A. Reliable Knowledge. Boston: Houghton Mifflin
D-1   Co., 1945.

C-4   Lasswell, Harold D. "The Method of Overlapping Observation in the
D-4   Study of Personality and Culture," Journal of Abnormal and So-
       cial Psychology, XXXII (1937), 240-43.

C-4   _____. "The Contribution of Freud's Insight Interview to the Social
D-4   Sciences," American Journal of Sociology, XLV (1939), 375-90.

D-1   Lawrence, Paul. Interaction Process Analysis: A Method for the
       Study of Small Groups. Cambridge, Mass.: Addison-Wesley Pub-
       lishing Co., Inc., 1950.

D-3   Lazarsfeld, Paul F. "The Art of Asking Why," National Marketing,
       I (1935), 1.

D-4   _____. "The Controversy over Detailed Interviews—An Offer for Ne-
       gotiation," Public Opinion Quarterly, VIII (1944), 38-60.

D-5   Lazarsfeld, Paul F., and Robinson, W. S. "The Quantification of Case
       Studies," Journal of Applied Psychology, XXIV (1940), 817-25.

A   Lazarsfeld, Paul F., and Thielens, Wagner, Jr. The Academic Mind:
       Social Scientists in a Time of Crisis. With a Field Report by
       David Riesman. Glencoe, Ill.: Free Press, 1958.

C-4   Lee, Alfred McClung. "Individual and Organizational Research in So-
D-1   ciology," American Sociological Review, XVI (1951), 701-7.

A   Leighton, Alexander H. The Governing of Men: General Principles
D-1   and Recommendations Based on Experiences at a Japanese Relo-

cation Camp. Princeton, N. J.: Princeton University Press, 1945.

D-1 Lerner, Daniel. "Attitude Research in Modernizing Areas," Public Opinion Quarterly, XXII (1958). Special Issue.
A round-up of public opinion research, including discussion of "Research Experiences, Problems, Methods," in areas and nations undergoing economic and cultural change. Problems for future exploratory study which are more sociological and anthropological than matters of "public opinion measurement" are stressed.

D-1 Lewin, Kurt. "Action Research," in Resolving Social Conflicts: Selected Papers on Group Dynamics, ed. G. W. Lewin. New York: Harper & Bros., 1948.

A   Lewis, Oscar. Life in a Mexican Village: Tepotzlan Restudied. Urbana: University of Illinois Press, 1951.
D-1

D-1 ———. "Controls and Experiments in Field Work," in Anthropology Today, ed. A. L. Kroeber. Chicago: University of Chicago Press, 1953.

D-6 Lindeman, Edward C. Social Discovery. New York: Republic Press, 1923.

D-1 Lindzey, Gardner (ed.). Handbook of Social Psychology. 2 vols. Cambridge, Mass.: Addison-Wesley Publishing Co., 1954.

D-4 Link, H. "An Experiment in Depth Interviewing," Public Opinion Quarterly, VII (1943), 267.

D-1 Linton, Ralph. The Cultural Backgrounds of Personality. New York: Appleton-Century Co., 1945.

D-1 Linton, Ralph (ed.). The Science of Man in the World Crisis. New York: Columbia University Press, 1945.

A   Little, Kenneth L. The Mende of Sierra Leone: A West African People in Transition. London: Routledge & Kegan Paul, Ltd., 1951.
C-3
See pp. 11-16 especially for evaluations of information ("secrets," etc.) and ethics of reporting.

D-6 Lohman, Joseph D. "The Participant Observer in Community Studies," American Sociological Review, II (1937), 890-97.

D-4 Lorie, J. H., and Roberts, H. V. Basic Methods of Marketing Research. New York: McGraw-Hill Book Co., 1951.
See especially Part IV, "Communication and Observation."

D-4 Ludeke, H., and Inglis, R. "A Technique for Validating Interview Methods," Sociometry, V (1942), 109.

D-1 Lundberg, George A. A Study in Methods of Gathering Data. New York: Longmans, Green, 1929.
See especially chapter titled, "Field Work: The Interview and the Social Survey."

D-1 ———. Social Research. New York: Longmans, Green, 1942.

D-2 Lundberg, George A., and Larsen, O. N. "Characteristics of Hard-

to-Reach Individuals in Field Surveys," Public Opinion Quarterly, XIII (1949), 487-94.

D-1 Luszki, Margaret Barron (ed.). Interdisciplinary Team Research:
Methods and Problems. New York: New York University Press,
1958.

A   Lynd, R. S., and Lynd, H. M. Middletown. New York: Harcourt,
Brace & Co., 1929.

A   _____. Middletown in Transition. New York: Harcourt, Brace & Co.,
1937.
A further study of the community described in Middletown
(1929). For a discussion of the problems encountered in returning to a community where publication of the earlier findings was
received with much resentment, see the preface, pp. xi-xiii.

-M-

D-4 Maccoby, Eleanor E., and Maccoby, Nathan. "The Interview: A Tool of
Social Science," in Handbook of Social Psychology, ed. G. Lindzey. Cambridge, Mass.: Addison-Wesley Publishing Co., 1954.

A   Malinowski, Bronislaw. Coral Gardens and Their Magic: A Study of
the Methods of Tilling the Soil and of Agricultural Rites in the
Trobriand Islands. 2 vols. London: Allen & Unwin, 1935.

A   _____. Argonauts of the Western Pacific. With a Preface by Sir
James G. Frazer. New York: E. P. Dutton & Co.; London: Routledge & Kegan Paul, 1950.

A   _____. "The Problem of Meaning in Primitive Languages," Supplement I in The Meaning of Meaning, by C. K. Ogden and I. A. Richards. 3d rev. ed. New York: Harcourt, Brace & Co., 1930. 10th
ed. London: Routledge & Kegan Paul, 1953.

A   _____. "Preface" to The Sorcerers of Dobu by Reo Fortune. London:
G. Routledge & Sons, 1932.

A   _____. "Preface" to Facing Mount Kenya by Jomo Kenyatta. London:
Secker & Warburg, 1938.

D-7 Maller, J. B. "Personality Tests," in Personality and the Mental
Disorders, ed. J. McV. Hunt. New York: Ronald Press, 1944.

D-1 Mark, Mary Louise. Statistics in the Making: A Primer in Statistical
Survey Method. Columbus, O.: Bureau of Business Research, College Commerce and Administration, Ohio State University, 1958.

D-4 Marshall, S. L. A. Island Victory. Washington, D. C. and New York:
The Infantry Journal and Penguin Books, 1944.
See the appendix, "Conducting the Interview after Combat."

D-5 Maxcy, Ellis C. "Understanding People in Work Relationships," Personnel, XVIII (1942), 371-76.

D-1 Mayer, Joseph. Social Science Principles in the Light of Scientific
Method: With Particular Application to Modern Economic
Thought. Durham, N. C.: Duke University Press, 1941.

D-8 McCormick, Thomas C., and Francis, Roy G. Methods of Research

in the Behavioral Sciences. New York: Harper & Bros., 1958.
Pays most attention to problems of interest to sociologists
(survey-research design, sampling, measurement, etc.).

C-4   McLaughlin, Isabella C. "History and Sociology: A Comparison of
Their Methods," American Journal of Sociology, XXXII (1926),
379-95.
Discusses the relation of cultural anthropology to sociology.

D-3   McNemar, Quinn. "Opinion-Attitude Methodology," Psychological
D-7   Bulletin, XXXVII (1940), 331-68; also XLIII (1946), 289-374.

D-1   Mead, George Herbert. Mind, Self, and Society from the Standpoint
of a Social Behaviorist. Ed. Charles W. Morris. Chicago: University of Chicago Press, 1934.

A   Mead, Margaret. The Changing Culture of an Indian Tribe. With a
Foreword by Clark Wissler. New York: Columbia University
Press, 1932.

A   _____. Male and Female: A Study of the Sexes in a Changing World.
D-1   New York: William Morrow & Co., 1949.

A   _____. New Lives for Old: Cultural Transformation—Manus, 1928-
1953. New York: William Morrow & Co., 1956.

A   _____. An Anthropologist at Work: Writings of Ruth Benedict. Boston: Houghton Mifflin Co., 1959.

D-1   _____. "More Comprehensive Field Methods," American Anthropologist, XXXV (1933), 1-15.

D-4   _____. "The Mountain Arapesh: The Record of Unabelin with Ror-
schach Analysis," Anthropological Papers of the American Museum of Natural History, Vol. XLI, Part III (1949).
Exemplifies the use of interviews of long duration.

D-1   _____. "The Training of the Cultural Anthropologist," American Anthropologist, LIV (1952), 343-46.

D-1   Mead, Margaret, and Métraux, Rhoda (eds.). The Study of Culture at
a Distance. Chicago: University of Chicago Press, 1953.

C-4   Merton, Robert K. Social Theory and Social Structure. Glencoe, Ill.:
D-1   Free Press, 1949; rev. ed., 1957.
This book reflects development of two sociological concerns:
first, that with the interplay of social theory and social research,
and second, the concern with progressively codifying both sub-
stantive theory and the procedures of sociological analysis, most
particularly of qualitative analysis.

C-4   _____. "Sociological Theory," American Journal of Sociology, L
D-1   (1945), 462-73.
The phrase "sociological theory" has been used to refer to
at least six types of analysis which differ significantly in their
bearings upon empirical research. These are methodology, general orientations, conceptual analysis, post factum interpretations, empirical generalizations, and sociological theory. The
distinctive limits and functions of each are described and illustrated. A typical case of the incorporation of an empirical generalization into a theoretic system is considered. The conven-

tions of formal derivation and codification are suggested as devices for aiding the integration of theory and empirical research.

C-4 Merton, Robert K. "Selected Problems of Field Work in the Planned
D-1   Community," American Sociological Review, XII (1947), 304-12.

C-4 _____. "The Bearing of Empirical Research upon the Development of
D-1   Social Theory,"American Sociological Review, XIII (1948), 505-
         15. Reprinted in his Social Theory and Social Structure (1949).

D-1 Merton, Robert K.; Broom, Leonard; and Cottrell, Leonard S., Jr.
     (eds.). Sociology Today—Problems and Prospects. New York:
     Basic Books, Inc., 1959.

D-4 Merton, Robert K.; Fiske, Marjorie; and Kendall, Patricia. The Fo-
     cused Interview: A Manual. 2d ed. New York: Bureau of Ap-
     plied Social Research, Columbia University, 1952.

D-4 Merton, Robert K., and Kendall, Patricia L. "The Focused Inter-
     view," American Journal of Sociology, LI (1946), 541-57.

A   Miller, Paul A. Community Health Action: A Study of Community
     Contrast. East Lansing: Michigan State College Press, 1953.

D-6 Miller, S. M. "The Participant Observer and 'Over-Rapport,'"
     American Sociological Review, XVIII (1952), 97-99.

B   Miner, Horace. Saint Denis: A French Canadian Parish. Chicago:
     University of Chicago Press, 1939.·

D-4 Moore, B. V. "The Interview in Industrial Social Research," Social
     Forces, VII (1929), 445-52.

C-4 Murdock, George P., et al. Outline of Cultural Materials ("Behavior
D-1   Science Outlines," Vol. I). 3d rev. ed. New Haven: Human Rela-
         tions Area Files, Inc., 1950.

D-1 Murdock, George P. "The Processing of Anthropological Materials,"
     in Anthropology Today, ed. A. L. Kroeber. Chicago: University
     of Chicago Press, 1953.

A   Myrdal, Gunnar. An American Dilemma. 2 vols. New York: Harper
     & Bros., 1944.
         A comprehensive study of the Negro in American society
     sponsored by the Carnegie Corporation. There is extensive doc-
     umentation and a methodological note on the "art" of interpreting
     data. See also Vol. II, pp. 1043-44 for the often-quoted sentence
     in the section on "Value Premises": ". . . there is no other de-
     vice for excluding biases in the social sciences than to face the
     evaluations and introduce them as explicitly stated, specific, and
     sufficiently concretised value premises. If this is done it will be
     possible to determine in a rational way, and openly account for,
     the direction of theoretical research."

D-4 Myrick, H. L. "The Non-Verbal Elements in the Interview," Social
     Forces, VII (1928), 561.

-N-

D-1 Nadel, S. F. The Foundations of Social Anthropology. Glencoe, Ill.:
     Free Press, 1951.

SELECTED BIBLIOGRAPHY

D-4 _____. "The Interview Technique in Social Anthropology," in The Study of Society, ed. F. C. Bartlett et al. London: Kegan Paul, Trench, Trubner, & Co., 1939.

D-4 National Opinion Research Center. Interviewing for NORC. Denver: NORC, 1945; rev. ed., 1947.

-O-

D-1 Odum, Howard. An Introduction to Social Research. New York: Henry Holt & Co., 1929.

C-3 Ogden, C. K., and Richards, I. A. The Meaning of Meaning. 3d rev.
D-1 ed. New York: Harcourt, Brace & Co., 1930.
D-4

D-4 Oldfield, R. C. The Psychology of the Interview. London: Methuen & Co., Ltd., 1941.

B Osgood, Cornelius. The Koreans and Their Culture. New York: Ronald Press, 1951.

D-4 Otis, Jay L. "The Improvement of Employment Interviewing," Journal of Consulting Psychology, VIII (1944), 64-69.

-P-

D-1 Palmer, Vivien. Field Studies in Sociology: A Student's Manual. Chicago: University of Chicago Press, 1928.

D-1 _____. "Field Studies for Introductory Sociology: An Experiment,"
D-6 Journal of Applied Sociology, X (1926), 341-48.

E Park, Robert E. Masse und Publikum, eine methodologische und soziologische Untersuchung. Bern: Lack & Grunau, 1904.

B _____. (Collected Papers) Race and Culture (1950). Human Commu-
D-1 nities: The City and Human Ecology (1952). Society (1954). Glencoe, Ill.: Free Press.
In the volume, Society (1954), see especially chapter vii, "News as a Form of Knowledge," and chapter ix, "News and the Human Interest Story," the latter being the Introduction, by Park, to Helen MacGill Hughes, News and the Human Interest Story (Chicago: University of Chicago Press, 1940).

C-4 _____. "The Concept of Position in Sociology," Publications of the American Sociological Society, XX (1926), 1-14.

D-2 _____. "Roundtable on the Technique of the Social Survey," Publications of the American Sociological Society, XXII (1928), 223-25.

D-1 Park, Robert E., and Burgess, Ernest W. Introduction to the Science of Sociology. 2d ed. Chicago: University of Chicago Press, 1924.
A systematic treatise containing excerpts from a wide range of sources. Each chapter is divided into four sections: the introduction, the readings, investigations and problems, and a selected bibliography. For many students, a landmark in the history of sociology.

D-3 Parry, H. J., and Crossley, H. M. "Validity of Responses to Survey Questions," Public Opinion Quarterly, XXII (1950), 60.

B   Parsons, Elsie C. Mitla, Town of Souls, and Other Zapoteco-speak-
         ing Pueblos of Oaxaca, Mexico. Chicago: University of Chicago
         Press, 1936.

D-1   Parten, Mildred Bernice. Surveys, Polls, and Samples. New York:
         Harper & Bros., 1950.

D-4   Paul, Benjamin D. "Interview Techniques and Field Relationships,"
         in Anthropology Today, ed. A. L. Kroeber. Chicago: University
         of Chicago Press, 1953.

D-3   Payne, S. L. The Art of Asking Questions. Princeton, N. J.: Prince-
         ton University Press, 1951.

B   Pierson, Donald. Negroes in Brazil: A Study of Race Contact at
         Bahia. Chicago: University of Chicago Press, 1942.

D-1   Piper, Raymond F., and Ward, R. F. The Fields and Methods of
         Knowledge. New York: F. S. Crofts & Co., 1930.

D-1   Pollack, Otto. Social Science and Psychotherapy for Children. New
         York: Russell Sage Foundation, 1952.
             A study concerned specifically with the possible contribu-
         tions of the behavioral sciences to practice in a psychoanalyti-
         cally oriented child guidance clinic, but of importance to the
         wider applications of social science disciplines.

A   Powdermaker, Hortense. After Freedom: A Cultural Study of the
         Deep South. New York: Viking Press, 1939.

-Q-

D-4   Queen, Stuart. "Social Interaction in the Interview," Social Forces,
         VI (1928), 545.

-R-

A   Radcliffe-Brown, A. R. The Andaman Islanders: A Study in Social
         Anthropology. Glencoe, Ill.: Free Press, 1948.

D-1   Radin, Paul. The Method and Theory of Ethnology. New York:
         McGraw-Hill Book Co., 1933.

D-4   Reckless, Walter, and Spelling, L. "A Sociological and Psychiatric
         Interview Compared," American Journal of Orthopsychiatry, VII
         (1937), 532.

B   Redfield, Robert. Tepotzlán, a Mexican Village: A Study of Folk Life.
         Chicago: University of Chicago Press, 1930.

A   _____. The Folk Culture of Yucatan. Chicago: University of Chicago
         Press, 1941.

A   Redfield, Robert, and Villa, R. A. Chan Kom: A Maya Village. Wash-
         ington, D. C.: Carnegie Institution of Washington, 1934.
             Appendix A consists of a journal written by R. A. Villa, and
         the Preface contains an account of the field work, especially of
         the manner in which the collaboration of this local "natural ob-
         server" was obtained.

D-4   Rice, Stuart A. "Contagious Bias in the Interview," American Journal of Sociology, XXXV (1929), 420-23.

D-1 Rice, Stuart A. (ed.). Methods in Social Science: A Case Book. (Social Science Research Council, Committee on Scientific Method
in the Social Sciences.) Chicago: University of Chicago Press,
1931.
A series of interpretations of the scientific methods employed by authors of significant contributions to the social sciences.

A   Richards, Audrey I. Hunger and Work in a Savage Tribe: A Functional Study of Nutrition among the Southern Bantu. With a Preface by Professor B. Malinowski. London: George Routledge &
Sons, Ltd., 1932.

D-1 Richardson, Stephen A. "Training in Field Relations Skills," Journal of Social Issues, VIII (1952), 43-50.

D-1 _____. "A Framework for Reporting Field Relations Experiences,"
Human Organization, XII (1953), 31-37.

D-1 Richmond, Mary E. Social Diagnosis. New York: Russell Sage Foun-
D-4 dation, 1917.
Although this book was written primarily for social workers,
it contains observations on the interview as a process of a developing relationship between participants involving a continuous
and reciprocal interaction, and other ideas that can be useful to
the field worker.

D-4 Riecken, Henry W. "The Unidentified Interviewer," American Journal of Sociology, LXII (1956), 210-12.
An account of the kind of complete participant role adopted
by the authors of Festinger et al., When Prophecy Fails (1956).

D-4 Riesman, David, and Benney, Mark. "The Sociology of the Interview,"
Midwest Sociologist, XVIII (1956), 3-15.

D-4 _____ (eds. in charge). "The Interview in Social Research," American Journal of Sociology, LXII (1956), 137-252. Entire issue devoted to this topic.

C-4 Rignano, Eugenio. "Sociology, Its Methods and Laws." Translated
by Howard Becker. American Journal of Sociology, XXXIV
(1928), 429-50; (1929), 605-22.
Static sociology studies the social and economic organization of society, dynamic sociology, its progress and evolution.
There are three methods of research: pure observation, experimentation, and comparison. Sociology depends on the organic
and inorganic sciences.

A   Roethlisberger, F. J., and Dickson, W. J. Management and the
D-4 Worker. Cambridge: Harvard University Press, 1943.

D-4 Rogers, Carl R. Counseling and Psychotherapy. Boston: Houghton
Mifflin, 1942.
Also see his earlier work, The Clinical Treatment of the
Problem Child (Boston: Houghton Mifflin, 1939).

D-4 _____. "The Nondirective Method as a Technique for Social Research," American Journal of Sociology, L (1945), 279-83.

A   Rogler, Charles C. Comerio: A Study of a Puerto Rican Town.
        Lawrence: University of Kansas Press, 1940.

D-4   Rose, Arnold M. "A Research Note on Experimentation in Interview-
        ing," American Journal of Sociology, LI (1945), 143-44.

D-1   Ross, E. A. World Adrift. New York: Century Co., 1928.
        See pp. 149-73 for "Getting at Significant Social Situations
        in Foreign Countries."

A   Rosten, Leo C. Hollywood: The Movie Colony, the Movie Makers.
        New York: Harcourt, Brace & Co., 1941.
        A sociological study of the manners and mores of Hollywood
        and of the movie producers, actors, directors, and writers. The
        preface and appendices give methodological notes. See especially
        Appendix B for a statement of the difficulties of getting answers
        to questionnaires and the kinds of information people will report.

D-1   Rowe, John Howland. "Technical Aids in Anthropology: A Historical
        Survey," in Anthropology Today, ed. A. L. Kroeber. Chicago:
        University of Chicago Press, 1953.

D-1   Ruesch, Jurgen, and Bateson, Gregory. Communications, the Social
D-4   Matrix of Psychiatry. New York: W. W. Norton & Co., 1951.

D-3   Rugg, D., and Cantrill, H. "The Wording of Questions in Public Opin-
        ion Polls," Journal of Abnormal and Social Psychology, XXXVII
        (1942), 469.

                                -S-

A   Salter, J. T. Boss Rule: Portraits in City Politics. New York:
        McGraw-Hill Book Co., 1935.

A   Sanders, Irwin T. Balkan Village. Lexington: University of Ken-
        tucky Press, 1949.

D-8   Sargent, S. S., and Smith, M. W. (eds.). Culture and Personality.
        New York: Libertarian Press, 1949.

B   Saunders, Lyle. Cultural Differences and Medical Care. New York:
        Russell Sage Foundation, 1954.

D-6   Schneider, Eugene V. "Limitations on Observation in Industrial So-
        ciology," Social Forces, XXVIII (1950), 279-84.

D-1   Searles, Herbert L. Logic and Scientific Method. New York: Ronald
        Press, 1948.

A   Seeley, John R.; Sim, R. A.; and Loosley, H. W. Crestwood Heights:
        A Study of the Culture of Suburban Life. New York: Basic Books,
        Inc., 1956.

A   Seeley, John R., et al. Community Chest: A Case Study in Philanthro-
        py. Toronto: University of Toronto Press, 1957.

D-1   Sells, Saul B., and Travers, R. M. W. "Observational Methods of Re-
        search," Review of Educational Research, XL (1945), 394-407.

D-1   Sewell, William K. "Field Techniques in Social Psychological Study
        in a Rural Community," American Sociological Review, XIII

(1949), 718-26.

D-5   Shaw, Clifford R. "The Case Study Method," Publications of the
      American Sociological Society, XXI (1927), 149-57.

D-2   Shaw, Clifford R., and McKay, Henry D. Juvenile Delinquency and
D-5   Urban Areas. Chicago: University of Chicago Press, 1942.

D-4   Sheatsley, P. B. "An Analysis of Interviewer Characteristics and
      Their Relationships to Performance," International Journal of
      Opinion and Attitude Research, IV (1950), 473-98; and V (1951),
      79-94, 191-220.

E   Shera, Jesse H., and Egan, M. E. (eds.). Bibliographic Organization:
      Papers Presented before the Fifteenth Annual Conference of the
      Graduate Library School. Chicago: University of Chicago Press,
      1951.

A   Sherman, Mandel, and Henry, T. R. Hollow Folk. New York: Thomas
      Y. Crowell, 1933.
            A study of mountain people in the Appalachians. The Pref-
      ace gives a brief methodological note.

C-4   Shils, Edward. The Present State of American Sociology. Glencoe,
D-1   Ill.: Free Press, 1948.

C-4   _____. "Social Science and Social Policy," Philosophy of Science,
D-1   XVI (1949), 219-42.
            Among the points discussed are: the development of social
      science, the different roles of the social scientist from mere
      consultation to participation in policy making, funds assigned to
      social research, the advantages and disadvantages of the prac-
      tical orientation of contemporary social science, the contribution
      of social science to practice.

C-4   Sibley, Elbridge. "Education in Social Science and the Selection of
D-1   Students for Training as Professional Social Scientists," Social
      Science Research Council Items, V (1951), 25-29.
            The well-educated citizen needs a general understanding of
      the nature of social science. This should be taken care of by col-
      leges providing more adequate undergraduate education in social
      science. Thus standards of training for professional social sci-
      entists can be raised, leading to the advancement of social sci-
      ence itself.

C-4   Simmel, Georg. The Sociology of Georg Simmel. Ed. Kurt Wolff.
D-1   Glencoe, Ill.: Free Press, 1950.

D-2   Skott, H. "Attitude Research in the Department of Agriculture," Pub-
D-4   lic Opinion Quarterly, IV (1943), 176.

D-7   Sletto, Raymond. Construction of Personality Scales by the Criterion
      of Internal Consistency. Hanover, N. H.: Sociological Press, 1937.

D-3   _____. "Pretesting of Questionnaires," American Sociological Re-
      view, V (1940), 193-200.

D-1   Small, Albion W. The Meaning of Social Science. Chicago: Univer-
      sity of Chicago Press, 1910.
            Indicates the scope of sociology, as viewed by the founder
      of the first Department of Sociology in the United States.

C-4   Small, Albion W. "A Prospectus of Sociological Theory," American
D-1   Journal of Sociology (1920), 29-59.

C-4   _____. "Technique as an Approach to Science," American Journal
           of Sociology, XXVII (1922), 646-51.

C-4   _____. "Some Researches into Research," Journal of Applied Psy-
           chology, IX (1924-25), 3-11, 98-107.

D-4   Smigel, Erwin O. "Interviewing a Legal Elite: The Wall Street Law-
           yer," American Journal of Sociology, LXIV (1958), 159-64.

C-4   Smith, T. V., and White, L. D. (eds.). Chicago: An Experiment in So-
D-1   cial Science Research. Chicago: University of Chicago Press,
           1929.
               See especially T. V. Smith's article therein, "Social Science
           Research and the Community."

D-1   Sorokin, Pitirim. "Main Methods, Principles and Techniques of So-
           ciological Research," Sociology and Social Research, XXXIII
           (1948), 6-7.

D-1   Spahr, Walter E., and Swenson, R. J. Methods and Status of Social
           Research. New York: Harper & Bros., 1930.

D-1   Spencer, Robert F. (ed.). Method and Perspective in Anthropology.
           Papers in Honor of Wilson D. Wallis. Minneapolis: University
           of Minnesota Press, 1954.

C-4   Spicer, E. H. "The Use of Social Scientists by the War Relocation
D-1   Authority," Applied Anthropology, VI (1946), 16-36.

D-4   Steiner, I. "Interpersonal Behavior and Accurate Social Perception,"
           Psychological Review, XLVII (1955), 51-57.
               Suggestive for a theory of role relationships in field work
           and accuracy of researcher's perceptions.

D-8   Stephenson, William. The Study of Behavior: Q-Technique and Its
           Methodology. Chicago: University of Chicago Press, 1953.

D-5   Stouffer, Samuel A. "Notes on the Case Study and the Unique Case,"
           in The Prediction of Personal Adjustment, ed. Paul Horst. New
           York: Social Science Research Council, 1941.

D-2   Stouffer, Samuel A., et al. The American Soldier. 4 vols. Prince-
           ton: Princeton University Press, 1949.

D-2   Streib, Gordon F. "The Use of Survey Methods among the Navaho,"
           American Anthropologist, LIV (1952), 30-40.

D-2   Stringfellow, Cyril D. "The Confidential Interview Method in Atti-
D-4   tude Surveys," International Journal of Opinion and Attitude Re-
           search, III (1949), 87-94.

D-4   Symonds, P. M. "Securing Rapport in Interviewing," Teachers Col-
           lege Record, XXXIX (1938), 707-22.

D-4   _____. "Research on the Interviewing Process," Journal of Educa-
           tional Psychology, XXX (1939), 346.

D-5   _____. "The Case Study as a Research Method," Review of Educa-
           tional Research, XV (1945), 352-59.

-T-

D-1   Tarde, Gabriel. Les lois sociales: esquisse d'une sociologie. Paris:
D-6   Ancienne Librarie Germer Baillière et Cie. Felix Alcan, Edi-
          teur. 108, Boulevard Saint-Germain. 1898.
             See also the translation by Howard C. Warren, published as
          Social Laws, an Outline of Sociology (New York, 1899). In the
          French edition see pp. 153-54 for Tarde's footnote suggestion
          that "a truly experimental" social science would require the col-
          laboration of a great number of "devoted observers," born in va-
          rious regions of France and overseas, who would record in great
          detail and in its local social context, every event, however minor
          it might seem, that reflected (and affected) social change: "the
          series of little changes in the political order, the economic or-
          der, etc." He suggested that "These narrative monographs would
          be entirely different from descriptive monographs and would be
          illuminating in a quite different way." He urged, at the outset, in-
          quiry into such apparently minor matters as the question of what
          persons introduced and spread among the peasants the new cus-
          tom of no longer bowing to wealthy landowners in the vicinity,
          "or under what influences there begin to be a loss of faith in sor-
          cery, were-wolves [loup-garous], etc."

A   Tax, Sol. "The Social Organization of the Fox Indians." Master's
          thesis, Department of Sociology and Anthropology, University of
          Chicago, 1932.
             See the "Introduction: The Ethnographic Procedure" for lim-
          itations of the study due to the short time spent among the group
          and the lack of knowledge of the native language. The introduction
          also describes methods of collecting and organizing the data.

B   Tax, Sol, et al. Heritage of Conquest: The Ethnology of Middle Amer-
          ica. Glencoe, Ill.: Free Press, 1951.

D-1   Taylor, Carl C. "Techniques of Community Study and Analysis as
          Applied to Modern Civilized Societies," in The Science of Man in
          the World Crisis, ed. Ralph Linton. New York: Columbia Univer-
          sity Press, 1948.

D-6   Thomas, Dorothy S., et al. Observational Studies of Social Behavior.
          New Haven: Yale University Press, 1933.
             Describes development of methods for the observation of
          nursery school children by classroom teachers (that is, by a kind
          of "participant observation").

A   Thomas, Dorothy S., and Nishimoto, R. S. The Spoilage. Berkeley
          and Los Angeles: University of California Press, 1946.
             A study of the processes of readjustment in a Japanese relo-
          cation camp. The preface illustrates some of the problems a re-
          search group meets when studying such processes in extremely
          tense and suspicious communities: the inability to get valid in-
          formation through attitude surveys or questionnaires, the need
          for using "insiders" or trained participant observers to get a
          record of what is going on, the problem of keeping informants
          anonymous, linguistic difficulties, etc.

A   Thomas, William, and Znaniecki, F. The Polish Peasant in Europe
          and America. New York: Alfred A. Knopf, 1927.
             A case study of social and personal disorganization and reor-
          ganization. See especially pp. 1-86 for the "Methodological Note."

D-4   Thompson, James D., and Demerath, N. J. "Some Experiences with the Group Interview," Social Forces, XXXI (1952), 148-54.

A   Thrasher, Frederic M. The Gang: A Study of 1,313 Gangs in Chicago.
D-1   Chicago: University of Chicago Press, 1926; rev. ed., 1936.

D-1   _____. "How To Study the Boys' Gang in the Open," Journal of Edu-
          cational Psychology, I (1928), 244-54.

D-7   Thurstone, L. L., and Chave, E. J. The Measurement of Attitudes.
          Chicago: University of Chicago Press, 1929.

C-2   Trice, H. M. "The 'Outsider's' Role in Field Study," Sociology and
D-1   Social Research, XLI (1956), 27-32.

-U-

D-4   Udow, Alfred B. "Interviewer Effect in Public Opinion and Market-
          ing Research," Archives of Psychology, No. 277. New York:
          Columbia University, 1942.

C-4   Useem, John. "Social Anthropology: Recent Trends and Significant
D-1   Literature," Social Education, XIV (1950), 347-54.

-V-

D-4   Van Kleeck, Mary. "The Interview as a Method of Research," Tay-
          lor Society Bulletin, XI (1926), 268-74.

D-3   Vernon, P. E. "Questionnaires, Attitude Tests, and Rating Scales,"
D-7   in The Study of Society, ed. F. S. Bartlett, et al. London: Kegan
          Paul, Trench, Trubner & Co., 1939, 1946.

-W-

A   Wagley, Charles, and Galvai, Edwards. The Tenetehara Indians of
D-4   Brazil: A Culture in Transition. New York: Columbia Univer-
          sity Press, 1949.
              A study of an aboriginal tribe which has made a successful
          adjustment to a new environment brought by contact with other
          cultures, while retaining much of its original culture. The pref-
          ace has methodological notes and brief biographies of the native
          informants.

A   Walker, C. R., and Guest, R. H. The Man on the Assembly Line.
          Cambridge, Mass.: Harvard University Press, 1952.

D-1   Waller, Willard. "Insight and Scientific Method," American Journal
D-5   of Sociology, XL (1934), 285-97.

A   Ware, Caroline F. Greenwich Village, 1920-1930: A Comment on
          American Civilization in the Post-War Years. Boston: Houghton
          Mifflin Co., 1935.

A   Warner, W. Lloyd. A Black Civilization: A Social Study of an Austra-
          lian Tribe. New York: Harper & Bros., 1937; rev. ed. 1958.

D-1   _____. "Contemporary Social Anthropology." A lecture given before
          the Division of the Social Sciences, University of Chicago, De-
          cember 8, 1936.

A   Warner, W. Lloyd, et al. "The Yankee City Series." The Social Life
D-1   of a Modern Community (1941). The Status System of a Modern

Society (1942). The Social Systems of American Ethnic Groups
(1945). The Social System of a Modern Factory (1947). The Living and the Dead: A Study of the Symbolism of Americans (1959).
New Haven: Yale University Press.

B   Warner, W. Lloyd, and Associates. Democracy in Jonesville: A Study
        in Quality and Inequality. New York: Harper & Bros., 1947.

A   Warner, W. Lloyd; Havighurst, R. J.; and Loeb, M. B. Who Shall Be
        Educated? New York: Harper & Bros., 1944.

A   Warner, W. Lloyd; Junker, Buford H.; and Adams, Walter A. Color
        and Human Nature. Washington, D. C.: American Council on Ed-
        ucation, 1941.

D-1   Warren, Roland L. Studying Your Community. New York: Russell
        Sage Foundation, 1955.
                An excellent handbook for interested citizens and beginning
        sociologists.

D-4   Webb, Beatrice. My Apprenticeship. New York: Longmans, Green
        & Co., 1926.

A   Webb, Sidney, and Webb, Beatrice. Problems of Modern Industry.
C-4   London: Longmans, Green & Co., 1898.
                See chapter i, pp. 1-19, "The Diary of an Investigator."

D-1   _____. Methods of Social Study. London: Longmans, Green & Co.,
        1932.

D-7   Wechsler, Irving R., and Bernberg, R. B. "Indirect Methods of Atti-
        tude Measurements," International Journal of Opinion and Atti-
        tude.Research, IV (1950), 209-28.

D-4   Wechsler, James. "Interviews and Interviewers," Public Opinion
        Quarterly, IV (1940), 258-60.

B   Weslager, C. A. Delaware's Forgotten Folks: The Story of the Moors
        and the Kanticokes. Philadelphia: University of Pennsylvania
        Press, 1943.

A   West, James. Plainville, U.S.A. New York: Columbia University
        Press, 1945.

D-1   White, Leonard D. (ed.). The State of the Social Sciences. Chicago:
        University of Chicago Press, 1956.

D-1   Whitehead, Alfred North. Science and the Modern World. ("Lowell
        Lectures, 1925.") New York: Macmillan Co., 1925; New York:
        New American Library, 1948.

A   Whitehead, T. North. Leadership in a Free Society. Cambridge,
        Mass.: Harvard University Press, 1936.

A   _____. The Industrial Worker. 2 vols. Cambridge, Mass.: Harvard
        University Press, 1938.
                A statistical study of human relations in a group of manual
        workers (data from the Western Electric researches, specifical-
        ly the experiments at Hawthorne Works, Chicago).

A   _____. "Social Relationships in the Factory: A Study of an Industrial
        Group," Human Factor, XVIII (1935), 381-94.

D-1   Whitney, Frederick L. Elements of Research. New York: Prentice-
        Hall, 1942; 1950.

A   Whyte, William Foote. Street Corner Society: The Social Structure
D-1   of an Italian Slum. Chicago: University of Chicago Press, 1941;
        2d ed., 1955.
            In addition to the Preface in the first edition, see the second
        for "a special added Appendix of eighty-two pages, in which the
        author describes the actual methods, procedures, and interview-
        ing techniques that he used in conducting his research."

D-1   _____. Man and Organization: Three Problems in Human Relations
        in Industry. Homewood, Ill.: Richard D. Irwin, Inc., 1959.

D-4   _____. "Small Groups and Large Organizations," in Social Psychol-
        ogy at the Crossroads, ed. J. H. Rohrer and M. Sherif. New
        York: Harper & Bros., 1951.

D-4   _____. "Interviewing for Organizational Research," Human Organi-
        zation, XII (1953), 15-22.

C-4   Wiese, Leopold von. Allgemeine Soziologie: I. Beziehungslehre.
D-1   München U. Leipzig: Verlag von Dunckler u. Humbolt, 1924.
            Makes an elaborate attempt to classify social relations and
        social processes, of possible use in attempting to codify field
        worker roles and relational contexts.

D-1   Willems, Emilio. "Neuere Tendenzen sozialanthropologischer Feld-
        forschung," in Soziologische Forschung in unserer Zeit, ed. K. G.
        Specht. Köln u. Opladen: Westdeutscher Verlag, 1951.

D-4   Williams, F. "The Use of Interviewer Rapport as a Method of De-
        tecting Differences between 'Public' and 'Private' Information,"
        Journal of Social Psychology, XXII (1945), 171-75.

A   Wilson, Godfrey, and Wilson, Monica (Hunter). The Analysis of So-
D-4   cial Change, Based on Observations in Central Africa. Cam-
        bridge: Cambridge University Press, 1945.
            See pp. 55-56 for an example of the "group interview."

A   Wilson, Monica Hunter. Good Company: A Study of Nyakusa Age Vil-
        lages. London: Oxford University Press, 1951.

D-1   _____. "Some Possibilities and Limitations of Anthropological Re-
        search." Inaugural lecture delivered at Rhodes University Col-
        lege. Grahamstown, Union of South Africa: Rhodes University
        College, 1948.
            Points out (p. 19) that professional field work in anthropol-
        ogy began only 50 years ago (c. 1898) with Boas; and mentions
        the Cambridge Expedition to the Torres Straits and the Jesup
        Expedition to the North Pacific. Social anthropology has two
        great contributions to make in the social field: (1) the study of
        comparative material, and (2) insistence upon synthesis (or so-
        cial system).

C-4   Wirth, Louis (ed.). Eleven Twenty-six: A Decade of Social Science
D-1   Research. Chicago: University of Chicago Press, 1940.
            A critical review of research studies by University of Chi-
        cago social scientists. Contains a bibliography of publications
        in the social sciences by those associated with the University
        of Chicago.

A   Wisdom, Charles. The Chorti Indians of Guatemala. Chicago: Uni-
       versity of Chicago Press, 1940.

D-1   Wissler, Clark. "Foreword" to The Changing Culture of an Indian
       Tribe by Margaret Mead. New York: Columbia University Press,
       1932.

D-1   Wolff, K. H. "A Critique of Bateson's Naven," Journal of the Royal
       Anthropological Institute, LXXIV (1944), 59-74.

D-1   _____. "A Methodological Note on the Empirical Study of Culture
       Patterns," American Sociological Review, X (1945), 176-84.

D-1   _____. "The Collection and Organization of Field Materials: A Re-
       search Report," Ohio Journal of Science, LII (1952), 49-61.

D-4   Womer, S., and Body, H. "The Use of a Voice Recorder in Selection
       and Training of Field Workers," Public Opinion Quarterly, XV
       (1951), 358.

D-4   Woodside, M. "The Research Interview," Sociological Review,
       XXXVII (1945), 28.

D-4   Woodworth, R. S. "Psychological Experience with the Interview,"
       Journal of Personnel Research, IV (1925), 162-65.

                                   -Y-

D-1   Young, Kimball. "Methods of Studying the Personality," in Person-
D-5   ality and Problems of Adjustment, by Kimball Young. New York:
       F. S. Crofts, 1940.

D-4   Young, Pauline V. Interviewing in Social Work. New York: McGraw-
       Hill Book Co., 1935.

D-1   _____. Scientific Social Surveys and Research. 2d ed. New York:
       Prentice-Hall, 1949.

                                   -Z-

A   Zaleznik, A.; Christensen, C. R.; and Roethlisberger, F. J. The Mo-
       tivation, Productivity, and Satisfaction of Workers: A Prediction
       Study. Boston: Harvard Graduate School of Business Administra-
       tion, Division of Research, 1958.
             A thorough-going report of an elaborately designed study in
       the field of human relations in industry, with methods and results
       carefully specified.

C-4   Znaniecki, Florian. The Laws of Social Psychology. Chicago: Uni-
D-1   versity of Chicago Press, 1925.

C-4   _____. The Method of Sociology. New York: Farrar & Rinehart, 1934.
D-1

C-4   _____. "Methodological Trends in Sociological Research," Sociology
D-1   and Social Research, XXXIII (1948), 10-14.

C-4   _____. Cultural Sciences: Their Origin and Development. Urbana:
D-1   University of Illinois Press, 1952.